TOEFL* CBT

by

Marilyn J. Rymniak

Janet B. Shanks

and the Staff of
Kaplan Educational Centers

Simon & Schuster
Sydney • London • Singapore • New York

*TOEFL is a registered trademark of Educational Testing Service (ETS), which is not affiliated with this product.

Kaplan Books
Published by
Simon & Schuster
1230 Avenue of the Americas
New York, NY 10020

Photo credits: Boston University, p. 155; Colgate University, p. 149; Earlham College, p. 159; Rhodes College, p. 157; Skidmore College, p. 151; Southwestern University, p. 163; SUNY Albany, p. 86; SUNY Stony Brook, p. 90; University of Pennsylvania, p. 153; University of the South, p. 146; and Wofford College, p. 161.

For bulk sales to schools, colleges, and universities, please contact the Vice President for Special Markets, Simon & Schuster, 1633 Broadway, 8th Floor, New York, NY 10019.

Project Editors: Julie Schmidt and Larissa Shmailo
Production Editor: Maude Spekes
Design: Jude Bond
Page Layout: Laurel Douglas and Hugh Haggerty
Managing Editor: Dave Chipps
Desktop Publishing Manager: Michael Shevlin
Executive Editor: Del Franz

CD-ROM Development Team
Producer: Robert Garrelick
Development Manager: Hristina Le Blanc
Project Manager: Karen Fallowes
Contributing Developer: Bill Shander
Content Development Team: Marilyn Rymniak, Yuriko Hirai-Hirsch, Pamela Vittorio, Patty MacKinnon, Janet Shanks, Laura Rowley, Christine Paul, and Stephen Shaffer
Audio Production: Charles Morrow Associates

Special thanks to: Sara Pearl

Manufactured in the United States of America
Published simultaneously in Canada

February 2000

10 9 8 7 6 5 4 3 2 1

ISBN: 0-684-87095-9

Table of Contents

About the Authors

Marilyn J. Rymniak

Marilyn J. Rymniak is the executive director of International Products and Programs at Kaplan Educational Centers. For over 25 years, she has been a foreign language/ESL specialist and a leader in the international education field, holding national and regional positions with NAFSA: Association of International Educators, and TESOL. A sociolinguist and international and comparative educator by training, she has taught, administered, and developed curricula for campus-based intensive English programs in California and New York, including those at the University of California at San Diego, the University of California at Los Angeles, University of California at Irvine, the California State University System, and Manhattanville College. She has held overseas teaching and curriculum development positions in Spain, France, England, Iran, and Saudi Arabia and has done ESL training in Poland. Rymniak, who was a Fulbright scholar to Germany, can communicate in six languages. She also sits on the Board of Directors of Metro International in New York City and is an intercultural communication trainer for BDx InterFace, Inc. of Connecticut.

Janet Shanks

Janet Shanks has taught English as a Second Language, TOEFL, and writing skills classes for over twenty years, and currently teaches ESL and TOEFL at the American Language Program, Columbia University. Educated in applied linguistics and English education, she also received a graduate student fellowship to Columbia University School of Journalism, Freedom Forum and a scholarship to the British Studies at Oxford Program.

A Special Note on Studying in the U.S.A.

If you are not from the United States, but want to attend a United States college or university, here are the steps you need to take:

- If English is not your first language, start there. You will probably need to take the TOEFL or show some other evidence that you are very proficient in English. Usually an applicant's TOEFL scores are submitted as part of the university application. You should, of course, prepare for the TOEFL itself, but TOEFL preparation alone is probably not going to give you the scores you need to get into an American university. A good base in all aspects of English is necessary.

- Depending on the university, some undergraduate applicants may also be required to take the SAT (formerly known as the Scholastic Assessment Test). Applicants for graduate programs may have to take the GRE (Graduate Record Exam); applicants for Masters in Business Administration programs may have to take the GMAT (Graduate Management Admissions Test); and law school applicants will probably have to take the LSAT (Law School Admissions Test).

- Selecting the correct school can be difficult. Get help from a counselor or use the information provided in a Kaplan book such as *Guide to College Selection* or *Graduate School Admissions Adviser*. Since admission to many undergraduate and graduate programs is competitive, you should select at least three or four programs and complete an application for each one. You need to begin the application process at least a year in advance, especially if you are overseas. Find out the application deadlines for the schools you are interested in, and plan accordingly.

- Higher education in the United States is generally very expensive in comparison to university education in other countries. International students generally have to show at the time that they apply that they have sufficient funds to pay for the costs of a year's studies in the United States. On the undergraduate level, there are few scholarships given to international students. Advanced-degree students, however, may find that there are opportunities for research grants, teaching assistantships, and practical training or work experience in U.S. graduate departments. To be eligible for these, a student will first have to be accepted into the college or university in question. For more information on funding for higher education in the United States, see Kaplan's *Scholarships* or *Yale Daily News Guide to Fellowships and Grants*.

- Finally, after you are accepted into a university, you will need to obtain an I-20 Certificate of Eligibility in order to receive an F-1 Student Visa to study in the United States. This can be obtained from the school that you are going to attend.

KAPLAN'S ENGLISH LANGUAGE PROGRAMS

If you need more help with English language learning, TOEFL preparation, or the complex process of university admissions, you may be interested in Kaplan's English language programs.

Kaplan created the Access America™ series of courses to assist international students and professionals who want to enter the United States university system. The program was designed for students who have received the bulk of their primary and secondary education outside the United States in a language other than English. Kaplan also has programs for obtaining professional certification in the United States. A brief description of some of the help available through Kaplan follows.

Kaplan's University Bridge Program

This English for TOEFL and university preparation is a comprehensive English language training program that prepares serious students for admission to an accredited American university. Using a content-based approach to studying English, this course trains students in three main areas:

- Academic English for university admissions
- TOEFL and other university entrance exam test-taking skills and strategies
- University admissions counseling and placement

This course is designed for international students at the high-intermediate, advanced, and super-advanced levels of English proficiency who have as their end goal admission into a university degree program. Some American universities will accept Kaplan's Certificates of Achievement in English for University Admissions in lieu of a TOEFL score. This means that they trust the Kaplan Certificate as a reliable evaluation of a student's readiness for university work. A list of schools providing TOEFL waivers for Kaplan's certificate will be provided upon request.

In this course, students use actual material written for native speakers of English and work on improving the following critical skills:

(1) Listening and lecture notetaking skills

(2) Extended and rapid textbook reading skills

(3) Vocabulary enhancement for developing native-like intuition about words

(4) Understanding and applying English grammar in a real context

(5) Effective use of a monolingual dictionary

(6) Time management skills for academic study

(7) Computer literacy and computer keyboarding skills

(8) Successfully taking the TOEFL (on paper and on computer) and other standardized test skills

(9) Functional conversation performance skills

(10) Learning strategies

Graduate School/GRE (Graduate Record Exam) Preparation

If your goal is to enter a master's or Ph.D. program in the United States, Kaplan will help you achieve a high GRE or GMAT score, while helping you understand how to choose a graduate degree program in your field.

USMLE (United States Medical Licensing Exam) and Other Medical Licensing

If you are an international medical graduate who would like to be certified by the Educational Commission for Foreign Medical Graduates (ECFMG) and obtain a residency in a United States hospital, Kaplan will help you achieve a passing score on all three steps of the USMLE.

If you are an international nurse who wishes to practice in the United States, Kaplan will help you achieve a passing score on the NCLEX (Nursing Certification and Licensing Exam) or CGFNS (Commission on Graduates of Foreign Nursing Schools) exam. Kaplan will also provide you with the English and cross-cultural knowledge you will need to be an effective nurse.

Business Accounting/CPA (Certified Public Accounting)

If you are an accountant who would like to be certified to do business in the United States, Kaplan will help you achieve a passing score on the CPA Exam, and will assist you in understanding accounting procedures in the United States.

Undergraduate Preparation

If you are seeking a B.A. or B.S. degree, Kaplan will help you achieve a high SAT score while guiding you through the college admissions process.

 ix

APPLYING TO KAPLAN'S ENGLISH LANGUAGE PROGRAMS

To get more information, or to apply for admission to any of Kaplan's programs for international students or professionals, you can write to us at:

Kaplan Educational Centers
International Admissions Department
888 Seventh Avenue
New York, NY 10106

You can call us at 1-800-527-8378 from within the United States, or at 1-212-262-4980 outside the United States. Our fax number is 1-212-957-1654. Our e-mail address is world@kaplan.com. You can also get more information or even apply through the Internet at http://www.kaplan.com/intl.

KAPLAN

User's Guide for the CD-ROM

Chapter at a Glance:

If you are worried because the new computer-based TOEFL (the TOEFL CBT) includes unfamiliar types of questions, you are in luck! *Kaplan's Mastering the Computer-Based TOEFL® Test* CD-ROM, combined with the information you will cover while working through this book, will give you the edge you need to conquer both your fears and the TOEFL CBT (as well as many other types of computer-based or computer adaptive tests). The CD-ROM attached to the back cover of this book is the result of months of research, development, and testing by Kaplan Educational Centers' expert Technology and ESL divisions.

Before you install the CD-ROM, read the User's Guide provided here. You should also check out the introductory sections on the TOEFL CBT test that precede each set of Power Lessons. These materials offer details about the new question types you will be asked to answer, and will help you master the mechanics of taking the test on the computer.

NOTE: This CD-ROM also includes audio recordings for the Listening Power Lessons and the Diagnostic Test. DO NOT attempt to play this disc on a regular music CD player.

NOTE: Technical Support for the CD-ROM is available Monday through Friday from 6 A.M. to 6 P.M. EST at 1-970-339-7142.

SYSTEM REQUIREMENTS

Windows™

Windows 3.1 or higher, 486 SX or higher, 50MHz, 8 MB hard disk space, 16 MB available RAM (64 MB of RAM is recommended for optimal performance of the audio files), 640x480/256 colors, 2x CD-ROM, 16-bit audio, speakers or headphones.

Macintosh®

Macintosh OS 7.0 or higher, 68040 or higher, 8 MB hard disk space, 16 MB available RAM (64 MB of RAM is recommended for optimal performance of the audio files), 640x480/256 colors, 2x CD-ROM, 16-bit audio, speakers or headphones.

INSTALLING AND LAUNCHING THE SOFTWARE

This application requires QuickTime™ software, which has been included on the CD-ROM. If you do not have QuickTime installed, or are not sure if you do or not, choose to install QuickTime.

Windows 3.1, 3.11

(1) Exit out of all open applications (make sure you have no applications running).

(2) Insert *Kaplan's Mastering the Computer-Based TOEFL Test* CD-ROM into your CD-ROM drive.

(3) Choose **Run** from the File menu of the Program Manager and type d:\Kapsetup.exe (where d: is your CD-ROM drive).

(4) Press **OK** and follow the prompts.

(5) You are now ready to use the software. You must have the CD-ROM in your computer when using the software, even though you have installed information onto your hard drive. To run the program after installation, choose the **Kaplan** program group from the Program Manager and select the *Mastering the Computer-Based TOEFL Test* icon.

(6) At the title screen, click the mouse once anywhere on the screen to go on. Use the right-facing arrow at the top right of the next few screens to go through the introduction and get to the Main Menu.

Windows 95 or Higher

(1) Exit out of all open applications; make sure you have no applications running.

(2) Insert *Kaplan's Mastering the Computer-Based TOEFL Test* CD-ROM into your CD-ROM drive.

(3) From the **Start Menu**, choose **Run** and type (or browse for) d:\Kapsetup.exe (where d: is your CD-ROM drive).

(4) Press **OK** and follow the prompts.

(5) You are now ready to use the software. You must have the CD-ROM in your computer when using the software, even though you have installed information on your hard drive. To run the program, go to the **Start Menu**, choose **Programs**, then **Kaplan**, then **Mastering the Computer-Based TOEFL Test**.

(6) At the title screen, click the mouse once anywhere on the screen to go on. Use the right-facing arrow at the top right of the next few screens to go through the introduction and get to the **Main Menu**.

Macintosh

(1) Quit out of all open applications; make sure you have no applications running.

(2) Insert *Kaplan's Mastering the Computer-Based TOEFL Test* CD-ROM into your CD-ROM drive.

(3) Double-click the **Kaplan Mastering TOEFL Install** icon.

(4) Follow the prompts.

(5) When Kaplan files are done installing, the installer will determine if you need to install QuickTime. If so, you will be prompted to do so.

(6) When QuickTime installation is complete, you will be forced to restart your computer.

(7) You are now ready to use the software. You must have the CD-ROM in your computer when using the software, even though you have installed information on your hard drive. To launch the program, double-click the **Mastering the Test** icon in the "Kaplan's Mastering the TOEFL" folder (installation default name).

(8) At the title screen, click the mouse once anywhere on the screen to go on. Use the right-facing arrow at the top right of the next few screens to go through the introduction and get to the Main Menu.

USING THE APPLICATION—MAJOR SECTIONS OF THE SOFTWARE

At the Main Menu, you will have three options:

- Familiarize yourself with the different types of questions and strategies for answering these questions
- Learn more about the English language programs provided by Kaplan Educational Centers and about computer-based testing
- Take a full-length practice TOEFL CBT test

Strategies and Practice

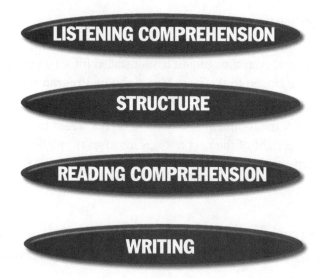

Kaplan Strategies for Listening, Structure, Reading, and Writing will walk you through strategies for approaching each section and answering its questions, and will provide a short set of practice questions. You will get feedback on your performance and the correct answers to the practice questions. For more information on the format of the test, you can contact ETS to receive a free copy of their CD-ROM Sampler, which includes information on question types found on the computer-based TOEFL test. Write to TOEFL Order Services, P.O. Box 6161, Princeton, NJ 08541-6161. You can also order the CD-ROM or download the tutorial from the Web at www.toefl.org.

These button descriptions will help you navigate through the strategies and practice questions.

Tutorial Screens:

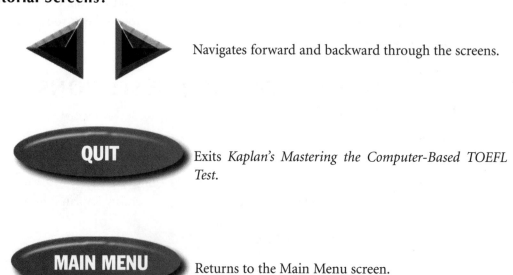

Navigates forward and backward through the screens.

Exits *Kaplan's Mastering the Computer-Based TOEFL Test*.

Returns to the Main Menu screen.

Question Screens:

Available in all test areas: click this to go on the next question. In the Listening Comprehension, Structure, and Writing sections, you can change your response after clicking **Next**, but you must confirm your response to go on to the next question.

Available in Listening Comprehension and Structure practice test areas: you must click this after clicking **Next** in order to go on to the next question. In Writing, click this when you've completed your essay. You cannot change your answer or return to the item after clicking on **Confirm**. **Confirm** saves your response, and sends you to the next item.

Available only in the Reading test area. Goes back to the previous question.

Review Screens:

You must complete the practice questions before you can access these screens.

Available from the **Feedback** and **Answers** areas. Goes to the beginning of the strategies for that section.

Shows analysis of your performance for the section of the practice questions you are reviewing.

Shows the questions, your responses to them, and the correct answers in the section you are reviewing.

Typing Test

This typing test goes with the Writing section of Kaplan's Mastering the Computer-Based TOEFL Test CD-ROM. Type the essay below as quickly and accurately as you can. After 5 minutes have passed, your essay will be checked for its accuracy, and your typing speed will be calculated by the CD-ROM. This information will help you decide whether you should hand write the essay portion of the TOEFL or type it directly onto the computer.

It is important for all TOEFL test-takers to be able to use the computer. Not only are computers used for the actual TOEFL test, they are an important part of everyday life for a student. From typing papers to finding out in which building your class is being held, computers are indispensable for today's university student.

Whether you are studying art history or zoology, business or medicine, the laws of man or the laws of nature, your professor will require you to turn in assignments that have been typed on a computer. Gone are the days of handwritten essays on notebook paper. Be sure to practice using an American keyboard whenever you can. The keys may be laid out differently from keyboards in your own country, so pay close attention. Also, word-processing programs vary from one to another. The TOEFL word-processing program is probably very different from any you have seen before. Make sure you use the "help" button on your screen if you do not know how to perform a particular function.

Many institutions disseminate a great deal of important information via the internet. You will be given an e-mail account when you begin your studies and will use it often to communicate with fellow students, professors and university administrators. Most universities also maintain a web page; that is, a particular site on the internet where you can find information ranging from a class syllabus to recreational activities on campus. For more information on many universities, you can check out Kaplan's web site at http://www.kaplan.com.

More about U.S. University Entrance Exams and Admissions

MORE INFORMATION

If you are considering studying or attending school in the United States, this section will give you valuable information about the U.S. educational system. It also contains information about Kaplan programs, and additional details about and strategies for taking computer-based exams.

These button descriptions will help you navigate through information in this section.

   Shows a list of all topics available to review.

   In subsections with video and text, plays the video.

   In subsections with video and text, displays the text.

Full-Length Practice Tests

Once you've worked with the strategies and practice questions and feel comfortable with the interface and mechanics of taking the test on the computer, you can take two full-length tests that follow the format of the actual TOEFL CBT exam. Each test will consist of all four sections and be timed in the same way the real exam is.

At the end of the test, your test will be scored and you will receive an analysis of your test performance in several key areas. Use this feedback to adjust your test-taking strategies and zero in on your weaker areas. The feedback is broken down as follows:

Overall

Shows the breakdown of correct, incorrect, not reached, and omitted items for each section. Test scoring and essay ratings are also provided.

Content

Shows the percentage of correct responses you received in key content areas. This can be a highly effective guide for further study; concentrate more on those areas in which you did not score well.

Timing

The pace of this test is the same as what you can expect on test day. If you're having trouble finishing the test, see whether your time investment is paying off. We'll identify the 5 questions on which you spent the most and the least time. How did you do on these questions? If you tend to miss these despite spending a large amount of time on them, consider a change in test-taking strategy.

To take a full-length test:

(1) Click the **Full-Length Test** button on the Main Menu.

FULL-LENGTH TEST

(2) Login window will appear. Click the button **Add New User.** Type in any 8-digit number (the number cannot begin with a zero) and click **OK.** You need to add yourself only once. To review, resume, or reset your test, select your ID from the list, click **Select User,** and enter your name.

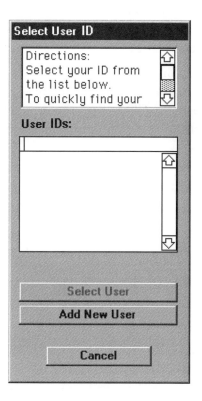

(3) At the next window, enter your name (remember exactly what you type; you will need it to access your test results at a later time). Click **OK.**

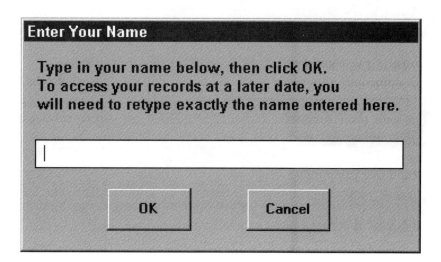

(4) You can now click **Continue** to begin a full-length test, or you can click **Main Menu** to take it at some other time. Follow all on-screen instructions.

(5) Since stamina is a big part of taking the TOEFL CBT test, you are encouraged to complete the test at one sitting with one short break in the middle, as you would if taking the actual test. However, we allow you to exit the test early and resume at a later time. There are two ways to exit early:

- From the middle of a section (Windows users press the Esc key or Control-Q, Macintosh users press Command-period). Your answers to that section will not be saved. All completed sections will be saved. You will quit out of the *Kaplan's Mastering the Computer-Based TOEFL Test* software completely (NOT RECOMMENDED).

- Between sections (click the **Exit** button at the end of a section instead of **Continue**). All of your work will be saved and you can resume taking the test at a later time. You will be returned to the Main Menu of the software.

(6) To resume taking the test, go to the login screen and click the 8-digit number you already entered, click **Select User**, and enter your name. A test will resume until it is completed, at which point the other test will become available.

These button descriptions will help you navigate through the full-length practice tests.

Question Screens:

After reading the directions, click this to begin the section.

Available in Reading only. Click this after scrolling through the passage to get to the first question.

Available in all test areas. Click this to go on the next question. In the Listening Comprehension, Structure, and Writing sections, you can change your response after clicking **Next**, but you must **confirm** your response to go on to the next question.

Available in Listening Comprehension, Structure, and Writing test areas. You must click this after clicking **Next** in order to go on to the next question. In Writing, click this when you've completed your essay. You cannot change your answer or return to the item after clicking on **Confirm**. **Confirm** saves your response, and sends you to the next item.

Available only in the Reading test area. Goes back to the previous question.

Review Screens

You must complete an entire test before you can use these buttons.

Available after completing a full-length test. Brings you to the **Overall Feedback** screen.

Shows the questions, your responses to them, and the correct answers in each section of the full-length test you took.

Shows an analysis of your content mastery and test-taking skills for each section of the full-length test.

Shows general feedback (number of correct, incorrect, not reached, and omitted questions) for all sections of the full-length test. Test scoring and essay ratings are also available.

Available in Listening Analysis only. Replays the audio so you can read the transcript for each question while listening to it.

AUDIO FOR BOOK PRACTICE

All of the audio files that are referenced throughout this book are located on the CD-ROM. **The CD-ROM must be played on a computer and cannot be used with a regular music CD player.**

(1) Insert *Kaplan's Mastering the Computer-Based TOEFL Test CD-ROM* into your CD-ROM drive.

(2) Navigate to the folder called "Audio" on the CD-ROM.

(3) Double-click the file referenced in the text of the book. The QuickTime MoviePlayer will launch (if you are prompted about purchasing QuickTime 3.0 Pro, click "Later"), and a control bar will appear:

The only button you will need on the control bar is: play/pause. Click the left arrow to begin playing the sound. If it is too loud or too soft, you'll need to adjust your computer's volume. On Windows, do this through **Sounds** in the Control Panel or, if available, on the Task Bar. On Macintosh, do this through **Sound** in the Control Panels. (If you use the volume button on the QuickTime controller, you will need to adjust the volume of each file individually.) There is no need to start/stop playback after each question. The audio file includes time to respond that approximates the pace of the actual test.

When you have finished listening to a file, you can open the next one by choosing **Open** from the File menu in the QuickTime MoviePlayer. (If you double-click the next file in Windows, the QuickTime MoviePlayer will relaunch.) Then, navigate to the Kaplan CD-ROM, and select the desired audio file. If you are done with audio files for now, you can **Quit** from the QuickTime movie player.

The audio files do not necessarily appear in the same order in the text as they do on the CD-ROM. The text will direct you to the appropriate audio track numbers on the CD-ROM.

The audio files for the Diagnostic Test are named:

Test_1A.mov

Test_1B.mov

Test_1C.mov

KAPLAN

The audio files for the Power Lessons are named:

Listening Power Lesson One (Short Conversations):

> Track_1.mov
>
> Track_2.mov
>
> Track_3.mov
>
> Track_4.mov
>
> Track_5.mov
>
> Track_6.mov
>
> Track_7.mov

Listening Power Lesson Two (Long Conversations):

> Track_8.mov
>
> Track_9.mov
>
> Track_10.mov
>
> Track_11.mov
>
> Track_12.mov
>
> Track_13.mov
>
> Track_14.mov
>
> Track_15.mov

Listening Power Lesson Two (Lectures):

> Track_16.mov
>
> Track_17.mov
>
> Track_18.mov
>
> Track_19.mov
>
> Track_20.mov
>
> Track_21.mov
>
> Track_22.mov

PART ONE:
Understanding the TOEFL CBT

Getting Started

At a Glance:

WHOM THIS BOOK IS FOR

This book was particularly written for students who are preparing for the computer-based Test of English as a Foreign Language (the TOEFL CBT) on their own. Self-study students will appreciate the clear, carefully written lessons as well as the fact that answer keys are provided for all of the exercises and practice tests. It can also be used effectively by English teachers in a formal, classroom-based setting.

TOEFL CBT is filled with information about the new computer-based TOEFL exam. Those who plan to take the paper-based test will also find it useful. However, if the computer-based TOEFL exam is not offered in your country, we recommend that you buy Kaplan's *TOEFL Workbook* in addition to this book. *TOEFL Workbook* provides information on the paper-based exam and offers numerous paper-based TOEFL test strategies and tips. Students will benefit from *TOEFL Workbook*'s extensive TOEFL content review lessons and practice tests whether they plan to take the paper-based TOEFL or the CBT.

This book assumes that the student using it has a good grasp of the English language. Students who have a previous paper-based TOEFL score of below 440 should probably improve their basic knowledge of the language before attempting to devote themselves to TOEFL preparation.

HOW THIS BOOK WILL HELP YOU

The authors of this book have spent years teaching TOEFL preparation and administering these exams. They have also read numerous studies of the TOEFL and of the kind of language that it tests. The organization of this book has been shaped by this experience.

Basically, *TOEFL CBT* is organized around the kinds of questions the TOEFL asks. For example, there is a section of this book designed to help students master the fact-based/inference type of question that is often asked in the Reading Comprehension section of the TOEFL CBT. Other sections teach students to recognize and be prepared for frequent distractors—that is, answers that look correct but are actually what the makers of the TOEFL use to mislead test takers.

The exercises and CBT practice tests on the CD-ROM will help you to familiarize yourself with the kinds of questions you will encounter on the TOEFL CBT. You will also find the explanations and extensive practice exercises in the book useful in this regard, although keep in mind that it is impossible to reproduce computerized question types exactly in a paper-based format.

WHAT IS THE TOEFL?

This section of the book is meant to give you a clear understanding of exactly what the Test of English as a Foreign Language is—and exactly what it is not. There is an expression in English that states, "Know thy enemy." This means that the best way to defeat an opponent is to know as much as possible about that opponent.

To get the best possible TOEFL score possible, you should know the TOEFL as well as the people at Kaplan do—and we know the TOEFL inside and out!

Some Basic Information on the TOEFL

The TOEFL is designed to test your ability to understand standard North American English. It is written and administered by the Educational Testing Service (ETS), a private, not-for-profit company based in Princeton, New Jersey. The TOEFL was developed to help American and Canadian colleges and universities evaluate the level of English language proficiency of the international students they want to admit. You may need a certain TOEFL score to get into a particular college or university. However, even a high TOEFL score does not guarantee that you will get into the college of your choice. Nor does a high TOEFL score guarantee academic success. To succeed in school, you also need to know how to communicate in English.

The TOEFL is one of several standardized tests that measure a student's proficiency level in English. A standardized test:

- Consists of different types of multiple-choice questions
- Is given to a large number of people at the same time
- Is graded by computer
- Is timed

Because Kaplan has studied and analyzed many TOEFL exams, we can explain to you the form of the test and the kinds of questions that will appear on it, as well as help you develop skills and strategies for taking it. This will allow you to work more efficiently when the time comes to take the actual TOEFL exam.

Since 1998, the TOEFL has been offered as a computerized test in many areas of the world. However, in certain countries, the paper-based TOEFL will continue to be used. In the pages that follow we will discuss in detail the differences between the paper-based and the computer-based TOEFL and what you can expect from each.

Basic Sections of the TOEFL

In both the paper-based and the computer-based TOEFL exams, each section tests particular skills in English communication:

Listening Comprehension

The questions in the Listening Comprehension section test your understanding of English grammar, idioms, and vocabulary. They also test your ability to distinguish between words with similar sounds. And since you have only about 12 seconds to answer each question, your ability to concentrate is also very important.

Structure and Written Expression (Called Structure on the TOEFL CBT)

The questions in the Structure section focus primarily on grammar and word choice. Though this section stresses grammar, having a broad vocabulary plays a large role in your doing well here, especially when you are asked to make a correct word choice.

Reading Comprehension

In the Reading Comprehension section, you must read a number of passages and answer questions about what you have read in each passage. You will be asked about the content of what you read and about the meanings of words as they are used in the passage.

Test of Written English or TWE (Called Writing on the TOEFL CBT)

The TWE (or Writing) part of the TOEFL is a 30-minute section that tests your ability to write well in English. This includes the ability to organize your ideas well, support these with specific examples and/or evidence, and write in standard English in response to the assigned topic. You must also demonstrate a broad vocabulary and ease in using idiomatic English.

THE PAPER-BASED TOEFL

The paper-based TOEFL will continue to be administered until at least the year 2000 in a number of countries. In addition to these countries, all Institutional TOEFLs will continue to be paper-based, regardless of the country in which they are administered. The Institutional TOEFL, as its name implies, is given by an institution or school to its own students. This exam has the same form, content, and level of difficulty as the official paper-based TOEFL and is also produced and distributed by ETS, but is considered unofficial by ETS for college or university admissions from overseas. Some universities will, however, accept the score of an Institutional TOEFL conditionally while waiting for your official score.

Again, for more in-depth information on the paper-based TOEFL, you should consult Kaplan's *TOEFL Workbook*.

Form and Content

The paper-based TOEFL is approximately two hours long and consists of 140 multiple-choice questions. If you include the time it takes to fill in forms and listen to directions, you will spend about three hours at the test site.

Paper-based TOEFL questions are divided into three sections: Section I, Listening Comprehension; Section II, Structure and Written Expression; and Section III, Reading Comprehension. Each section is timed separately. You have approximately 30 to 40 minutes to work on Section I, 25 minutes to work on Section II, and 55 minutes to work on Section III. Once you are done with a section, you cannot return to it.

Listening Comprehension

In Section I, which consists of 50 questions, you listen to spoken English and answer questions that test how well you understood what you heard. This section consists of three parts: A, B, and C. In part A, you hear 30 short conversations and answer a question about each one. In part B, you hear three or four longer conversations and answer a few questions about each one. In part C, you listen to three or four talks or lectures of about a minute each, and answer several questions about each one.

KAPLAN

Structure and Written Expression

In Section II, which consists of 40 questions, you are asked to either complete a sentence or identify an error in a sentence. The first 15 questions are sentence completion, in which you will see a sentence with a blank space. You will be presented with four answer choices from which you will choose one. The remaining 25 questions are error identification, in which each question consists of a sentence that contains four underlined words or phrases, labeled A, B, C, and D. One of these four words or phrases is incorrect, and you must identify it.

Reading Comprehension

In Section III, you must read 5 or 6 reading passages and answer 50 questions about what you have read. You will be asked about the content of what you read and the meanings of the words as they are used in a passage. The questions include four answer choices from which you select the best answer.

TWE

The TWE (Test of Written Expression) is required on the CBT but is an optional section of the paper-based TOEFL. The TWE tests your ability to respond to a question in essay form using standard English. You are given a choice of two topics, from which you pick one. You must write your essay by hand.

THE COMPUTER-BASED TOEFL (TOEFL CBT)

The computer-based TOEFL uses two types of computerized testing: computer adaptive testing (CAT) and computer-linear testing. Before we take a closer look at the different sections of the computer-based TOEFL, let's clarify the major differences between these two types of testing.

Computer Adaptive Testing

Computer adaptive testing is a complex system for determining your proficiency level in the English language. The following is a very simplified explanation of how computer adaptive and computer-based testing determine your TOEFL score.

Computer adaptive tests, or CATs, are quite different from the paper-and-pencil standardized tests you have probably seen in the past. For example, you might have taken the TOEFL before July 1998 early on a Friday or Saturday, in a huge room full of other test takers, all of whom were given identical tests with questions that ranged in difficulty from easy to hard. The CAT is a computer-based test that you take at a special test center, by yourself, at a time you schedule.

The major difference between the tests is that the CAT "adapts" to your performance. That is, each test taker is given a different mix of questions depending on how well he or she is doing on the test. This means the questions get harder or easier depending on whether you answer them correctly or not. Your score is not directly determined by how many questions you get right, but by the difficulty level of the questions you answer correctly.

Computer Adaptive Test Scoring

When you start a section, the computer:

- Assumes you have a medium level score as defined by ETS's TOEFL division
- Gives you a question of medium difficulty; that is, about half the people who take the test would probably get this question right, and half would get it wrong.

What happens next depends on whether you answered the question correctly. If you answer the question correctly:

- Your score goes up
- You are given a slightly harder question

If you answer a question incorrectly:

- Your score goes down
- You are given a slightly easier question

This pattern continues for the rest of the test. Every time you answer a question correctly, the computer raises your score, then gives you a slightly harder question. Conversely, every time you get a question wrong, the computer lowers your score, then gives you a slightly easier question.

Sample Computer Adaptive Test

To do your best on a CAT, you must have a basic understanding of the mechanics which it uses to find your score. Look at the adaptive test on the following pages. It follows the same sort of rules the CAT does in assigning a score and a new question.

As you answer the questions, notice what happens to your score as you answer questions correctly or incorrectly, and note what happens to the difficulty level of the questions if you get them right or wrong.

WORLD CAPITALS ADAPTIVE TEST

Instructions

a) Pick an answer for question 1, then check the answer on the page following the test.

b) Each time you get a question right, follow the ✓ arrow.

c) Each time you get a question wrong, follow the ✗ arrow.

d) Your current score is the value in the oval.

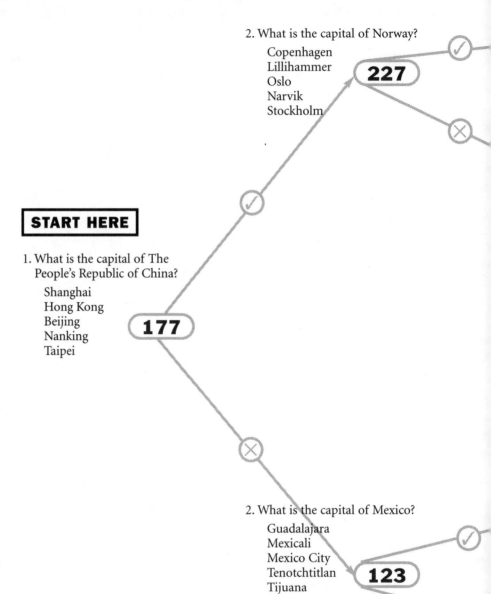

2. What is the capital of Norway?

Copenhagen
Lillihammer
Oslo
Narvik
Stockholm

227

START HERE

1. What is the capital of The People's Republic of China?

Shanghai
Hong Kong
Beijing
Nanking
Taipei

177

2. What is the capital of Mexico?

Guadalajara
Mexicali
Mexico City
Tenotchtitlan
Tijuana

123

3. What is the capital of Australia?

Canberra
Melbourne
Perth
Porpoise Spit
Sydney

263

✓

4. What is the capital of Eritrea?

Asmara
Berbera
Bosasu
Masawa
Mogadishu

287

✓ → **300**

✗ → **277**

✗

4. What is the capital of Brazil?

Amazonia
Brasilia
Buenos Aires
Rio de Janiero
Sao Paulo

237

✓ → **247**

✗ → **223**

3. What is the capital of Portugal?

Florence
Madrid
Le Paz
Lisbon
Sao Paulo

187

✓

4. What is the capital of Kenya?

Harare
Kampala
Lusaka
Mombassa
Nairobi

213

✓ → **223**

✗ → **200**

✗

4. What is the capital of Vietnam?

Bangkok
Hanoi
Ho Chi Minh City
Hue
Phnom Penh

160

✓ → **173**

✗ → **150**

3. What is the capital of Spain?

Barcelona
Bilbao
Granada
Madrid
Seville

163

✓

4. What is the capital of Iceland?

Ålborg
Birkenstock
Reykjavik
Trondheim
Björk

187

✓ → **200**

✗ → **173**

✗

4. What is the capital of Austria?

Berlin
Bonn
Prague
Linz
Vienna

140

✓ → **150**

✗ → **127**

3. What is the capital of France?

Madrid
Marseilles
Louisville
Paris
The Hague

83

✓

4. What is the capital of Japan?

Helsinki
Kyoto
Nakasone
Osaka
Tokyo

113

✓ → **127**

✗ → **100**

✗

4. What is the capital of the U.S.A.?

Washington, D.C.
Chicago
New York
Ottawa
Austin

53

✓ → **67**

✗ → **40**

Answer Key for Sample Test

Question 1: The capital of the People's Republic of China is Beijing.

Question 2: The capital of Norway is Oslo.
The capital of Mexico is Mexico City.

Question 3: The capital of Australia is Canberra.
The capital of Portugal is Lisbon.
The capital of Spain is Madrid.
The capital of France is Paris.

Question 4: The capital of Eritrea is Asmara.
The capital of Brazil is Brasilia.
The capital of Kenya is Nairobi.
The capital of Vietnam is Hanoi.
The capital of Iceland is Reykjavik.
The capital of Austria is Vienna.
The capital of Japan is Tokyo.
The capital of the U.S.A. is Washington, D.C.

How Does This Test Relate to the Real CAT Sections of the TOEFL?

So, how did you do on our World Capitals test? Of course, you will never see questions like this on the TOEFL; we used this example to illustrate a few important points about the computer adaptive test. Here's what you might have noticed:

1. The questions got progressively easier or harder depending on your performance.

The first question was of average difficulty (about half of test takers should get it right). Thereafter, the computer assigns questions based on your responses to previous questions. The test "adapts" to your ability as you take it. So, if you get the first question right, the second question should be a little harder, and if you get the first question wrong, the second question should be a little easier, and so on.

2. The more hard questions, the better.

Every question counts equally to your final score. However, harder questions generate higher scores and easier questions lower scores. So, you want to answer as many hard questions as possible. It's important to get to the hard questions early by answering questions right. The sooner you start to see harder questions, the higher your final score is likely to be.

Work systematically at the beginning of a TOEFL CAT section. Use scratch paper to help you organize your thinking. If you eliminate choices, cross them off and guess intelligently. The first 10–15 questions of a TOEFL CAT section are crucial in determining your ability estimate, so invest the necessary time to try and answer these questions correctly.

Make sure, however, that you pace yourself so that you have time to mark an answer for every question in the section. You will be penalized for questions you don't reach.

3. You must answer each question in the order it is given to you.

The structure of the test means you must take the questions one at a time, as they are given to you. You can't skip around on the CAT sections of the TOEFL; if you are stuck, you have to guess an answer if you want to move on.

Computer-Linear Testing

Computer-linear testing is similar to computer adaptive testing in that you record your answer on the computer; however, in computer-linear testing, the test does not adjust for your level. You will be given a set number of questions to answer. In a computer-linear testing situation, you can skip a question and come back to it later, but we don't recommend doing this as it is very easy to lose your place in the exam.

Form and Content of the Computer-Based TOEFL

The length of the computer-based TOEFL is more flexible than the paper-based TOEFL. You will have up to three-and-a-half hours to complete the exam, which includes time for a break. Your appointment for the exam will cover a four-and-a-half hour time slot; this is to allow ample time to do the necessary paperwork. When you begin a section, the total number of questions will appear at the top of the screen. On each question screen, you will be provided with information telling you which question you are currently on and how many questions there are in total.

Computer-based TOEFL questions are divided into four sections: Section I, Listening Comprehension; Section II, Structure; Section III, Reading Comprehension; and Section IV, Writing. Each section is timed separately. You have 40 or 60 minutes to work on Section I, 15 or 20 minutes to work on Section II, 70 or 90 minutes to work on Section III, and 30 minutes to work on Section IV. Once you are done with a section, you cannot return to it.

The following is a general overview of each section of the computer-based TOEFL. For more detailed information on what you can expect from the computer-based versions of these different sections, check out the Listening, Structure, Reading, and Writing Power Lessons later in this book.

Listening Comprehension

The Listening Comprehension section of the TOEFL CBT is computer adaptive. You will have 40 or 60 minutes to complete Section I, Listening Comprehension. This section consists of 30 or 50 questions in which you listen to spoken English and answer questions that test how well you understood what you heard. This section consists of two parts: A and B. In part A, you will hear a number of short conversations, anywhere from 6 to 20 seconds long, and be asked to answer a question about each one. In part B, you will hear 2 or 3 longer conversations, from 30 seconds to 1 minute, and a few long talks that are 1.5 to 2.5 minutes long. You will be asked to answer 4 or 5 questions about each one. The subject matter for these questions is academic or university-related. Computer-based listening comprehension questions may appear in the following formats:

- Four-choice
- Multiple answer (pick two of four choices)
- Ordering or matching questions (click on one element, then click on another to create a match)
- Graphic region selection (click on a picture or element in a picture)

Structure

The Structure section of the computer-based TOEFL, Section II, is computer adaptive. You will have 15 or 20 minutes to complete this section. It consists of 20 or 25 questions in which you either complete a sentence or identify an error.

There are two question formats mixed together here:

- Four-choice
- Click on underlined word

Reading Comprehension

The Reading Comprehension section of the computer-based TOEFL, Section III, is computer linear. You will have 70 or 90 minutes to complete it. You must read 5 to 8 academic reading passages and will be asked a number of questions about the content of what you have read and the meanings of the words as they are used in the passage. The total number of questions will be either 44 or 60. The computer-based Reading Comprehension section includes slightly longer passages than the paper-based test. You must read from the screen and scroll in order to read the entire passage. There are four question formats:

- Four-choice
- Click on word, paragraph, or sentence
- Insert text
- Graphic region choice (click on a picture or element in a picture)

Assessment of Written English

The Writing section of the TOEFL CBT is required. You will have 30 minutes to write an essay in response to a single topic that appears on the screen. You can either type your answer on the computer or write your essay by hand on a separate sheet of paper. The results from this section will be combined with those from the Structure section to give a final scaled score. The computer does not figure out your grade on this section; it must be graded the old-fashioned way—by human beings who are specifically trained to score your essay.

ADMINISTRATION OF THE TOEFL CBT

Recent changes in the administration of the TOEFL include:

- When and where students take the TOEFL
- The number of questions a student must answer
- The duration of the exam
- The overall scaled score
- Format

ETS has a contract with Sylvan Technology Centers and some university computer centers to administer the computer-based TOEFL exam. Each of the centers is set up according to strict regulations. Even the furniture, color of the walls, and number of computers available are the same in each center!

One of the major changes is that you can now take the TOEFL any day of the year (except Sundays and holidays), and you have a choice of morning or afternoon to take your test. You should register early to take the test: Sylvan Technology Centers can accommodate only up to 15 test takers at one time, and you may be taking your exam next to other students who are taking other ETS standardized tests. You can still take the test once per calendar month, but if you register for a test twice in one month, you will not receive a score for the second exam and your money will not be refunded.

You cannot eat, drink, or smoke while taking the test. Your personal belongings can be stored in a locker provided to you by the testing center. You should not bring anything but yourself into the testing center—no pencils, pens, paper, calculators, books of any kind, dictionaries, electronic equipment, watches with calculators, pagers, or translators. Finally, you will not get any scratch paper and you are not permitted to take notes during the exam. If you choose to hand write your essay, you will be given paper at that time.

How to Register for the TOEFL

To register to take the TOEFL, you need to fill out the form in the *Information Bulletin*, which also contains a list of all the test dates for the TOEFL, the TWE, and the TSE. Copies of the *Bulletin* are available at many United States educational commissions, United States Information Service (USIS) offices and libraries, binational centers, and private English language schools. You will be charged for the test. Check the *Bulletin* for details or contact ETS.

If you cannot get a copy of the *Information Bulletin* locally, you can write to:

TOEFL/TSE Publications
P.O. Box 6154
Princeton, NJ 08541-6154 USA
Phone: (609) 771-7100
Fax: (609) 771-7500
E-mail: toefl@ets.org
www.toefl.org

Test Day Tips

(1) Arrive at the test center at least a half hour before your scheduled test time in order to check in. If you arrive late for your appointment, you may not be able to take the test at that time and your registration fee will not be refunded.

(2) Make sure you bring proper photo identification with you to the testing center. There are strict requirements for the Photo Identification section. In the United States, you can use your passport as official photo identification (exceptions apply to U.S. citizens, naturalized citizens, immigrants, refugees, or members of the U.S. Armed Forces). If you are taking the exam outside of the United States, you can use your passport as a photo ID. Be sure to read the latest ETS bulletin to see what the acceptable alternative identifications are for the region in which you are taking the exam, if you do not currently hold a passport.

(3) You will also need your appointment confirmation number, which is given to you when you register for the exam.

(4) Compose a list of institutions to which you would like your test scores sent. You can have scores automatically sent to four institutions at no additional charge.

SCORING

When you take the official TOEFL CBT, you will be able to know your score immediately before leaving the test center. ETS will send reports of your score directly to the institutions you have chosen, and to you, about 2–3 weeks after you have taken the test. You will receive four scores, one for each of the three TOEFL sections, and most importantly, a three-digit total score.

Your total score is based on the number of correct answers you identified, and adjusted (the technical word for this is *scaled*) for the difficulty level of the particular TOEFL items you answered. The total score for the computer-based TOEFL is reported on a 40–300 scale, and the scores for each section are reported on a scale of 2–30. Most students get a total score of between 120 and 240. For the paper-based TOEFL, scores range from 310–677, with scores for each section reported on scales from 31–68. Most students get a total score of between 440 and 580.

The chart on the following page will give you an idea of how TOEFL scores measure English proficiency. Remember that the lowest possible computer-based TOEFL score is 40 (310 on the paper-based TOEFL), and the highest possible score is 300 (677 on the paper-based TOEFL).

TOEFL SCORE (CBT/ Paper-Based)	PROFICIENCY LEVEL	PROFICIENCY DESCRIPTION
83 (380)	Elementary Proficiency	Able to satisfy basic survival requirements, maintain very simple face-to-face conversations on familiar topics; thinks in native language and translates into English.
133 (450)	Intermediate Proficiency	Can initiate and maintain predictable face-to-face conversations; range and control of language limited; demonstrates emerging, but not consistent, basic grammar; can read very simple English texts.
213 (550)	Working Proficiency	Able to satisfy routine social demands; facility with concrete subject matter and language; however, needs more practice in academic-level reading.
267 (630)	Advanced Working Proficiency	Approaching native proficiency in English; able to satisfy most university-level academic requirements with language usage that is often, but not always, acceptable and effective; however, effective use of language may deteriorate under tension or pressure.

Passing TOEFL Score

There is no "passing" or "failing" score on the TOEFL. The test measures English language proficiency only and it is up to the individual college or university to set its own minimum TOEFL score for admission. Minimum scores can vary from a low of 133 (450 on the paper-based TOEFL) to a high of 267 (630 on the paper-based TOEFL) or more. A score of 300 (677 on the paper-based TOEFL) is considered perfect.

Keep in mind that schools with low TOEFL admissions score requirements may also have lower academic standards. In many colleges, to major in communications, journalism, public relations, marketing, advertising, and English/American literature, you need a TOEFL CBT score of 250 (which is the equivalent of a score of 600 on the paper-based TOEFL). The most prestigious American universities require a TOEFL score of 250 (600 on the paper-based TOEFL) or more for all students admitted. Most top-tier master of business administration (MBA) programs require a TOEFL score of 250 (600) in addition to good GMAT scores.

Paper-Based Scores versus Computer-Based Scores

The concordance table on the following pages will tell you how paper-based TOEFL scores compare with computer-based TOEFL scores. For more details on how each section is scored, read through the introductory pages of each Power Lesson section carefully.

TOEFL Concordance Table Total Score Comparison

Paper-Based TOEFL	Computer-Based TOEFL	Paper-Based TOEFL	Computer-Based TOEFL	Paper-Based TOEFL	Computer-Based TOEFL
677	300	553	217	430	117
673	297	550	213	427	113
670	293	547	210	423	113
667	290	543	207	420	110
663	287	540	207	417	107
660	287	537	203	413	103
657	283	533	200	410	103
653	280	530	197	407	100
650	280	527	197	403	97
647	277	523	193	400	97
643	273	520	190	397	93
640	273	517	187	393	90
637	270	513	188	390	90
633	267	510	180	387	87
630	267	507	180	383	83
627	263	503	177	380	83
623	263	500	173	377	80
620	260	497	170	373	77
617	260	493	167	370	77
613	257	490	163	367	73
610	253	487	163	363	73
607	253	483	160	360	70
603	250	480	157	357	70
600	250	477	153	353	67
597	247	473	150	350	63
593	243	470	150	347	63
590	243	467	147	343	60
587	240	463	143	340	60
583	237	460	140	337	57
580	237	457	137	333	57
577	233	453	133	330	53
573	230	450	133	327	50
570	230	447	130	323	50
567	227	443	127	320	47
563	223	440	123	317	47
560	220	437	123	313	43
557	220	433	120	310	40

TOEFL Concordance Table Total Score Range Comparison

Paper-Based TOEFL	Computer-Based TOEFL	Paper-Based TOEFL	Computer-Based TOEFL
660–677	287–300	460–477	140–153
640–657	273–283	440–457	123–137
620–637	260–270	420–437	110–123
600–617	250–260	400–417	97–107
580–597	237–247	380–397	83–93
560–577	220–233	360–377	70–80
540–557	207–220	340–357	60–70
520–537	190–203	320–337	47–57
500–517	173–187	310–317	40–47
480–497	157–170		

TOEFL Concordance Table Section Scaled Scores

Listening Comprehension		Structure/Writing		Reading	
Paper-Based TOEFL	Computer-Based TOEFL	Paper-Based TOEFL	Computer-Based TOEFL	Paper-Based TOEFL	Computer-Based TOEFL
68	30	68	30	67	30
67	30	67	29	66	29
66	29	66	28	65	28
65	28	65	28	64	28
64	27	64	27	63	27
63	27	63	27	62	26
62	26	62	26	61	26
61	25	61	26	60	25
60	25	60	25	59	25
59	24	59	25	58	24
58	23	58	24	57	23
57	22	57	23	56	22
56	22	56	23	55	21
55	21	55	22	54	21
54	20	54	21	53	20
53	19	53	20	52	19
52	18	52	20	51	18
51	17	51	19	50	17
50	16	50	18	49	16
49	15	49	17	48	16
48	14	48	17	47	15
47	13	47	16	46	14
46	12	46	15	45	13
45	11	45	14	44	13
44	10	44	14	43	12
43	9	43	13	42	11
42	9	42	12	41	11
41	8	41	11	40	10
40	7	40	11	39	9
39	6	39	10	38	9
38	6	38	9	37	8
37	5	37	9	36	8
36	5	36	8	35	7
35	4	35	8	34	7
34	4	34	7	33	6
33	3	33	7	32	6
32	3	32	6	31	5
31	2	31	6		

FREQUENTLY ASKED QUESTIONS

Q: How will studying from a book help me prepare for the computer-based TOEFL?

Naturally, the CD-ROM that accompanies this book will allow you to review for the TOEFL CBT in true CBT-like environment but you'll also find the book useful for this purpose. Even though the format of the test is different on the TOEFL CBT—for example, you may be asked to click on a graphic element or choose two out of four answer choices—the skills being tested remain the same as those on the paper-based TOEFL, and this book provides you with ample opportunity to practice them. The Listening Comprehension section has several question types that are not easily reproduced in a book, but the Listening Power Lessons offer you practice in two of them. The Structure section of the TOEFL CBT is virtually identical to the paper-based exam, except that sentence completion and error identification questions are not segregated. The types of questions you'll encounter on the Reading Section of the CBT can be found—in a somewhat modified form—in the Reading Power section of this book. Reading is actually a little easier on the computer-based exam, as the computer will highlight or otherwise indicate the section of the passage in which the answer can be found for certain question types. As for the Writing section, it is your choice whether you will keyboard or hand write your response, and this book provides a great deal of focused writing practice.

Q: How often can I take the computer-based TOEFL?

You can take the computer-based TOEFL only once per calendar month. If you register for the TOEFL CBT twice in one month, your second score will not be recorded and you will have wasted your time and money. Be sure to check with ETS when scheduling your exam to make sure a sufficient amount of time has passed since your last exam.

Q: Is the TOEFL written or administered by the U.S. government's Department of Education?

No. The U.S. government has nothing to do with the TOEFL. The TOEFL is administered by the Educational Testing Service. ETS is a private, nongovernmental, not-for-profit organization that writes, manages, and administers standard exams for American college and university entrance. Look up their Web site at www.ets.org for more information.

Q: Is it possible to use a TOEFL score from a test taken a long time ago?

Not usually, no. Admissions officers want to know what your current English level is, so most admissions officers require a recent TOEFL score taken within the previous six months when they consider a candidate for admission.

Schools frequently have this rule because TOEFL scores can drop significantly if a person takes a break of longer than two months from intensive English study. This is especially true if a student's level of English proficiency has not yet reached the 550 level (213 on the CBT).

Q: Can students prepare for the TOEFL in the same way that they study for a typical college exam?

No. Most exams test a student's knowledge of a set of information. There may or may not be a lot of information that the student needs to know, but it is always a finite amount. A student can make a list of information that he or she must learn and study it item by item.

The TOEFL, on the other hand, tests English proficiency. A language cannot be summed up in a list. The best way to improve your TOEFL scores is by improving your overall proficiency in the language. Another way to improve your TOEFL score is to become very familiar with the exam. You should take several practice exams and you should know what kinds of questions and general topics to expect. You can also learn certain test-taking strategies—ways of finding the correct answer more quickly. This book will help you do both.

YOU'RE IN CHARGE!

This section is entitled "You're in Charge!" because we want to emphasize that you must take control of your own English learning. In addition to introducing you to the TOEFL, giving you practice tests, and suggesting test-taking strategies, this book will show you how to take charge of your own English learning.

The Limitations of Test Preparation Without Intensive English Study

For a good TOEFL score, it is essential that you become familiar with the test and the kinds of questions the test asks. This is true whether you are taking the paper-based or the computer-based TOEFL. A student who takes the test without this kind of preparation will not do as well as he or she would have with test preparation. So test preparation helps. The creators of this course have seen students' scores jump as much as 40 points (or approximately 50 points on the paper-based TOEFL) (paper-based TOEFL equivalents appear in parentheses) in a short, ten-week, 40-hour course.

The problem is that an increase of 20 (30), 30 (40), or even 40 (50) points may not be enough. If a student starts with a proficiency level of 123 (440), a jump of 40 (50) points will not be sufficient for him or her to get into a university that requires a score of 213 (550) for admission. Even worse, a second or third TOEFL preparation course almost never improves a student's score as much as the first. So our imaginary student, who jumped from a 133 (450) to a 163 (490) after just ten weeks of TOEFL preparation, may have only a score of 173 (500) after two or three more courses—still not enough to get into the university he or she wants to attend.

What this student needs is more knowledge of English, not more TOEFL preparation. Too many learners of English don't understand this, and they continue to spend more money on too many TOEFL-preparation courses, or worse, they become frustrated and abandon their dreams of studying in the United States.

ETS, the makers of the TOEFL exam, once conducted a study that showed that, on average, an increase of 30 (40) points on the TOEFL requires about 300 hours of intensive English study. The details of the study are shown in the graph on the following page.

Average Hours of Study Needed in Order to Reach Your Goal

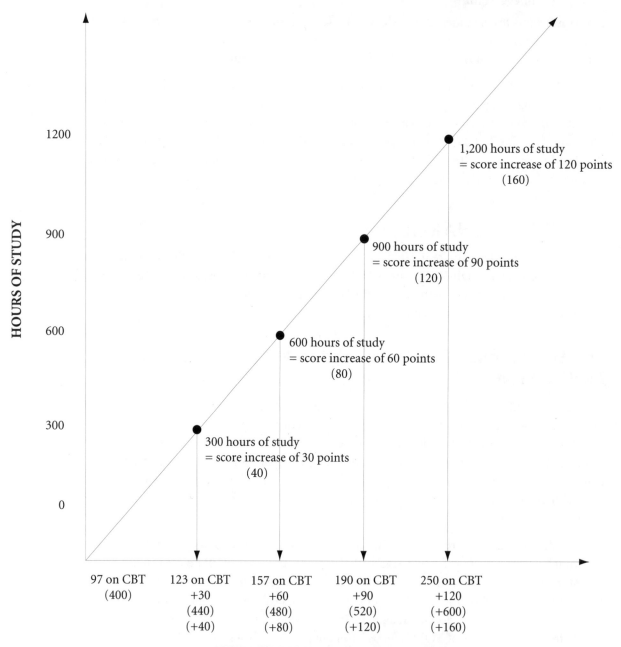

HOURS OF STUDY

1200

900

600

300

0

1,200 hours of study
= score increase of 120 points
(160)

900 hours of study
= score increase of 90 points
(120)

600 hours of study
= score increase of 60 points
(80)

300 hours of study
= score increase of 30 points
(40)

97 on CBT	123 on CBT	157 on CBT	190 on CBT	250 on CBT
(400)	+30	+60	+90	+120
	(440)	(480)	(520)	(+600)
	(+40)	(+80)	(+120)	(+160)

AVERAGE INCREASE IN TOEFL POINTS

The Importance of Vocabulary

Look at the sentences below. They could all easily appear on the TOEFL exam. Do any of the underlined words seem incorrect to you?

She wants to marry <u>as tall a man</u> as possible.

You'll just have to <u>make do with what</u> you have.

KAPLAN

Don't <u>talk with your mouth full</u>.

The French <u>founded</u> the city in 1678.

The fact is, there is nothing wrong with any of these sentences, no matter how strange they may look to a nonnative English speaker.

The point of the little test you just took is to show that even though no section of the TOEFL is called "Vocabulary," there is no doubt that vocabulary plays an important—perhaps the most important—role in every section.

Perhaps you're thinking, "Sure, I can see why vocabulary is important in the Reading Comprehension section, but why is it so important in the Listening Comprehension or Structure sections?"

Of course, the Listening Comprehension section tests your listening skills. But how can you expect to answer questions about what you have heard if you do not know the meaning of what is said? Moreover, in the Structure section (the grammar section) of the TOEFL, getting the correct answer often depends more on your knowledge of English idioms than your knowledge of English grammar. Even more often, it depends on your knowing whether something "sounds right" or not.

Look at the sentences above again. Do the underlined words "sound right" to you? If one or more of them sounds wrong, then you need to add that expression to your English vocabulary.

Keep in mind that vocabulary does not involve only individual words. It also includes idioms (like *to keep your head*, meaning "not to panic"), phrasal verbs (like *do something over*, meaning "to do something a second time"), and collocations (words that often appear together, like *sparsely populated*, meaning "having a low population"). Vocabulary, for the purposes of TOEFL, means using words the way real people use them.

Take charge of your own vocabulary building by collecting English words and expressions that you encounter in films, TV shows, magazines, books, and newspapers.

The Importance of Reading

Like vocabulary, reading is at the heart of the TOEFL exam, basically because it is at the heart of good academic skill preparation. Success on the TOEFL, and in any American college or university, depends heavily on a student's ability to read well.

Many students find the Reading Comprehension section of the TOEFL extremely difficult. To make matters worse, the Reading Comprehension section comes at the end of the exam, when concentration requires real effort. The best way to prepare for this section, and for your academic studies in general, is to do a lot of reading in English on your own.

Varying the content of your reading as much as possible is strongly recommended. This means that your reading should not be limited to one topic or style. For example, if you read a lot of literature, you should try to read science articles from a general-interest magazine like *Newsweek*. On the other hand, if you love science, read some short stories or a Hemingway novel. As you may already know from your native language, these are two very different types of reading.

The reason for this advice is that the Reading Comprehension section of the TOEFL requires the test taker to read an extremely varied amount of topics, from literature to geology to American history. If you can't read many different types of writing well—if you aren't familiar with different styles of writing and the different kinds of vocabulary belonging to different topics—you will probably not do well on the TOEFL.

Here is a list of the topics most often found in the reading section of the TOEFL, with a percentage indicating how frequently they appear.

- Natural and physical sciences (40%)
- American and natural history (30%)
- Biography (15%)
- Social science (10%)
- General interest (5%)

To get started, look for the chapter entitled "Recurring TOEFL Topics and Related Vocabulary" later in this book. But remember that this is only a start: It's your job to *take charge* by going out and reading as much and as widely as you can in English.

THE TOEFL STUDY PLAN

In this section we offer a plan to the self-study student who is preparing for the TOEFL by himself or herself. To be as prepared as possible for the TOEFL, a student should go through every section of this book. The TOEFL Study Plan below offers advice on how to do that. How long it takes the student to go through all the lessons depends on how much time he or she spends on them per day.

(1) Study the chapter "TOEFL Test Strategies," and the "computer-based TOEFL" sections at the beginning of the Listening, Structure, and Reading Power Lessons.

Test strategies are suggestions on how to take the TOEFL. They can improve student scores significantly. The computer-based TOEFL sections will tell you how to tackle different types of questions on this exam.

(2) Take the paper-based Diagnostic Test.

Use the answer key and the conversion chart after the test to give yourself a grade for each section as well as an overall grade for the test. Decide on your areas of weakness.

(3) Begin a program of extensive reading in English.

Read widely—about many different topics, including the topics given in the "Recurring TOEFL Topics and Related Vocabulary" section towards the back of the book. Begin collecting vocabulary words and expressions from the reading. You should do this even if the Reading Comprehension section was not the part of the exam you did most poorly in.

(4) Go through half of the Power Lessons.

The Power Lessons can be done in any order: listening first, then structure, then reading; or, alternatively, a student could do one listening lesson and three structure lessons, followed by one reading lesson. And don't forget the writing exercises in the Writing Power chapter.

As you go through the Power Lessons of this book, you should take charge of your English acquisition by doing additional work in these areas. If the Listening Comprehension section was very difficult for you, schedule time to watch movies or TV programs in English, or to listen to English-language cassettes. If the Structure section was especially difficult, get a good reference grammar book and learn more about the grammar structures you got wrong on the practice test. If the Reading Comprehension section was your problem, go through the practice test and identify the topics that gave you the most trouble. Then go to an English language library or bookstore to get books and/or magazines on the troublesome topics.

(5) Take one of the computer-based TOEFL practice tests on the CD-ROM.

Try one of the full-length computer-based practice tests on the CD-ROM included with this book. Use the answer key and the conversion chart at the back of the book and/or the concordance charts on pages 19–20 to give yourself a grade for each section as well as an overall grade for the test.

Are your areas of weakness the same as after the first practice test? If so, you need more practice. Identify a new set of areas of weakness, and devote additional time to these.

(6) Finish the Power Lessons.

Don't forget to continue doing additional reading and vocabulary building as you work through the Power Lessons.

(7) Take the other computer-based TOEFL practice test on the CD-ROM.

(8) Do the "Recurring TOEFL Topics and Related Vocabulary" section towards the back of the book.

Make sure your outside reading covers these topics.

TOEFL FACT SHEET

The following is an overview of the differences between the paper-based TOEFL and the TOEFL CBT.

Paper-Based TOEFL

Total number of questions: 140
Duration: 2–2.5 hours (3–3.5 hours at test site)
Overall scaled score: 300 to 677
Format: Three scored sections, each with a subscore of 30 to 68

Section I: Listening Comprehension

Number of questions: 50
Duration: 30 or 40 minutes
Part A—Short conversations (30 questions)
Part B—Longer conversations (8 questions)
Part C—Talks (12 questions)

Section II: Structure and Written Expression

Number of questions: 40
Duration: 25 minutes
Part A—Sentence completion (15 questions)
Part B—Error identification (25 questions)

Section III: Reading Comprehension

Number of questions: 50
Duration: 55 minutes
5 or 6 reading passages (8–12 questions per passage)

Computer-Based TOEFL

Total number of questions: varies
Duration: varies—2.25–3 hours (up to 4.5 hours at test site)
Overall scaled score: 0 to 300
Format: Four sections. Sections I, II, and III have subscores of 0 to 30. Section IV has subscores of 0 to 6.

Section I: Listening Comprehension

Number of questions: 30 or 50
Duration: 40 or 60 minutes
Part A—Short conversations
Part B—Longer conversations and talks
Computer adaptive

Section II: Structure

Number of questions: 20 or 25
Duration: 15 or 20 minutes
Sentence completion and error identification questions are mixed together.

Section III: Reading Comprehension

Number of questions: 44 or 60. The test taker will see the total number of questions displayed on screen prior to beginning this section.
Duration: 70 or 90 minutes
5 to 8 reading passages (8 to 12 questions per passage)

Section IV: Writing

Number of questions: 1
Duration: 30 minutes

Kaplan's TOEFL CBT Test Strategies

An examination is meant to test a person's knowledge or skills in a particular area. But sometimes two people with the same knowledge may not receive the same score on an exam. This is because only one of them knows how to do well on the exam.

That's what test-taking strategies are: methods of taking exams that lead to greater success. This book is designed to give you every advantage on the TOEFL. Of course, we want to improve your English proficiency—that's the job of the Power Lessons. But we also want to give you the test-taking strategies you need in order to get the very best TOEFL score possible.

In this section, we offer you a number of different types of test strategies. These strategies will help you to improve your score dramatically on both the paper-based and the computer-based versions of the TOEFL exam. For more specific information on how to do your best on each section of the TOEFL CBT, turn to the introductory pages of the Power Lessons. For example, to find out more about listening comprehension computer-based test strategies, turn to the "Listening Comprehension for the TOEFL CBT" section of the Listening Power Lessons.

To benefit as much as you can from all of these strategies, you should review them before you take every practice exam. Review them again before you take the official TOEFL.

The basic TOEFL CBT Strategies you should keep in mind are as follows:

- Know the directions ahead of time.
- Know how to use the computer ahead of time. Practice scrolling and using the mouse and the keyboard.
- Leave no blanks. Guess if you don't know the answer.
- Budget your time.
- Read all the answer choices before selecting the best one.
- Develop your stamina (this version of the test is much longer than the paper-based test).

Know the Directions Ahead of Time

Make absolutely sure you know the directions for each section of the TOEFL CBT. Read and reread the directions given on the CBT practice tests on the CD-ROM, or on the computer-based TOEFL tutorial CD-ROM distributed by ETS. Contact ETS at 1 (609) 771-7100 for a free copy of this CD-ROM; you can also visit their Web site at http://www.toefl.org. Once you learn how to do the questions, you won't have to read the directions during the real TOEFL exam. This means that on the Structure sections as well as the Reading Comprehension section, you can begin the test immediately instead of reading the directions. This will save you a lot of time.

Know How to Use the Computer Ahead of Time

Try to use computers whenever possible. Most Kaplan centers are equipped with computer equipment and will have some TOEFL practice programs for you to work on. You can also practice the skills you will need for taking the TOEFL CBT on any computer that uses a mouse. Public libraries in most cities will have computers that you can use for free. Surfing the Internet is a great way to practice the computer skills you will need for this test because many sites ask you to click on buttons or pictures, have long blocks of text that require you to scroll, and have audio clips and places in which you can write your own text. Plus, since most of the Internet is in English, this is a great opportunity to practice your language skills as well!

Leave No Blanks; Guess If You Don't Know the Answer

On the TOEFL CBT, you will not be permitted to leave "blanks" in the Listening Comprehension and Structure sections of the exam. In fact, if you fail to click on at least one answer, you will not be permitted to go on to the next question, and the computer will give you a message saying that you must make a selection. Meanwhile, for the Reading Comprehension section, you are allowed to leave blanks and skip questions, but this is not a good idea as you risk forgetting to answer a question. Failure to complete the Writing section will result in a score of zero. As a general rule, you should avoid leaving blanks. Remember that you are not penalized for getting a wrong answer—in fact, you have a 25 percent chance of getting the question right, compared to 0 percent if you leave it blank.

In computer adaptive testing, your goal is to answer as many questions as possible at the highest level of difficulty. Because the bigger jumps in your score are determined by the earlier questions in these tests, it is better to spend a little more time on the first third of the set of questions. If you still have some questions left at the end and you have very little time left, try clicking on either of the two middle choices. If you must click on two, try the second and fourth answer choice. If it is a matching question, drag the first item to the middle slot, the second item to the third, and the third item to the first. These are only guessing strategies, so don't rely on them throughout the test—only use them if you absolutely do not know the answer and cannot make an educated guess!

A wise test taker will make educated guesses on the TOEFL. This means using what you already know to eliminate answers that you know are wrong. Each section of this book will help you with strategies for making educated guesses on the various sections of the test. Another point to consider when making an educated guess is that you will rarely see more than four consecutive identical answers. If you are certain about your answers to questions 21–24, and they are all (C), but in question 25 you are not sure if the answer is (C) or (D), you should select (D).

Suppose that on the entire exam you get six or seven questions correct by guessing. That can raise your score by 25 to 30 points. In fact, guessing is so important that we suggest that in the last two minutes of every section of the test, you stop working on the questions and make guesses for every unanswered question on the answer sheet. When you do this, always guess (B) or (C), because on past TOEFLs these have been the most common answers.

Read All the Answer Choices Before Selecting the Best One

Don't pick the first answer choice that "looks good." Read all the answer choices and then pick the best answer. Many of the wrong answers on the TOEFL have been purposely written to confuse you. We call these types of wrong answers "distractors." In order to distinguish the distractors from the right answer, you must always read all the answer choices.

Develop Your Stamina

The TOEFL CBT allows a ten-minute break between the Listening Comprehension section and the remainder of the test. Section III is long. You need to keep working even if you are tired. Take as many practice tests as you can as if they were real tests. Do not let yourself be distracted. Try to stick to the amount of time that it takes for each section. Do not get up for a break, or a snack or even to use the bathroom! You need to increase your ability to sit in one place for an extended period.

Other Tips

Eat a good breakfast on the day of your test, but nothing greasy or unusual. The test is long and hunger can be very distracting. If you are a person who gets hungry easily, it might be a good idea to eat an apple or some bread just before the test begins. Don't drink too much coffee or tea beforehand; a lot of caffeine (or any other drug, for that matter) is a bad idea. Finally, remember that if you are taking the TOEFL CBT, there is no food or drink allowed in the testing center.

PART TWO:
TOEFL
Diagnostic Test

Directions for the TOEFL Diagnostic Test

This diagnostic test is intended as a tool to help guide you in your TOEFL preparation. Ideally, you should take this test before you go through any of the Power Lessons or the computer-based practice tests on the CD-ROM.

Although this diagnostic test is paper-based, it tests the same basic content that is covered in the TOEFL CBT exam. Therefore, even if you plan to take the computer-based version of the exam, the Diagnostic Test will give you a good indication of the kinds of questions you can expect. It will also help you to identify potential areas of weakness. Based on how you do on the different sections of the Diagnostic Test, you can decide which areas you need to spend most time on in your TOEFL studies. For example, if your score is not as high as you would like it to be for the Reading Comprehension section of the Diagnostic Test, you should pay particularly close attention to the Reading Power Practice section of this book.

Make this practice test as much like a real TOEFL test as possible. This means that you must find a space of about two-and-a-half hours during which you can take the practice test completely uninterrupted. Do not take breaks between the three sections of the practice test; you are not allowed breaks during the real TOEFL, so you need to build up your mental stamina.

As you take the Diagnostic Test, give yourself only the allotted time for each section of the test. Stop when your time is up. Then use the answer key and conversion chart that follow the test to give yourself a TOEFL score. (Don't forget to check the Listening Comprehension script immediately following the test if you don't understand why you got a particular Listening Comprehension answer wrong.)

TOEFL Diagnostic Test Listening Comprehension

SECTION I

🕐 **Time allowed for this section: 30 or 40 minutes**

Directions: Listening Comprehension Section

In this section of the test, you will demonstrate your ability to understand conversations and talks in English. You will find the audio tracks for this section on the CD-ROM included with this book. There are three parts to this section, with different directions for each part. Answer all the questions according to what the speakers say or imply. When you take the actual TOEFL test, you will not be allowed to take notes or write in your test book. Try to work on this sample test in the same way.

PART A

Listen to Test_1A.mov.

<u>Directions:</u> In Part A, you will hear two people having short conversations. After each conversation, you will hear a question. The conversations and questions will not be repeated. After you hear a question, read the four possible answers and choose the best answer.

Here is an example.

> **On the recording, you hear: (Listen to the CD-ROM)**
>
> **In your book, you read:**
> - ● He is too tired to walk in the park.
> - Ⓑ He agrees to go walking in the park with her.
> - Ⓒ He is not Jim. His name is Pete.
> - Ⓓ He doesn't know what to do.

You learn from the conversation that the man is "beat," an idiomatic expression meaning "very tired." Therefore, the best answer to the question, "What does the man say?" is (A).

1. Ⓐ It's a bad idea.

    Ⓑ She can't understand where he got such an idea.

    Ⓒ It's a good idea.

    Ⓓ It's insane.

2. Ⓐ It sounds like a bird.

    Ⓑ It reminds her of a movie.

    Ⓒ It's for the birds.

    Ⓓ He should have been cited.

3. Ⓐ the woman's roommate

    Ⓑ Jane

    Ⓒ the man

    Ⓓ Jane's sister

4. Ⓐ She doesn't understand the idea.

    Ⓑ She's surprised to hear this.

    Ⓒ She doesn't like the idea.

    Ⓓ She didn't know where the chapel was.

5. Ⓐ out in the fields

    Ⓑ on a trip to the fields

    Ⓒ playing field hockey

    Ⓓ on a class outing

6. Ⓐ She dares him to skip class.

    Ⓑ She would dare to skip a class.

    Ⓒ She will go to class.

    Ⓓ She dared not skip a class.

7. Ⓐ only if she can't find a job

    Ⓑ only if she can't get in

    Ⓒ only if she is working

    Ⓓ she didn't get in

8. Ⓐ She didn't understand it.

    Ⓑ She caught the joke.

    Ⓒ The speaker was too loud.

    Ⓓ He is always kidding.

9. Ⓐ to keep a diary

    Ⓑ to become a journalist

    Ⓒ to become an adviser

    Ⓓ to stop writing creatively

10. Ⓐ Her writing is lovely.

    Ⓑ Her writing is illegible.

    Ⓒ She would be a good typist.

    Ⓓ He doesn't have time to read it.

11. Ⓐ He shouldn't be upset.

    Ⓑ He needs to find a place to settle down in and get a job.

    Ⓒ He should sit down.

    Ⓓ The matter is settled.

12. Ⓐ pick up their daughter first

    Ⓑ come with their daughter

    Ⓒ pick a day camp for their daughter

    Ⓓ come after they leave their daughter at camp

13. Ⓐ in a bookstore

    Ⓑ in a library

    Ⓒ in a classroom

    Ⓓ at a street fair

14. Ⓐ an exploding idea

    Ⓑ She has a good idea.

    Ⓒ She doesn't know.

    Ⓓ a loud explosion

15. Ⓐ go if she can find a coat

    Ⓑ go for a higher fare

    Ⓒ go if she can afford to

    Ⓓ go to another coast

16. Ⓐ She forgot to warn him.

    Ⓑ She knew it would fill up quickly.

    Ⓒ He should never take that class.

    Ⓓ The class contains a warning.

17. Ⓐ in a dressing room

    Ⓑ at a theater

    Ⓒ at a train station

    Ⓓ in a classroom

18. Ⓐ waitress

    Ⓑ physics teacher

    Ⓒ physical education teacher

    Ⓓ army officer

19. Ⓐ They've bitten off more than they can chew.

    Ⓑ She feels famished.

    Ⓒ She can't see over her head.

    Ⓓ She sees an overhead projector.

20. Ⓐ It's a great chance.

    Ⓑ He should go away for a while.

    Ⓒ He should forget about it.

    Ⓓ It's a ridiculous idea.

21. Ⓐ He hates both of them.

    Ⓑ He can't make up his mind.

    Ⓒ He's made up his mind.

    Ⓓ He's really torn up inside.

22. Ⓐ Who is Norman?

    Ⓑ Where is Norman?

    Ⓒ What will be discussed next time?

    Ⓓ Why did she say Norman Conquest?

23. Ⓐ a traffic jam

    Ⓑ he had an accident

    Ⓒ the coast was clear

    Ⓓ he got lost

24. Ⓐ when the professor will return

    Ⓑ when the exam will take place

    Ⓒ why the exam was called off

    Ⓓ where Dr. Jones will be

25. (A) He assumes it's the same as previous breaks.

    (B) He broke up last March too.

    (C) He plans to stay there for spring break.

    (D) He has no idea.

26. (A) to ask to see the manager

    (B) to see a busboy

    (C) to look at a menu

    (D) to look for a menu

27. (A) out of town

    (B) off campus

    (C) Jones Hall

    (D) Riley Hall

28. (A) by Butler Hall

    (B) It's not on the map.

    (C) Neither of them knows.

    (D) It's in a new building too.

29. (A) They should stop working for a while.

    (B) They should stop breaking for a while.

    (C) They should get some breakfast.

    (D) They should break up.

30. (A) He slept in the classroom.

    (B) It was boring.

    (C) He didn't go.

    (D) Professor Weiss slept right through it.

PART B

Listen to Test_1B.mov.

Directions: On this part of the test, you will hear slightly longer conversations. After each conversation, you will hear several questions. Neither the conversations nor the questions will be repeated.

After you hear a question, read the four possible answers in this book and choose the best one. Then, on your answer sheet, find the number of the question and fill in the space that corresponds to the letter of the answer you have chosen.

Remember *that you cannot take notes or write on the test pages in any way.*

31. Ⓐ professor
    Ⓑ teaching assistant
    Ⓒ receptionist
    Ⓓ tour guide

32. Ⓐ in a library
    Ⓑ in a grammar school playground
    Ⓒ in a college or university
    Ⓓ in an office building

33. Ⓐ She needs advice on her paper.
    Ⓑ She wants to advise him on her paper.
    Ⓒ She wants a part-time job.
    Ⓓ She wants to drop his class.

34. Ⓐ 443-3655
    Ⓑ 334-3655
    Ⓒ 343-5666
    Ⓓ She didn't say.

35. Ⓐ the last day of class
    Ⓑ the middle of the term
    Ⓒ the first day of class
    Ⓓ during preregistration

36. Ⓐ a graduate student
    Ⓑ a professor
    Ⓒ an undergraduate student
    Ⓓ a receptionist

37. Ⓐ a graduate course
    Ⓑ a beginning class
    Ⓒ an abnormal class
    Ⓓ a class for psychiatric patients

38. Ⓐ if she can take his class
    Ⓑ what his name is
    Ⓒ if she is in the right class
    Ⓓ if he is abnormal

PART C

Listen to Test_1C.mov.

<u>Directions:</u> On this part of the test, you will hear several talks. After each talk, you will hear some questions. Neither the talks nor the questions will be repeated. After you hear a question, read the four possible answers in this book and choose the best one.

Here is an example.

> **On the recording, you hear: (Listen to the CD-ROM)**
>
> **In your book, you read:**
> Ⓐ Dinosaurs of the Sahara
> Ⓑ Tyrannosaurus Rex
> ⬤ A New Species of Dinosaur
> Ⓓ Bipedal Carnivorous Dinosaurs

The best answer to the question, "What would be a good title for this talk?" is (C), "A New Species of Dinosaur."

Remember *you should not take notes or write on your test pages.*

39. Ⓐ All stress is bad.
    Ⓑ Stress is unmanageable.
    Ⓒ Stress is avoidable.
    Ⓓ Stress is inevitable.

40. Ⓐ getting a divorce
    Ⓑ having a baby
    Ⓒ taking a nap
    Ⓓ marriage

41. Ⓐ decreasing caffeine intake
    Ⓑ cutting down on exercise
    Ⓒ cutting out vitamins
    Ⓓ getting stressed out

42. Ⓐ abnormal, tense
    Ⓑ normal, unavoidable
    Ⓒ abnormal, irregular
    Ⓓ necessary, avoidable

43. Ⓐ euphoric

    Ⓑ pleasant

    Ⓒ upsetting

    Ⓓ dependent

44. Ⓐ Drugs are a dangerous way of handling stress.

    Ⓑ Stress is not inevitable.

    Ⓒ Stress cannot be dealt with.

    Ⓓ Drugs have helped some people who have severe stress.

45. Ⓐ a student

    Ⓑ an administrator

    Ⓒ Mr. Stromm

    Ⓓ Mr. Wingfield

46. Ⓐ at City Hall

    Ⓑ in the gymnasium

    Ⓒ in Butler Library

    Ⓓ In Butler's Continuing Ed. Department

47. Ⓐ during graduation

    Ⓑ in the middle of the semester

    Ⓒ before the semester begins

    Ⓓ during the last week of the semester

48. Ⓐ It opens at nine every day.

    Ⓑ All students can use it.

    Ⓒ Well-trained assistants are on hand.

    Ⓓ The equipment is archaic.

49. Ⓐ $5.30

    Ⓑ an ID

    Ⓒ an expired computer pass

    Ⓓ nothing

50. Ⓐ a former vice-president

    Ⓑ a former professor of computer science

    Ⓒ Dr. Jane Robertson

    Ⓓ a former student

Structure and Written Expression

⊘ **Time allowed for this section: 25 minutes**

Directions: Structure and Written Expression Section

This section is designed to measure your ability to recognize language that is appropriate for standard written English. There are two types of questions in this section, with special directions for each type.

Part A

<u>Directions</u>: Questions 1–15 are incomplete sentences. Beneath each sentence you will see four words or phrases, marked (A), (B), (C), and (D). Choose the one word or phrase that best completes the sentence.

Example I:

> Geysers have often been compared to volcanoes _____ they both emit hot liquids from below the earth's surface.
>
> Ⓐ due to
> ● because
> Ⓒ in spite of
> Ⓓ regardless of

The sentence should read, "Geysers have often been compared to volcanoes <u>because</u> they both emit hot liquids from below the earth's surface." Therefore, you should choose answer (B).

Example II:

> During the early period of ocean navigation, _____ any need for sopisticated instruments and techniques.
>
> Ⓐ so that hardly
> Ⓑ when there was hardly
> Ⓒ hardly was
> ⬤ there was hardly

The sentence should read, "During the early period of ocean navigation, <u>there was hardly</u> any need for sophisticated instruments and techniques." Therefore, you should choose answer (D).

Now begin work on the questions.

1. _____ the Boston Red Sox have often been outstanding, they haven't won the World Series since 1918.

   Ⓐ However

   Ⓑ Yet

   Ⓒ That

   Ⓓ Although

2. _____ many computer software programs that possess excellent word-processing capabilities.

   Ⓐ There are

   Ⓑ The

   Ⓒ There is a lot of

   Ⓓ Some

3. Many Americans still feel that the jury system is _____ the core of our democracy.

   Ⓐ in

   Ⓑ with

   Ⓒ by

   Ⓓ at

4. I believed him when he said he would _____ here on time.

   Ⓐ is

   Ⓑ be

   Ⓒ are

   Ⓓ will be

KAPLAN

5. _____ of English 101 with a grade of B or better will exempt you from English 102.

    Ⓐ The complete

    Ⓑ Completing

    Ⓒ A completing

    Ⓓ The completion

6. Whenever the weather is nice, I _____ to work.

    Ⓐ walking

    Ⓑ walk

    Ⓒ to walking

    Ⓓ walked

7. _____ in the Midwest.

    Ⓐ Corn is grown usually

    Ⓑ Usually grown is corn

    Ⓒ Corn usually grown

    Ⓓ Corn is usually grown

8. _____ wrote the opera *Aida*.

    Ⓐ That was Verdi who

    Ⓑ Verdi who

    Ⓒ Since it was Verdi

    Ⓓ It was Verdi who

9. Some of my favorite recipes are _____ I learned from my great-grandmother.

    Ⓐ those

    Ⓑ them

    Ⓒ they

    Ⓓ their

10. In the _____ years, my old computer will become obsolete.

    Ⓐ few next

    Ⓑ a few next

    Ⓒ next few

    Ⓓ some next

11. During one's first few months in a new culture, one should learn the manners that are customary and _____.

    Ⓐ the spoken there language

    Ⓑ the language that is spoken there

    Ⓒ to be speaking language

    Ⓓ the language that is speaking

12. Picasso _____ one of the greatest artists of the 20th century.

    Ⓐ considered

    Ⓑ considered to be

    Ⓒ is considered to be

    Ⓓ is consideration

13. Due to _____ , the subways were closed all morning.

    Ⓐ its flooding

    Ⓑ floods

    Ⓒ are flooded

    Ⓓ flood

14. _____ he had been lied to, he got really angry.

    Ⓐ John discovered

    Ⓑ When John discovered

    Ⓒ Having discovered

    Ⓓ If John discovered

15. The main purpose of our group sessions is _____ by people who have lost a loved one.

    Ⓐ to reduce stress experienced

    Ⓑ reduce the experienced stress

    Ⓒ to reduce stress experiencing

    Ⓓ reducing the stress experience

PART B

<u>Directions:</u> In questions 16–40 each sentence has four underlined words or phrases. The four under-lined parts of the sentence are marked (A), (B), (C), and (D). Identify the one underlined word or phrase that must be changed in order for the sentence to be grammatically correct.

Example I:

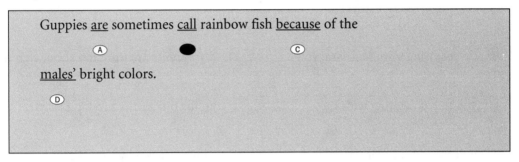

The sentence should read, "Guppies are sometimes <u>called</u> rainbow fish because of the males' bright colors." Therefore, you should choose (B).

Example II:

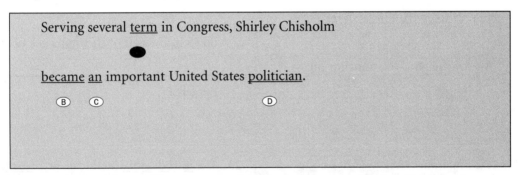

The sentence should read, "Serving several <u>terms</u> in Congress, Shirley Chisholm became an important United States politician." Therefore, you should choose answer (A).

Now begin work on the questions.

16. I <u>heard</u> that enrollment <u>is up</u> almost
     Ⓐ   Ⓑ

   fifteen percent <u>from</u> fall semester last
             Ⓒ

   <u>years</u>.
   Ⓓ

17. If you <u>requiring</u> a student visa, you
       Ⓐ

   <u>must</u> set up <u>a meeting</u> with <u>the</u>
   Ⓑ   Ⓒ   Ⓓ

   foreign student adviser.

18. It is <u>unlegal</u> for universities and
      Ⓐ

   colleges <u>to discriminate</u> on the basis
          Ⓑ

   <u>of sex</u>, religion, or national <u>origin</u>.
   Ⓒ   Ⓓ

19. It is imperative that <u>you are paying</u>
               Ⓐ

   your tuition <u>on time</u> if you <u>want</u> to
        Ⓑ   Ⓒ

   secure a place <u>in</u> the course.
          Ⓓ

20. The computer lab <u>will be close</u> all <u>of</u>
           Ⓐ   Ⓑ

   next week <u>while</u> the new computers
        Ⓒ

   <u>are being installed</u>.
   Ⓓ

21. My parents <u>are</u> thinking <u>about</u> signing
        Ⓐ   Ⓑ

   <u>up for one</u> of the life-long learners
       Ⓒ

   <u>course</u> offered by the school.
   Ⓓ

22. If you <u>wish</u> to drop <u>a course</u>, you must
      Ⓐ   Ⓑ

   <u>do so in</u> the end <u>of the first</u> week of
   Ⓒ   Ⓓ

   the term.

23. The <u>introductory</u> math course <u>is worth</u>
      Ⓐ   Ⓑ

   four credits <u>while</u> my philosophy
          Ⓒ

   course <u>are</u> only three points.
        Ⓓ

24. The MBA program boasts a reputation
    Ⓐ   Ⓑ
    of being considered a best on the
    Ⓒ   Ⓓ
    West Coast.

25. The health center offers several
                        Ⓐ
    program to help students deal with
    Ⓑ   Ⓒ
    stress and other emotional concerns.
                                  Ⓓ

26. The term etiquette originated of
        Ⓐ   Ⓑ
    France in the seventeenth century, but
           Ⓒ
    it is also a common term today in
              Ⓓ
    English.

27. The news are usually depressing, so I
              Ⓐ   Ⓑ
    tend not to watch the news shows.
       Ⓒ   Ⓓ

28. That was one of the most interested
        Ⓐ   Ⓑ
    lectures I have heard in a long time.
            Ⓒ   Ⓓ

29. Choose from a wide variety of subject
    Ⓐ   Ⓑ
    areas, you are allowed to up to three
          Ⓒ   Ⓓ
    elective courses.

30. The renovation of the building will
                  Ⓐ
    taken about three months more than
    Ⓑ   Ⓒ
    what had been previously estimated.
        Ⓓ

31. Recycling is mandatory in most major
                Ⓐ   Ⓑ
    cities today, and violators may
                   Ⓒ
    penalize up to five hundred dollars.
    Ⓓ

32. Today, <u>elderly is</u> the <u>fastest</u> growing
    Ⓐ   Ⓑ
    <u>demographic</u> group <u>in many</u>
    Ⓒ   Ⓓ
    developed countries.

33. <u>Solar</u> energy <u>has never</u> really
    Ⓐ   Ⓑ
    <u>caught on</u> like <u>to many</u>
    Ⓒ   Ⓓ
    environmentalists had predicted.

34. <u>Heat</u>, humid weather <u>can make</u> an
    Ⓐ   Ⓑ
    asthma <u>sufferer's</u> condition
            Ⓒ
    <u>much worse</u>.
        Ⓓ

35. If <u>one's basic</u> nutritional <u>needs</u> are
        Ⓐ   Ⓑ
    <u>being</u> met, <u>they</u> should not need to
    Ⓒ   Ⓓ
    take vitamin supplements.

36. <u>A cardiologist</u> is a physician <u>who's</u>
    Ⓐ   Ⓑ
    specialty <u>is dealing</u> with <u>heart disease</u>.
               Ⓒ   Ⓓ

37. I <u>was asked</u> to be <u>a juror</u> in the
      Ⓐ   Ⓑ
    <u>mock trial</u> which <u>take place</u> at the
    Ⓒ   Ⓓ
    law school next week.

38. <u>As soon</u> I looked <u>through</u> my first
    Ⓐ   Ⓑ
    telescope, I <u>knew</u> that one day I
                  Ⓒ
    <u>would become</u> an astronomer.
        Ⓓ

39. <u>In</u> agricultural states, the
    Ⓐ
    <u>minimum age</u> required <u>get</u> a driver's
    Ⓐ   Ⓑ
    license used to be <u>fifteen years</u> old.
    Ⓒ   Ⓓ

40. Sometimes <u>I come to</u> school <u>by bus</u>,
              Ⓐ   Ⓑ
    but if the weather is nice <u>I prefer</u> to
                                Ⓒ
    come <u>by feet</u>.
         Ⓓ

Reading Comprehension

🕐 **Time allowed for this section: 55 minutes**

Directions: Reading Comprehension Section

<u>Directions:</u> In this section you will read several passages. Each one is followed by several questions about it. For this section, you are to choose the one best answer, (A), (B), (C), or (D), to each question. Answer all the questions following a passage on the basis of what is stated or implied in that passage.

Read the following passage.

One of the most successful communal experiments in the New World was that of the Shakers, a sect that fled from England *Line* to New York State in 1774 in order to (5) escape religious bigotry. In America, they adopted the name Shaker, once used derisively by the English to describe the dance they performed when in a state of religious ecstasy. At the movement's peak, in the (10) decade prior to the Civil War, there were 6,000 Shakers in 18 communities throughout the eastern states. Since then, however, the Shakers have almost dwindled away. Today, only two active Shaker communities (15) remain, with a total membership of eighteen, all female. The Shakers are resigned to the death of their sect, as they have never believed that everyone could be persuaded to share their beliefs.

Example I:

> Where did the Shaker movement begin?
> - (A) The eastern states
> - (B) The New World
> - (C) New York
> - ● England

Example II:

At present, the Shakers are represented by

Ⓐ 6,000 worldwide members
Ⓑ 18 active communities
⬤ two remaining all-female communities
Ⓓ two female members

According to the passage, only two active Shaker communities remain, with a total membership of 18, all female. Therefore, you should have chosen answer (C).

Now begin work on the questions.

Questions 1–9 refer to the following passage.

Thomas A. Edison is widely regarded as one of the most important inventors of all time. His discovery of the electric light is
Line what he is most renowned for, but he is also
(5) credited with the invention of the phonograph and the movie camera, among a host of other important discoveries.

Edison has been referred to as a child prodigy, having begun work on his first
(10) inventions at the tender age of twelve. His family was not at all affluent, so even as a youngster, he had to take whatever odd jobs he could find. During his childhood, he worked as a newspaper salesman on the
(15) trains to Detroit which ran from his hometown. It was on these endless journeys that Edison became familiar with the telegraph. He felt, however, that there must be a more expedient way to send messages, so he set
(20) out to discover a new and better way to communicate.

One of Edison's first discoveries, and the very first one for which he received a patent, was an electronic method for elec-
(25) tion vote counting. The young man was intensely excited about the prospects of his invention and knew that it could greatly speed up the election counting process. Sadly, though, he could not get the needed
(30) support to make his first major invention a hit. He went all the way to Washington with it, but nobody seemed willing to fully buy into his idea.

Remaining confident, Edison was not
(35) deterred but viewed the incident as a lesson. He realized that to make successful inventions he had to appeal to the public, and especially to those with purchasing power. That is, unless he found an audience
(40) for his inventions, all of his great ideas would gradually vanish and be forgotten.

1. The best title for the passage is
    - Ⓐ Edison's Failures
    - Ⓑ The Unfailing Determination of Edison
    - Ⓒ The Greatest Inventor Who Ever Lived
    - Ⓓ Who Invented Electricity?

2. In line 4, the word *renowned* is similar in meaning to
    - Ⓐ respected
    - Ⓑ feared
    - Ⓒ scandalized
    - Ⓓ famous

3. In line 6, the word *host* means
    - Ⓐ a greeter
    - Ⓑ a problem
    - Ⓒ a lot of
    - Ⓓ a mirage

4. From the reading, one can say that Edison's family was
    - Ⓐ affluent
    - Ⓑ well-to-do
    - Ⓒ upper class
    - Ⓓ struggling financially

5. Edison learned about the telegraph
    - Ⓐ by reading brochures
    - Ⓑ through a friend
    - Ⓒ while working on the trains
    - Ⓓ in a letter

6. Which of the following is NOT a true statement?
    - Ⓐ People best remember Edison for his invention of the electric light.
    - Ⓑ Edison's electronic method for election voting was received very favorably by the national government.
    - Ⓒ Edison had a wide range of jobs.
    - Ⓓ Some of Edison's inventions went unrecognized while others changed the world.

7. One can infer from the reading that Edison had a lot of
    - Ⓐ insolence
    - Ⓑ perseverance
    - Ⓒ luck
    - Ⓓ trepidation

8. As a youngster, Edison was seen as being
    - Ⓐ very disobedient
    - Ⓑ advanced for his age
    - Ⓒ lazy
    - Ⓓ mentally disturbed

9. The word *hit* in line 31 could best be replaced by
    - Ⓐ blow
    - Ⓑ electronic method for vote counting
    - Ⓒ slap
    - Ⓓ success

Questions 10–17 refer to the following passage.

How one views "time" often depends on one's cultural background. That is, the definitions of what is considered to be "late" or
Line "on time" or even "early" can greatly vary
(5) from one region or group of people to another. Thus, it is important to know what a country's basic manners or attitudes are about acceptable time before moving to a foreign country.

(10) One thing is for sure: every nation places an emphasis on time in one regard or another. This can be seen through the myriad proverbs and expressions almost every culture has regarding time. Some of the
(15) American ones are so common they have become clichés: "Time is money," "My, how time flies," "Time waits for no one," "Time marches on," and so on.

You will seldom go into an American's
(20) home that is not full of various styles, sizes, and shapes of clocks. Nor are you likely to encounter an American who is not wearing a watch. Still, within the country, you will no doubt meet people with varying atti-
(25) tudes towards punctuality. While one person might become very irate if you are ten or fifteen minutes late for an appointment, another person may consider thirty minutes or more perfectly acceptable and not
(30) tardy at all. But, as is true of most customs, it is far better to be safe than sorry; it's hard to go wrong if you yourself arrive as close as possible to the designated time.

10. The main idea of the passage is
   Ⓐ Time Waits for No Man
   Ⓑ My, How Time Flies!
   Ⓒ The Importance of Time in a Culture
   Ⓓ Being Late Is a Sign of Bad Manners

11. The best synonym for *on time* is
   Ⓐ early
   Ⓑ punctual
   Ⓒ hurriedly
   Ⓓ hastily

12. According to the author,
   Ⓐ many cultures don't care about time
   Ⓑ one can never be too sorry
   Ⓒ one can never be too late
   Ⓓ all cultures have an attitude about time

13. This passage would most likely appear in
   Ⓐ an American history textbook
   Ⓑ a cross-cultural studies book
   Ⓒ a literature textbook
   Ⓓ a psychology textbook

14. From the passage, one can infer that a *cliché* is

    Ⓐ an overused expression

    Ⓑ an approach to time

    Ⓒ a new and trendy term

    Ⓓ an ancient saying

15. Within the boundaries of the United States, there seem(s) to be

    Ⓐ a general consensus about lateness

    Ⓑ no tolerance for tardiness

    Ⓒ many diverse attitudes about time

    Ⓓ few people who are punctual

16. The author's advice about time is

    Ⓐ go early, stay late

    Ⓑ waste not, want not

    Ⓒ better late than sorry

    Ⓓ try to be on time

17. The expression *time flies* refers to time

    Ⓐ passing quickly

    Ⓑ standing still

    Ⓒ running out

    Ⓓ being up in the air

Questions 18–26 refer to the following passage.

Religion has played a major role in the United States ever since it became a separate and independent country. Although there
Line have been a number of changes in religious
(5) attitudes and practices since the early days of colonialism and Puritanism, religion is still a major force in U.S. culture today.

Although there are well over a hundred different religions in the United States at pre-
(10) sent, more than half of those questioned in a recent survey declared themselves to be of a Protestant faith. Included in Protestantism are Baptists, Methodists, Presbyterians, Lutherans, and Episcopalians. Of the
(15) remaining Americans, almost 30 per cent are Catholics, and about two percent are Jewish. In New York City, there is a larger Jewish community than in Israel, so in specific areas of the United States one will find a predom-
(20) inance of one religion that may have relatively few, if any, members of that religion in another area. There are also Muslims, Buddhists, Hindus, and several other religious groups well represented, especially in
(25) the metropolitan areas of the country.

One of the most controversial issues involving religion in the United States regards what is known as the "separation of church and state." The American Constitution clearly
(30) states that religious worship and governmental activities shall not be intertwined. In spite of this, throughout much of the 20th century, many public schools held prayers in class, and students and their teachers celebrated
(35) various religious holidays. Recent court decisions forbidding such practices have motivated some parents to send their children to private schools that are exempt from such governmental restrictions.

(40) Whatever a person's religious or spiritual beliefs might be, it appears that the United States is still basically a country of believers. A 1990 survey found that over 80 percent of those polled claimed to believe in
(45) "God," and almost 70 percent stated that they engage in religious ceremonies and rituals on a regular basis.

18. This reading would most likely appear in
   Ⓐ a philosophy textbook
   Ⓑ an American history textbook
   Ⓒ a book on New Age religions
   Ⓓ a psychology textbook

19. The passage mainly discusses
   Ⓐ the importance of believing
   Ⓑ conflicts between church and state
   Ⓒ why Protestants are popular in America
   Ⓓ the role of religion in the United States

20. Which of the following is NOT a true statement?
   Ⓐ Religion still plays a role in most Americans' lives.
   Ⓑ Puritans settled recently in the United States.
   Ⓒ There is a debate about whether to allow praying in public schools.
   Ⓓ Catholicism is not considered to be a Protestant faith.

21. One can infer from the passage that

    Ⓐ many Protestants live in Israel

    Ⓑ many American Jews live in New York City

    Ⓒ it is illegal to practice Muslim rituals in America

    Ⓓ praying has always been illegal in the United States

22. In the expression *church and state* (lines 28–29), the word *state* refers to

    Ⓐ the 50 states

    Ⓑ only municipal government

    Ⓒ the government

    Ⓓ public schools

23. In line 38, the word *exempt* means

    Ⓐ excluded

    Ⓑ included

    Ⓒ explosive

    Ⓓ incorporated

24. According to a poll taken recently, the majority of Americans say that they

    Ⓐ are atheists

    Ⓑ are agnostic

    Ⓒ believe in God

    Ⓓ seldom worship

25. In line 47, the word *ritual* is closest in meaning to

    Ⓐ a right way to think

    Ⓑ a rite or tradition

    Ⓒ a writ mandated by the government

    Ⓓ a practice of atheists

26. According to the passage, religion in America today is

    Ⓐ highly controversial

    Ⓑ rarely accepted

    Ⓒ a major force in society

    Ⓓ in a state of fluctuation

Questions 27–34 refer to the following passage.

The invention of the television was made possible through the development of the electron tube. For this reason, the TV is
Line also known informally as the "tube." The
(5) term "couch potato"—the slang expression often associated with people who watch a lot of television—is said to refer to the potato because it is a tubular vegetable, with eyes (the little black specks on the
(10) potato) to symbolize someone's eyes, glued to the tube. Whether this was said in jest or not, it is a term that has stuck and is now a part of the lexicon of modern American culture.

(15) Though these so-called couch potatoes are often the butt of jokes or regarded as being "unintelligent," such a characterization is unfair. And very few of us can honestly claim that we are not "guilty" of indulging
(20) in and enjoying this form of entertainment. It is estimated that over 98 per cent of American households own a TV set. In fact, today most own more than one and at least half own a VCR as well. The latter
(25) makes it possible for people to record their favorite shows if they are not at home at the time they air, and they can save money by renting the movies they missed at the box office, often only a few weeks after they first
(30) came out.

Although many intellectuals make snide remarks about TV viewing, there are a number of "high-brow" shows. These may include classical music concerts, serious
(35) drama, science programs, and language-teaching shows. Television is also frequently used in schools as an educational tool, for students of all ages and in many different fields.

(40) It is up to the viewer to decide which programs are worth their while to watch. And many parents do place strict limits on the kinds of shows their children may see and the number of hours allowed for television
(45) viewing. TV itself should not be seen as bad; it all depends on what—and how—one watches!

27. The main point of the author is that
   Ⓐ TV receives unfair negative criticism
   Ⓑ censorship of television is too weak
   Ⓒ television viewing should be unregulated
   Ⓓ people were better off before the TV came along

28. The author's attitude towards television appears to be one of
   Ⓐ scorn
   Ⓑ appreciation
   Ⓒ ridicule
   Ⓓ confusion

29. According to the article, a *couch potato* best describes someone who
   Ⓐ watches television while sitting on a sedan
   Ⓑ eats potatoes while watching shows
   Ⓒ watches a lot of television
   Ⓓ is lazy and wastes a lot of time

30. In line 16, the *butt* of a joke refers to someone who is

    Ⓐ the joke teller

    Ⓑ being made fun of

    Ⓒ very funny

    Ⓓ not funny

31. A "*high-brow show*" (line 33) might be which of the following?

    Ⓐ a taped concert of the Boston Symphony

    Ⓑ a Saturday morning cartoon

    Ⓒ local news and weather reports

    Ⓓ soap operas

32. The author would probably think of someone who enjoys "high-brow" shows as having what kind of taste?

    Ⓐ acidic

    Ⓑ asinine

    Ⓒ sophisticated

    Ⓓ amorphous

33. According to the author, who should decide what shows we watch?

    Ⓐ the government

    Ⓑ censors

    Ⓒ we ourselves

    Ⓓ our children

34. In line 42, the word *strict* is closest in meaning to

    Ⓐ lenient

    Ⓑ unfair

    Ⓒ rigid

    Ⓓ amusing

Questions 35–42 refer to the following passage.

Of all organs in the body, perhaps the most mysterious one is the brain. Scientists, physicians, and psychologists have often
Line been at odds about how the brain func-
(5) tions. Still, today we do know that not only is the brain the center of the nervous system, it is considered the seat of one's emotions, memory, and ideas as well.

In the past, it was popular for both doctors
(10) and laymen to often talk about the left and right hemispheres of the brain, as if each had very specifically assigned functions. Today, this is not considered nearly as cut and dried as it once was. That is to say, we
(15) now know much more than we did a decade ago, and realize that though each area of the brain is associated with certain skills or functions, no one particular area of the brain is thought of as fully responsible
(20) for one specific function.

In very loose terminology, the right hemisphere of the brain controls the left side of the body (the arm, leg, hand, etcetera); likewise, the left hemisphere controls the right
(25) side of the body. In general, it is believed that the left hemisphere primarily controls language learning skills, and the right side controls creative activities. One reason, however, that there is much less emphasis
(30) on whether a person is considered to be "right-" or "left-brained" is that there is such an overlap in these areas. For example, a person who is greatly skilled at language learning may also be highly creative or
(35) imaginative, or possess musical ability, which is considered to be "right-brained" also.

Much has been learned about the functioning of the brain through recent medical
(40) and scientific research on the subject, and by studying brain-damaged patients. And from these studies, great strides have been made in treating patients with epilepsy, brain tumors, and a host of other brain dis-
(45) orders and diseases. Still, the brain is a great unknown in myriad ways, and remains one of the most challenging and fascinating areas in the medical field.

35. The best choice of a title for this passage is

    Ⓐ How We Think

    Ⓑ Left or Right Brain: Which Is Better?

    Ⓒ The Mystery of the Brain

    Ⓓ What Makes Us Smart?

36. In line 4, the term *at odds* means

    Ⓐ an even chance

    Ⓑ in dialogue

    Ⓒ in disagreement

    Ⓓ in debate

37. One can assume that the term *laymen* in line 10 refers to

    Ⓐ physicians

    Ⓑ researchers

    Ⓒ scientists

    Ⓓ none of the above

38. Which of the following is NOT true about the brain?

    Ⓐ It must be cut and dried.

    Ⓑ There are many unknowns about it.

    Ⓒ Each of its areas is associated with a function or skill

    Ⓓ Specialists in the field have disagreements among each other about it.

39. The word *subject* in line 40 refers to

    Ⓐ a brain-damaged patient

    Ⓑ brain functions

    Ⓒ treating patients

    Ⓓ brain disorders

40. In the past, one often assumed that someone who was multi-lingual was highly

    Ⓐ right-brained

    Ⓑ balanced

    Ⓒ left-brained

    Ⓓ even-handed

41. One can infer from the reading that much progress has been made in all of the following EXCEPT

    Ⓐ solving the mysteries of the brain

    Ⓑ improving the lives of epileptics

    Ⓒ advancements in removing brain tumors

    Ⓓ treating many neurological disorders

42. The word *myriad* in line 46 means

    Ⓐ multiple

    Ⓑ divided

    Ⓒ restricted

    Ⓓ brilliant

Questions 43–50 refer to the following passage.

The word *archaeology* comes from Greek, meaning "the study of beginnings." More specifically, it is the scientific and academic study and research of the material remains of past human cultures. These remains may date from the earliest of times all the way up to modern history. Hand-made (or rather human-made) tools have often been considered an important artifact in determining the sophistication of a culture. Only recently was it discovered that the earliest sophisticated tools were made in Africa.

Prior to this discovery, it had long been thought that the earliest ones were found in Europe. However, in the mid-1990s, archaeologists digging in Zaire uncovered advanced tools made of animal bones. These were highly ornate, with elaborate barbs and points on them. They have been determined to be at least 75,000–90,000 years old, which is about 60,000 years older than the ones that had been found in Europe.

Although some scientists have voiced skepticism at some of the claims surrounding these findings, the archaeologists on the seven-year dig stated that they have subjected their findings to stringent and numerous tests, conducted by many well-known experts in the field. The researchers say that their work just adds further support to the already widely held notion that humans first appeared in Africa. Just exactly when, how, and why they migrated to other areas still remains a mystery.

Line (5)
(10)
(15)
(20)
(25)
(30)
(35)

43. The main idea of the passage is to discuss
    Ⓐ the origins of man
    Ⓑ a recent discovery in the field
    Ⓒ false claims in the field
    Ⓓ an overview of the field

44. According to the article, man first appeared in
    Ⓐ Greece
    Ⓑ Africa
    Ⓒ Europe
    Ⓓ Nobody has any idea.

45. One of the most significant artifacts in determining the sophistication of a culture is the _____ they created.
    Ⓐ ornate clothes
    Ⓑ sophisticated art
    Ⓒ sophisticated tools
    Ⓓ hands

46. The artifacts recently found in Zaire are thought to be from
    Ⓐ 60,000 years ago
    Ⓑ 70,000 B.C.
    Ⓒ 70,000–90,000 years ago
    Ⓓ A.D. 60,000

47. The pronoun *these* in line 27 refers to which findings?

    (A) the Europeans'

    (B) recent ones from Zaire

    (C) ones made 60,000 years ago

    (D) ones made 75,000–90,000 years ago

48. According to the passage, there is general consensus that these findings

    (A) are consistent with some generally held ideas about the origin of man

    (B) are clearly bogus

    (C) have been obviously overhyped

    (D) were done in haste

49. The word *stringent* in line 29, describing the kinds of tests the findings have gone through, is closest in meaning to

    (A) rigid, tight

    (B) cold, mean

    (C) unfair

    (D) lenient

50. The word *skepticism* in lines 25–26 is closest in meaning to

    (A) disbelief

    (B) honor

    (C) elaboration

    (D) ignorance

END OF TEST. *Turn to the answer key and score conversion chart following the Listening Comprehension script to find out how you did on this Diagnostic Test. Check the Listening Comprehension script on the pages that follow if there was anything in the Listening Comprehension section of this test that you could not understand.*

SCRIPT FOR LISTENING COMPREHENSION
PART A (TEST_1A.MOV)
M=Man   W=Woman   N=Narrator

1. **M:** If I were you, I'd go through pre-registration and avoid the lines.

    W: Not a bad idea!

    N: What does the woman think of the man's suggestion?

2. **M:** We sighted over half a dozen pigeons flying around our classroom.

    W: Sounds like something out of that film *The Birds*!

    N: What was the woman's reaction?

3. **M:** Jane's sister is an associate professor of nursing at the school uptown.

    W: I think my roommate had her as a teacher last year.

    N: Who was a student at the nursing school last year?

4. **M:** Every day at noon the school symphony puts on a concert in the chapel.

    W: I had no idea.

    N: What does the woman mean?

5. **M:** Where were you this afternoon?

    W: Didn't I tell you? Our class went on a field trip.

    N: Where was the woman?

6. **M:** What do you feel like doing?

    W: Honestly, I feel like skipping class, but I wouldn't dare.

    N: What does the woman say?

7. **M:** Will you go to business school?

    W: Not unless I can't find a job out there.

    N: Does the woman plan to go to business school?

8. **M:** Did you catch the assignment?

    W: Are you kidding? That loudspeaker never works properly.

    N: What did the woman mean?

9. **M:** What are you writing?

    W: Oh, I've decided to start keeping a journal on the advice of my creative writing instructor.

    N: What did the woman's teacher suggest?

10. **M:** I'm afraid I can't read this. Can you type?

    W: I wish I could.

    N: What does the man imply?

KAPLAN

11. **M:** If we don't hurry we'll miss the first half of the movie.

    W: Settle down. It will only be previews then anyway.

    N: What is the woman's reaction?

12. **M:** Do you know when John and Mary will pick us up?

    W: Just as soon as they drop off their daughter at day camp.

    N: What will John and Mary do?

13. **M:** Excuse me, can you tell me where the philosophy section is?

    W: It's over there, behind the row of sale books, on the middle aisle.

    N: Where did this conversation take place?

14. **M:** What was that?!

    W: I have no idea—it sounded like some sort of explosion.

    N: What did the woman hear?

15. **M:** Would you be interested in going to the county fair with us?

    W: Well, it depends—how much does the fair cost?

    N: What does the woman plan to do?

16. **M:** Had I known how quickly this class would fill up, I would have gone through preregistration.

    W: Well, I tried to warn you.

    N: What does the woman imply?

17. **W:** Come on in, folks. Hurry up. Curtain goes up in five minutes.

    M: Oh, no—I can't find my ticket!

    N: Where did this conversation probably take place?

18. **W:** For our first class, we will just concentrate on your serve.

    M: I thought this was supposed to be a more advanced class than this!

    N: What is the woman's profession?

19. **W:** Let's face it. We're in this way over our heads.

    M: I'll say!

    N: What does the woman mean?

20. **W:** I think your professor just offered you a window of opportunity.

    M: So, you think I should go for it, right?

    N: What does the woman think of the professor's offer?

21. **W:** What are you majoring in?

    M: I'm torn between chemistry and biology.

    N: What does the man mean by this?

22. **W:** We'll pick up next week with the Norman Conquest.

    M: Excuse me, but what did you say?

    N: What does the man want to know?

23. **W:** What took you so long to get here?

    M: Traffic was backed up for over an hour because of some accident.

    N: Why was the man late?

24. **W:** When will our mid-term be?

    M: Dr. Jones said it would be week after next.

    N: What does the woman want to know?

25. **W:** Do you know when our spring break is?

    M: Oh, I hope it will be the second week of March again because I've already bought my plane ticket for home.

    N: What is the man's response?

26. **W:** Has anyone taken your order yet?

    M: We don't even have any menus.

    N: What does the man want?

27. **W:** Where are you living now?

    M: For the moment I'm in Riley Hall, but I'll be moving out to Jones Hall next week.

    N: Where does the man live?

28. **W:** Excuse me—can you tell me which one is the history building?

    M: Sorry, I'm new here too, but I think you can find it on the map in front of Butler Hall.

    N: Where is the history building?

29. **W:** I'm worn out—how about you?

    M: Well, we've been going at this algebra problem for over an hour—why don't we stop and take a break?

    N: What does the man suggest?

30. **W:** How was Professor Weiss's seminar today?

    M: I hate to say it, but I overslept again.

    N: What did the man say about the lecture?

SCRIPT FOR LISTENING COMPREHENSION PART B (TEST_1B.MOV)

N: *Questions 31–34 are based on the following talk.*

W: Excuse me. Is this Professor Wilson's office?

M: Yes, it is, but she's on another line. Would you like to hold?

W: About how long do you think she will be? I just want to set up an appointment to discuss my research paper with her.

M: It's hard to say. If you leave your name and number, though, I can have her T.A. call you back and arrange an office visit. I know she usually has hours on Tuesday and Thursday afternoons, from 3 to 5.

W: Yes, that would be great. This is Meg Phillips, at (512) 334-3655.

M: Okay, that's Ms. Phillips at (512) 334-6675?

W: No, it's 334-3655.

M: Thank you—I'll give her the message.

31. What is the man's profession?

32. Where does the man work?

33. Why does the woman want to talk to the professor?

34. What is the woman's phone number?

N: *Questions 35–38 are based on the following talk.*

M: Good morning. Welcome to Psychology 101. I'm Professor Aitkins and this is my teaching assistant, John Walters, who's a graduate student in the department. He will pass around a sign-in sheet so that I can check and make sure that all of you here are listed on my roster. Yes?

W: I'm not sure if I'm in the right place— is this Abnormal Psychology?

M: That's two doors down the hall, Professor Greene's class.

W: Is this Intro to Psychology required before Abnormal?

M: Generally, yes, but you'll need to see your professor about that. It all depends on what year you are, your GPA and so forth. Now, if there are no further interruptions, I'd like to give you a brief overview of what I'll expect out of you this semester.

35. When did this conversation take place?

36. Who is John Walters?

37. What kind of course does Professor Aitkins teach?

38. What does the woman want to know?

SCRIPT FOR LISTENING COMPREHENSION PART C (TEST_1C.MOV)

Questions 39–44 are based on the following talk.

How many people do you know who would describe their life as being unstressful? Probably very few, if any at all. Being "stressed out" seems to be the number one epidemic of the modern age. According to many mental health workers, almost any event in one's life can be classified as stress-inducing.

Not only do unpleasant experiences create anxiety for most people, but even pleasant experiences may be considered stressful if they cause a major change in one's life. For example, most psychologists consider marriage and the birth of one's first child as two of the most stressful events one will ever encounter—in spite of the fact that these can also bring a great deal of joy to the individuals involved. These kinds of stresses are sometimes called "eustress."

More often "negative" stresses, or "distress," is what comes to most people's mind when they hear the word "stress." These types of stress can include anything from the tension one may feel when waiting for someone who is half an hour late to having to deal with serious illness or even the death of a loved one.

Still, all types of stress are normal and are an unavoidable part of all of our lives. So what is necessary is for people to find better ways of coping with stressful events. For some people, simply beginning a regular exercise program or cutting down on caffeine may do the trick. But, for others, the stress can become so overwhelming that seeing a mental health therapist becomes necessary. Thousands today claim that pharmaceuticals have done wonders, helping them manage stress better on a day-to-day basis. The key point to remember is that since stress cannot be avoided, it is essential to find the best ways to deal with the conflicts and tensions we all must face.

39. Mental health experts would probably agree with which of the following statements?

40. Which of the following events would probably not be labeled "stressful," according to the lecturer?

41. Which of the following might help a person cope with stress?

42. Which of the following adjectives does the lecturer associate with stress?

43. A synonym for *distressing* is

44. Which of the following is a TRUE statement, according to the lecture?

Questions 45–50 are based on the following talk.

Welcome to the Fall '99 Orientation of the Adult and Continuing Education Program at Butler College. We are very proud of the fact that our adult education program was one of the first of its kind in America and the first in our state.

For the last 75 years, we have lead the way in many special programs, such as our Life-Long Learners classes, our "Arts in the City" program, and our business courses for Continuing Ed. And as many of you already know, we have just cut the ribbon on our Adult Education Computer Center, made possible through the generous donations of the Stromm and Wingfield Family Foundation. We hope that if you weren't able to attend last week's opening reception, you will find time in the very near future to tour this state-of-the-art facility. With your school I.D., you will be able to get a computer pass, free of charge. The labs will be open Monday through Thursday, 9 to 9, and on Friday and Saturday, from 9 to 5:30. We have hired computer experts and graduate students from our Computer Science Program, so you will always have knowledgeable people to train you on the latest technology, which we have in our lab.

Now, without further ado, I'd like to introduce you to Dr. Jane Robertson, vice president of Continuing Ed., who will introduce the professors and give a brief synopsis of their programs. Then, she will introduce you to Jeremy Wells, one of our former students, who has put together an excellent slide presentation for you about the department.

45. Who is the speaker?

46. Where is the talk most likely being given?

47. When do you think this talk was given?

48. Which of the following is NOT true about the new computer center?

49. What do you need to be able to use the computer lab?

50. Who will show a slide presentation?

DIAGNOSTIC TEST ANSWER KEY

LISTENING COMPREHENSION SECTION

1. C	14. C	27. D	40. C
2. B	15. C	28. C	41. A
3. A	16. B	29. A	42. B
4. B	17. B	30. C	43. C
5. D	18. C	31. C	44. D
6. C	19. A	32. C	45. B
7. A	20. A	33. A	46. D
8. A	21. B	34. B	47. C
9. A	22. C	35. C	48. D
10. B	23. A	36. A	49. B
11. A	24. B	37. B	50. D
12. D	25. A	38. C	
13. A	26. C	39. D	

STRUCTURE AND WRITTEN EXPRESSION SECTION

1. D	11. B	21. D	31. D
2. A	12. C	22. C	32. A
3. D	13. B	23. D	33. D
4. B	14. C	24. D	34. A
5. D	15. A	25. B	35. D
6. B	16. D	26. B	36. B
7. D	17. A	27. A	37. D
8. D	18. A	28. B	38. A
9. A	19. A	29. A	39. C
10. C	20. A	30. B	40. D

READING COMPREHENSION SECTION

1. B	14. A	27. A	40. C
2. D	15. C	28. B	41. A
3. C	16. D	29. C	42. A
4. D	17. A	30. B	43. B
5. C	18. B	31. A	44. B
6. B	19. D	32. C	45. C
7. B	20. B	33. C	46. C
8. B	21. B	34. C	47. B
9. D	22. C	35. C	48. A
10. C	23. A	36. C	49. A
11. B	24. C	37. D	50. A
12. D	25. B	38. A	
13. B	26. C	39. B	

Diagnostic Test Score Conversion Chart

To determine your approximate TOEFL Diagnostic Test score, follow these steps.

1. After finishing the test, check your answers by using the answer key. Determine the total number of correct answers for each section of the test. This is called your *raw score*.

2. Once you have obtained your raw score, use the conversion table on the next page to get a *scaled*, or *converted score*, for each section of the TOEFL. This is all you need to do to work out your score on the Diagnostic Test in this book.

3. To find out how you did on the computer-based TOEFL practice tests on the CD-ROM, use the scoring function on the CD-ROM. You may also go through steps one and two above and then turn to the TOEFL Concordance Tables provided in the chapter in the introduction entitled "Getting Started." These tables will tell you how your converted scores compare to scores on the computer-based exam.

For example, suppose your raw scores were:

Listening: 39

Structure and Written Expression: 25

Reading: 28

In this case you would use the conversion chart to get converted scores of:

Listening: 54

Structure and Written Expression: 49

Reading: 44

To calculate your overall cumulative TOEFL score for this exam, do the following:

- Add the converted scores you achieved for each of the three sections.
- Multiply this number by 10.
- Then, divide this number by 3.

Following our example, we would get:

$$54 + 49 + 44 = 147$$

$$147 \times 10 = 1470$$

$$1470 \div 3 = 490$$

This imaginary test taker's approximate TOEFL score on the paper-based exam is 490. On the computer-based exam, according to the TOEFL Concordance Table in the Introduction (page 18), the test taker would have scored approximately 160.

CONVERSION CHART

Section I Listening Comprehension		Section II Structure and Written Expression		Section III Reading Comprehension	
Raw Score	Converted Score	Raw Score	Converted Score	Raw Score	Converted Score
50	68	40	68	50	67
49	64	39	68	49	65
48	62	38	68	48	63
47	60	37	62	47	62
46	59	36	60	46	60
45	58	35	58	45	59
44	57	34	56	44	58
43	57	33	55	43	57
42	56	32	54	42	56
41	55	31	53	41	55
40	55	30	52	40	54
39	54	29	52	39	53
38	53	28	51	38	52
37	53	27	50	37	52
36	52	26	49	36	51
35	52	25	49	35	50
34	51	24	48	34	49
33	51	23	47	33	48
32	50	22	47	32	47
31	50	21	46	31	46
30	50	20	45	30	45
29	49	19	45	29	45
28	49	18	44	28	44
27	48	17	43	27	43
26	48	16	42	26	43
25	47	15	42	25	42
24	47	14	41	24	41
23	46	13	39	23	40
22	46	12	38	22	39
21	45	11	36	21	38
20	45	10	34	20	37
19	44	9	31	19	36
18	44	8	27	18	35
17	43	7	26	17	34
16	42	6	25	16	33
15	41	5	24	15	32
14	40	4	23	14	30
13	39	3	21	13	29
12	38	2	20	12	29
11	35	1	20	11	28
10	33	0	20	10	28
9	32			9	27
8	31			8	26
7	30			7	25
6	29			6	24
5	28			5	24
4	28			4	23
3	27			3	22
2	26			2	21

PART THREE:

Mastering the TOEFL CBT

Listening Power

The Listening Comprehension section of the TOEFL CBT has two parts: Section A (short conversations) and Section B (long conversations and talks). Our Power Lessons guide you through each of these parts. Here you will become acquainted with typical questions and distractors ("TOEFL traps") that appear in each section. Each lesson contains notes that refer to tracks on the CD-ROM that accompanies this book. Listen to these tracks when you are prompted, so that you will be able to answer the questions about the spoken conversations and lectures.

Before you start to work on the Listening Power Lessons, read through "Listening Comprehension for the TOEFL CBT" on the following pages. These pages will give you more details on what to expect on the Listening Comprehension section of the TOEFL CBT.

The Bigger Picture: Listening Beyond the TOEFL

It will help your TOEFL preparation to understand why the makers of the TOEFL at ETS place such emphasis on listening skills and why they test listening skills in the way that they do.

Remember that the TOEFL is meant to help American colleges and universities determine whether the English of a non-native speaker of English is of a high enough level for that person to function in an American university setting. For this reason, the TOEFL tests a student's ability to understand lecture-like talks given at a natural speed. In U.S. colleges and universities, students are expected to attend and take notes in class. Classroom lectures supplement the reading assignments; that is, they do not necessarily repeat the information in the reading homework, but add to it. On exams, students are expected to show that they have learned the information given in the lectures as well as the information given in the readings. Therefore, a successful international student must be able to understand his or her professors' lectures.

But successful students must be able to comprehend more than just university lectures. It is common for many American college and university classrooms to be centered around "group discussion," in which students talk about a subject at a fairly informal level. Also, you may have to ask one of your classmates to repeat an idea the professor mentioned in class, or ask a complete stranger how and where you register for a class. Finally, you will certainly want to make American friends. To accomplish these tasks, you need to understand what is often called "survival English." For this reason, the TOEFL also tests your ability to understand very short conversations about topics commonly found on an American college campus.

Listening Comprehension for the TOEFL CBT

Since July, 1998, the TOEFL has been administered by computer. The Listening Comprehension section of the TOEFL CBT differs from that of the paper-based TOEFL both in the way that test takers experience the conversations and talks and the way that they record their answers.

On test day, prior to taking the exam, you will have the opportunity to work through a tutorial that will show you, step-by-step, how to use a mouse, how to scroll, and how to use the testing tools. In addition, before each of the four sections, you will be shown how to answer the types of questions that you will encounter in that section. Remember, the more comfortable you are with computers, the less you will have to worry about on test day!

The following are some unique features of the Listening Comprehension section of the TOEFL CBT:

COMPUTER ADAPTIVE

The Listening Comprehension section is "computer adaptive." This means that the difficulty of each question that you see is based on whether or not you answered the previous question correctly. Every computer adaptive section of the test will begin with a few mid-level difficulty questions. If you answer most of them correctly, then the difficulty of the question that you receive next will increase. If you answer most of the first few questions incorrectly, the questions that follow will become easier.

> **Your goal is to answer as many questions as possible at the highest difficulty level. This is how the test determines your final score!**

Because each question that you receive is based on the questions that come before it, you cannot leave any questions unanswered or skip questions to answer them later.

VOLUME OF AUDIO

You will be able to control the volume for the Listening Comprehension section. *Before* the test begins, you have an opportunity to adjust the volume. During the tutorial, you will hear a phrase repeated over and over. You will see two arrows on the screen—one pointing up and the other pointing down. The up arrow makes the volume louder; the down arrow lowers the volume. Click on the arrows until the voice is clear and at a comfortable level for you.

It is very important that you set the volume at the right level before the test begins! Once the Listening Comprehension section starts, you will not be able to change the volume, and the staff at the testing center will not be able to help you.

TIME

In addition to being able to control the volume, you can also set the pace of the Listening Comprehension section. The time you have to take the test will vary from one test taker to another, but it will be either 20 or 30 minutes. The actual amount of time that you are allowed to take will appear on the screen before you begin. The time that you spend listening to the conversation or talk is not counted against your total time, only the time spent answering the question. The actual amount of time you spend in front of the computer to complete the Listening Comprehension section will be up to 40 or 60 minutes.

However, unlike the paper-based exam, in which all test takers listen to the audio at the same time and have exactly the same amount of time to answer each question, you decide when to go on to the next question. All this really means is that the Listening Comprehension section on the TOEFL CBT is now more like the other sections in this regard.

GRAPHIC ELEMENT

Each short conversation and long conversation will include a picture of two people talking. These pictures are there to focus your attention. They do not necessarily provide information that will help you answer the question correctly—you are being tested on your listening comprehension, *not* your visual comprehension.

The talks, however, will include graphic elements to which you should pay attention. Many of these elements will simply be a word, phrase, or name that looks like it is written on a blackboard. Make a mental note of the information on this kind of graphic; you will most likely get a question based on it. Other types of graphics will include pictures or illustrations, such as a map, a technical drawing, a photograph of an animal, or a diagram, to name just a few examples.

These graphics are there to help you understand what the speaker is talking about, and are typical of the kinds of visual aids a professor in a university classroom might use. You may encounter these or similar graphics as part of the actual questions themselves.

CONTENT

All of the items in the Listening Comprehension section of the computerized TOEFL will be set in an academic or university context. For this reason, it is essential that you become very familiar with common academic terminology.

Part A

Short conversations include a 6- to 20-second exchange between a man and a woman. The pair might be two students, a student and a professor, or a student and a university administrator. This section typically tests your ability to make inferences from word choice and tone of voice, for example, and to understand idiomatic expressions.

Part B

Longer conversations and talks range anywhere from 30 seconds to 2 minutes and 30 seconds long. The longer conversations might be between two students, a student and a professor, or a student and a university administrator.

The talks are typical academic lectures. They can be on any number of subjects drawn from physical and natural sciences and the humanities. You need not have any prior knowledge of the topic that is discussed, however; subjects dealing with the humanities, such as history and biography, will be based on American culture. In other words, you will not hear a lecture about a Japanese poet or an art movement that occurred in Russia, as these would bias the test toward test takers from those cultures.

Some of the talks include interruptions, such as a student asking a question, or the professor soliciting information from his or her students. These interruptions serve to make them more like talks that might occur in real-life classroom situations.

QUESTION FORMAT

The TOEFL CBT has introduced some significant changes in the format of the questions. On the paper-based exam, you are given four choices, from which you pick one and fill in the corresponding oval. On the computerized test, you record your answer directly on the screen. Unlike the paper-based exam, in which you merely hear the question, on the computer-based test you read the question on the screen after you hear the audio portion. The answer choices do not appear until after the audio has finished.

Remember, you are not permitted to leave any listening comprehension question unanswered, so you cannot come back to it later!

You may change your answer choice for all questions as often as you like until you click on **Next** and **Confirm Answer**. Once you have clicked on these boxes, you will hear the next audio clip.

Standard Multiple-Choice

For this type of question, you will click on the oval next to the correct answer.

Example:

You will hear the following conversation and a question:

MAN:	Did you go to chemistry class today? When I got there, nobody was there!
WOMAN:	Didn't you remember the announcement Professor Barnes made last week? We took a field trip to the river to take water samples.
MAN:	Oh, I was sick last week, so I didn't know.
NARRATOR:	Why didn't the man go on the field trip?

You will read the following question on screen:

TOEFL – LISTENING

Why didn't the man go on the field trip?

Ⓐ He was sick.

Ⓑ He didn't remember Professor Barnes.

Ⓒ He went to a barn.

● He was absent the week before and didn't hear about it.

KAPLAN

The questions on the short converstions in Part A are standard multiple-choice only. For the long conversations and talks in Part B, you will be asked questions in a variety of formats. Many of them will be the typical four-choice answer, as in the short conversations, but some will not. Other types of question formats include:

Matching

You must click on one element (a word, phrase or picture) and then click on the element to which it corresponds.

For example:

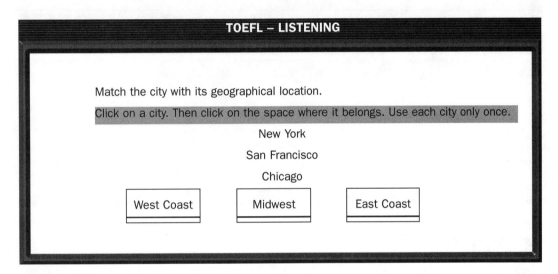

Multiple Answer

You must click on two or more boxes to complete your answer.

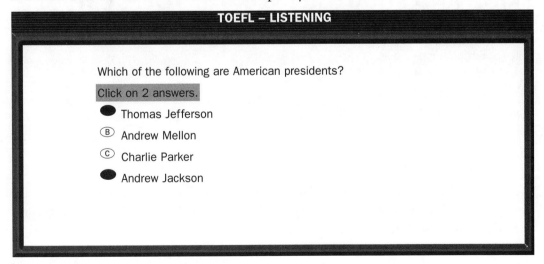

If you do not click on the number of choices that the question asks you to, you will not be able to proceed to the next question.

Graphic Element

You must click on a picture, or a region within a picture in order to select your answer.

SCORING

The Listening Comprehension section of the TOEFL CBT will be scored on a scale of 0 to 30.

SKILLS AND STRATEGIES FOR THE TOEFL CBT

Specific skills that you will practice throughout this section are:

- Restatement
- Identifying the main idea
- Identifying the main topic
- Determining time and sequence
- Identifying facts
- Making inferences
- Understanding the speakers' tone

Even though the Listening Comprehension section has been adapted for the computer, the same general skill is being tested as on the paper-based exam—listening. Below we offer some strategies to help you "test your best" on the TOEFL CBT Listening Comprehension section.

Strategies

Use the Graphics to Help You Focus

The photos of men and women talking in the short and longer conversations are there to help you focus. In the talks, the graphics are used to illustrate and clarify what the lecturer is discussing. You will always see the title of the lecture and a photo of the person lecturing. Once the lecture has begun, you will see graphics that illustrate content points in the lecture—perhaps a difficult vocabulary word or a person's name that appears to be written on a chalkboard, or pictures or charts that give an example of what the lecturer is describing—a chart, a map, a technical drawing, or an example of an artist's style, for example.

You will not receive new information in the graphic nor will you be given information that the lecturer doesn't also describe verbally. Don't worry if the voice doesn't seem to match the picture. Sometimes you will hear what sounds like a much older person's voice and see a picture of a younger adult; don't let that distract you. Remember, the Listening Comprehension section of the TOEFL CBT is not testing your visual comprehension, it is testing your ability to make sense of what you hear.

The Kaplan EASEL Method

(1) Engage

Engage your brain. Be ready to listen to discussions and talks that you would expect to find in a university setting.

(2) Anticipate

Think ahead. What kind of vocabulary would you expect to hear from two people talking on a campus? When the title of the talk appears, what kind of words or ideas do you think might come up?

(3) Summarize

You are not permitted to write during the TOEFL CBT exam, but you can mentally summarize what you have already heard. Listen for pauses in the talks; this probably means that the speaker is moving on to a new thought. In your mind, note what the speaker has just finished saying. Hint: The TOEFL often asks you to do this when it gives you Main Topic, Main Idea, and Restatement questions.

(4) Evaluate

What did you think of what the speaker just said? Did you agree or disagree? Was the speaker convincing? What was the tone of the speaker's voice? Hint: The TOEFL asks you to do this when it gives you Inference questions.

(5) Learn

What ideas or facts do you remember from the talk? After all, that is why you listen in the first place, isn't it? Hint: The TOEFL asks you to do this when it gives you Fact, Sequence, and Reference questions.

CHUNK!

Linguistic research shows that native speakers of a language do not learn the language word by word. Instead, they first hear and then learn language in "unanalyzed chunks." This ability to remember multiword chunks is what produces meaningful patterns in your, the speaker's, mind. When you speak your first language, you are remembering these patterns and chunks rather than analyzing them. You probably have a repertoire of thousands of these multiword chunks in your heads which you pull from your memory storage whenever they are needed. If you have learned English as a second language in a traditional, grammar-based way, you are probably doing something very different from this with the English language when you speak. That is, you are more than likely analyzing vocabulary word-for-word based on rules you have learned in the past: "Do I use the preposition *of* or *at*?" "Do I use the past tense of the verb or the present?" and so on.

Chunking helps you develop an intuition about the language, which is similar to a native speaker. Americans speak in chunks and the people you will hear in the Listening Comprehension section of the TOEFL CBT are no different. If you study in chunks, identifying the correct response without having to analyze each individual word becomes much easier.

Here is an example:

MAN:	How are your classes this year?
WOMAN:	Let me tell you, it seems like this semester will never end!
NARRATOR:	What does the woman mean?

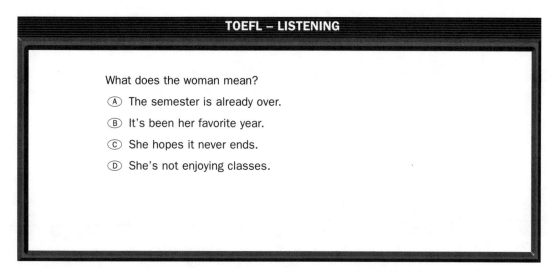

In this exchange, you can see a couple of chunks which will help you find the answer:

- *Let me tell you* (expresses annoyance or dissatisfaction)
- *It seems like this. . . will never end* (expresses the feeling that an activity is difficult)

If you were studying in chunks, you would be able to figure out that the woman is not enjoying her classes (answer D) from either of the chunks above.

A Note on the Practice Exercises

In the exercises that follow, we have attempted, to the fullest extent possible, to include all of the question types found on the Listening Comprehension section of the TOEFL CBT. However, it is impossible to accurately reproduce computerized question types in a paper-based format such as this book, and we recommend that you turn to the *Mastering the Computer-Based TOEFL* CD ROM for more practice in a truly CBT-like environment.

Listening Power
Lesson One

FOR LISTENING PART A OF THE TOEFL CBT

At a Glance:

This part of the TOEFL consists of a series of very short dialogues followed by a question. The student then selects one of four possible items as the best answer to the question.

For this lesson it is important to know what a *distractor* is:

A *distractor* is a wrong answer that looks correct. Test makers use distractors to trap you into choosing the wrong answer.

There are seven different types of distractors found in the Listening section:

- Homophones
- Synonyms
- Negatives
- Pronouns
- Time and sequencing
- Unreal situations
- Multiple referents

Remember that the TOEFL test makers use distractors to trick you into getting the question wrong.

SESSION A: HOMOPHONE DISTRACTORS

Homophone distractors are words or phrases that sound the same as or similar to words or phrases heard in the conversation.

Here is a TOEFL question that has a homophone distractor in the answer set.

Suppose you hear:

WOMAN: It's so hot—will fall ever get here?

MAN: It's just around the bend.

TOEFL – LISTENING

What does the man mean?

(A) It is close.

(B) He'll have to be flexible to make it to the meeting.

(C) It's just been to the fall.

(D) He will fall soon.

Answer (C) contains a homophone. *Just been* is a homophone that sounds similar to *just around the bend*, which was said in the original conversation. You should not be distracted into choosing that answer simply because it sounds similar.

In this case, (A) is the correct answer because *just around the bend* is an idiomatic expression that means *nearby* or *soon*. You will also notice that (A) sounds the most different from the original conversation. Keep in mind that there is no guarantee that the correct answer on the TOEFL exam will always be the one that sounds the most different, but it is usually a complete rephrasing of the conversation.

Similar-sounding answers are often wrong.

SESSION B: SYNONYM DISTRACTORS

Synonym distractors are words and phrases that seem to mean the same thing as a word or phrase in the conversation.

Can you identify the synonym distractor in the answer set of this example?

WOMAN: How did you do on the biology final?

MAN: Not great. I think I might have failed it.

TOEFL – LISTENING

What is the woman asking the man?

Ⓐ how he is feeling today

Ⓑ if he likes biology

Ⓒ if he had taken the last biology class of the semester

Ⓓ how he did on his biology exam

Answer (C) contains a synonym distractor. *Last* is substituted for *final* in the original conversation. *Last* and *final* are often synonyms for each other, but you have to remember that synonyms in one context may not be synonyms in another. Here you must pay special attention to the context in which the word *final* is used in the conversation—in this case it means "the final exam of the semester." (D) is the correct answer.

Don't be fooled by answers that use synonyms for the words in the dialogue. Read all the answer choices carefully before making your selection.

SESSION C: NEGATIVE DISTRACTORS

Negative distractors are answers in the negative that seem to mean the same as a statement in the conversation, but in reality mean the opposite.

Can you identify the negative distractor in this example?

WOMAN: Are you going to the bookstore tonight?

MAN: No way! I've got a date.

TOEFL – LISTENING

What does the man say?

- Ⓐ that he will be away
- Ⓑ that he will be late
- Ⓒ that he is not going on a date
- Ⓓ that he is meeting someone that night

In this question, answer choice (C) is a negative distractor. A student who is not paying careful attention might hear the negative in the man's answer—"No way!"—and incorrectly choose an answer that also contains a negative.

Answers (A) and (B) are homophone distractors ("away" sounds like "way," and "late" sounds like "date") . Therefore, (D) is the correct answer.

Another variation of the negative distractor is the use of a negative tag question in the conversation. On the TOEFL, when a person responds with a negative tag question, he/she is voicing agreement.

MAN: It's really hot today.

WOMAN: Isn't it, though?

The woman's response means that she agrees with him. Take a look at how this question might look on the TOEFL below. The correct answer to the following question is (B).

MAN: Jill's quite a card.

WOMAN: Isn't she, though?

TOEFL – LISTENING

What does the woman mean?

(A) She thinks Jill is not talented.

● She agrees with the man.

(C) She has not played cards with Jill.

(D) She did not hear his comment.

SESSION D: PRONOUN DISTRACTORS

Pronoun distractors are pronouns that either reverse the gender of the person being referred to or that confuse the interrogative pronouns *who*, *which*, or *what*.

Can you identify the pronoun distractor in this example?

MAN: Are you sure John's store is closed?

WOMAN: Oh, yes. My brother heard it from him directly.

TOEFL – LISTENING

How does the woman know the store is closed?

(A) he got it from her brother

● she heard it from her brother

(C) his brother didn't hear John

(D) John told it to the woman

(A) and (C) are pronoun distractors. Answers (A) and (C) contain pronouns that have the wrong gender. The man in the conversation did not hear about the store first, as (A) implies. (D) confuses John, the subject of the conversation, with the woman's brother, who was the one who actually gave the information to the woman. (B) is the correct answer.

Can you identify the interrogative pronoun distractor in this example?

WOMAN: What are you going to take next term?

MAN: World History and Art History, but I haven't decided about my other courses.

TOEFL – LISTENING

What does the woman ask the man?

(A) which courses he will take

(B) who he will take this semester

(C) what he will take to Art History

(D) what he will do this afternoon

Answers (B), (C), and (D) all confuse the interrogative pronoun. Notice that (C) especially causes a distraction because it repeats the same interrogative question. But (C) is asking what object he will take to Art History, which has a different meaning from the question in the conversation.

Always listen carefully to determine "who is doing what" in TOEFL dialogues.

"What are you taking?" is a common way of asking someone, "Which courses will you be taking?" So the correct answer is (A).

KAPLAN

SESSION E: TIME AND SEQUENCING DISTRACTORS

Time and *Sequencing distractors* offer confusing alternatives to the order of events in the conversation.

Can you identify the time/sequencing distractors in the following example?

MAN: When did you start your classes?

WOMAN: The week before last.

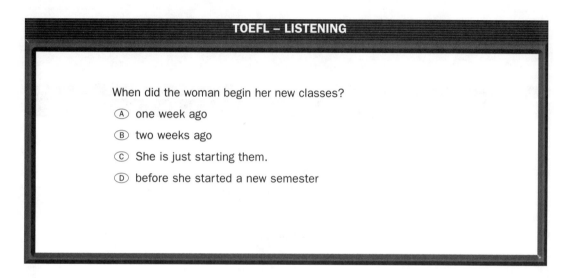

Answer (B) is correct. "The week before last" is another way of saying "two weeks ago." Answer (A) refers to "one week," which can be confused with the woman's response "The week," and answer (D) repeats the word *before* in a different context than it is used in the conversation.

SESSION F: UNREAL SITUATION DISTRACTORS

Unreal situation distractors try to make you think that an unreal or imaginary situation truly happened.

These unreal situations may be in the future or in a conditional if clause. Sometimes, to answer the question correctly, the student will have to make an inference and ignore information given directly in the conversation.

Can you identify the unreal situation distractor in this example?

WOMAN: If I had bought that lampshade, I would have gotten the green one.

MAN: Well, it's not as though there was a large selection.

TOEFL – LISTENING

What does the man tell the woman?

(A) He's happy with the aftershave that he bought.

(B) He's sorry that the woman bought the lampshade.

(C) He will purchase the lampshade next time.

(D) There were a limited number of lampshades.

Answer (B) is the unreal situation distractor. The woman did not buy the lampshade. When she says, "If I had bought that lampshade," she is using a conditional clause to describe an unreal situation. (See Structure Power Lesson Three, Session C for help on conditionals.) In his answer, the man justifies his choice by saying that there wasn't a large selection of lampshades. For that reason, (D) is the correct answer.

Let's take a look at another example of an unreal situation distractor. Can you find it?

WOMAN: Would you pick up some milk?

MAN: Why not? I've been sitting around all day. What kind do you want?

TOEFL – LISTENING

Where does the conversation probably take place?

(A) in a supermarket

(B) at the man's home

(C) at the man's place of work

(D) at a table

In this example, (A) is the unreal situation distractor. A student who hears the word *milk* might think that the conversation takes place in a supermarket. Here, the phrasal verb to pick up means to purchase it at a store. To get this question right, you must infer that the speakers are at home, and not be confused by the word *milk*.

SESSION G: MULTIPLE REFERENT DISTRACTORS

Multiple referent distractors occur when several people or items are mentioned and the answers then repeat all or some of the characters in an attempt to confuse you. Comparisons are often used to present this type of distractor problem.

Can you identify the multiple referent distractors in this example?

MAN: My job is harder than yours.

WOMAN: But mine is harder than John's!

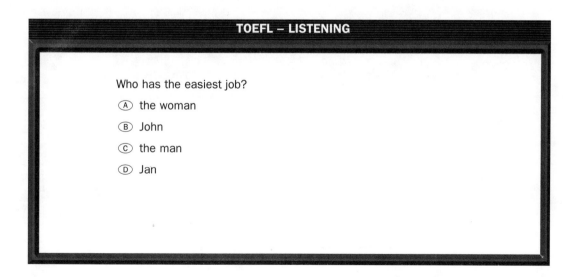

TOEFL – LISTENING

Who has the easiest job?

(A) the woman

(B) John

(C) the man

(D) Jan

Answer (B) is correct. If the man's job is harder than the woman's, and if the woman's job is harder than John's, then John's job is easier than the woman's and the man's. Therefore, John has the easiest job. Both (A) and (C) are multiple referent distractors. A student who is not listening carefully might select one of these as the answer.

Be careful to avoid the homophone distractor Jan [*dzæn*] for John [*dzan*] in (D).

PRACTICE 1: HOMOPHONE DISTRACTORS

Listen to Track_1.mov. Then select the correct answer choice for each question.

TOEFL – LISTENING

1. What does the woman mean?

   Ⓐ John could be seen by a boy in class yesterday.

   Ⓑ She didn't see John in class yesterday.

   Ⓒ John made a spectacle of himself in class yesterday.

   Ⓓ John wasn't in class until yesterday.

TOEFL – LISTENING

2. What did the man say?

   Ⓐ It's not unusual for the lab to smell peculiar.

   Ⓑ He sent something strange to the lab.

   Ⓒ It's not so strange for her to be sent to the lab.

   Ⓓ He sent something strong to the lab.

TOEFL – LISTENING

3. What is the man's response?

   Ⓐ It's a great idea.

   Ⓑ The weather's great.

   Ⓒ The weather's not so good.

   Ⓓ She looks gray today.

---

4. What does the man say?

Ⓐ He did not do very well.

Ⓑ He did okay.

Ⓒ He didn't take the quiz.

Ⓓ He quizzed her on what she said.

5. What did Mark do?

Ⓐ He accepted the accusations.

Ⓑ He charged the fighters.

Ⓒ He decided to break up the fight.

Ⓓ He pleaded with them to stop fighting.

6. What does the man mean?

Ⓐ It was a quiet noise.

Ⓑ It wasn't quite noisy.

Ⓒ It was really loud.

Ⓓ She was quite nosy.

TOEFL – LISTENING

7. How does the man feel about physics?

Ⓐ It isn't suited to him.

Ⓑ He must try to find a way to fit in.

Ⓒ He needs a new fit.

Ⓓ It suits him well.

TOEFL – LISTENING

8. What does the man say about Lee's class?

Ⓐ It's very tough.

Ⓑ It's inconsistent in difficulty.

Ⓒ It's difficult to get in to.

Ⓓ He can't say anything.

TOEFL – LISTENING

9. What does the man say about Willy?

Ⓐ He knows how to hit hard.

Ⓑ It never hit him before.

Ⓒ He's glad he didn't hit her.

Ⓓ He's glad they got along.

TOEFL – LISTENING

10. What does the man say about the algebra class?

Ⓐ The lessons should get less difficult.

Ⓑ The lessons are really tough.

Ⓒ The lessons will get more difficult later on.

Ⓓ It's always very tough.

KAPLAN

PRACTICE 2: SYNONYM DISTRACTORS

Listen to Track_2.mov. Then select the correct answer choice for each question.

TOEFL – LISTENING

1. What does the woman mean?
   - Ⓐ She bets on football games.
   - Ⓑ He better believe in her.
   - Ⓒ She will definitely go to the game.
   - Ⓓ He better go to class.

TOEFL – LISTENING

2. What does the man say about their T.A.?
   - Ⓐ He's very helpful.
   - Ⓑ He's far out.
   - Ⓒ He lives far away from them.
   - Ⓓ He's not very helpful.

TOEFL – LISTENING

3. What does the woman mean?
   - Ⓐ She'll discuss it next week.
   - Ⓑ He should start to study it more.
   - Ⓒ It won't be discussed next term.
   - Ⓓ It will be discussed next term.

TOEFL – LISTENING

4. Why did Jill drop out of school?
   - (A) She made a lot of money.
   - (B) She bought a market.
   - (C) She dropped a market.
   - (D) Her grades were very bad.

TOEFL – LISTENING

5. What does the man want to do?
   - (A) buy old textbooks
   - (B) receive his books
   - (C) turn in the books he now has
   - (D) keep his receipts

TOEFL – LISTENING

6. What will the woman do?
   - (A) consult a campus brochure for a recommendation
   - (B) ask her guide what he does
   - (C) go see a campus guy
   - (D) go far from campus

TOEFL – LISTENING

7. What does the woman want to do?
   (A) go away with the man
   (B) study in another place
   (C) take a break from the weekend
   (D) take a break from her studies

TOEFL – LISTENING

8. What does the woman say about Mary?
   (A) She's been acting bizarrely.
   (B) She's stated her mind lately.
   (C) She's not weird.
   (D) She's been in another state lately.

TOEFL – LISTENING

9. What does the teacher say about the man's request?
   (A) It's a good question.
   (B) He can submit his paper late.
   (C) He can't submit his paper late.
   (D) He's questionably late.

TOEFL – LISTENING

10. What does the woman say?

    Ⓐ All requests should be thrown away.

    Ⓑ There should be no required courses.

    Ⓒ Math is not worth getting rid of.

    Ⓓ She wishes they would get rid of the math instructors.

PRACTICE 3: NEGATIVE DISTRACTORS

Listen to Track_3.mov. Then select the correct answer choice for each question.

TOEFL – LISTENING

1. What does the man say about class?

    (A) It's chancy.

    (B) She should take a chance.

    (C) It will be canceled.

    (D) It won't be canceled.

TOEFL – LISTENING

2. What does the woman say about the lecture?

    (A) She thought it was interesting.

    (B) She hated it.

    (C) She didn't go to it.

    (D) She doesn't understand what he thinks.

TOEFL – LISTENING

3. What does the woman respond?

    (A) She's disappointed in the man.

    (B) She disagrees with the man.

    (C) She's doesn't believe the man.

    (D) She's surprised that they made the team.

TOEFL – LISTENING

4. What does the woman mean?

  Ⓐ She wants him to repeat what he said.

  Ⓑ She won't say it again.

  Ⓒ She agrees with him.

  Ⓓ She meant what she said.

TOEFL – LISTENING

5. How does the woman feel about the day?

  Ⓐ It's a fine day.

  Ⓑ The weather is not so good.

  Ⓒ He doesn't know what he's talking about.

  Ⓓ She's dismally late today.

TOEFL – LISTENING

6. How does the woman feel about the test?

  Ⓐ It couldn't be easier.

  Ⓑ It won't be difficult.

  Ⓒ It will be tough.

  Ⓓ She can't agree with the man's comments.

TOEFL – LISTENING

7. Will the woman go to summer school?

   Ⓐ in a way

   Ⓑ in her own way

   Ⓒ She'll go way out of her way.

   Ⓓ She won't go.

TOEFL – LISTENING

8. What does the man need?

   Ⓐ the woman's assistance

   Ⓑ the woman's applause

   Ⓒ a woman's touch

   Ⓓ to borrow one hand

TOEFL – LISTENING

9. What is the woman's response?

   Ⓐ She'll be part of the group.

   Ⓑ She won't participate.

   Ⓒ You can count on her.

   Ⓓ She'll count down the days.

TOEFL – LISTENING

10. How does the woman feel about the man's suggestion?

Ⓐ It's not a bad idea.

Ⓑ He should say something.

Ⓒ He shouldn't have said anything.

Ⓓ She doesn't understand what he said.

KAPLAN

PRACTICE 4: PRONOUN DISTRACTORS

Listen to Track_4.mov. Then select the correct answer choice for each question.

TOEFL – LISTENING

1. Who wants the man to go to the game?
   - Ⓐ Jan's mother doesn't.
   - Ⓑ Jan does.
   - Ⓒ The woman wants him to go with her instead of with Jan.
   - Ⓓ Jan's mother invited him.

TOEFL – LISTENING

2. Who will grade the tests?
   - Ⓐ They will.
   - Ⓑ the teacher
   - Ⓒ the teacher's assistant
   - Ⓓ the test takers

TOEFL – LISTENING

3. What does the man think?
   - Ⓐ She'll get Jim a tutor.
   - Ⓑ Jim would make a good tutor.
   - Ⓒ She needs the means to hire a tutor.
   - Ⓓ She should accept Jim's suggestion.

TOEFL – LISTENING

4. Who will the man probably vote for?

    Ⓐ He'll support Kay.

    Ⓑ He stay out of this one.

    Ⓒ He'll vote for Grant.

    Ⓓ He hasn't made up his mind.

TOEFL – LISTENING

5. What does the man think about the woman's suggestion?

    Ⓐ It's a great idea.

    Ⓑ He'll be out on the town then.

    Ⓒ It's out of the question.

    Ⓓ He needs to see his adviser then.

TOEFL – LISTENING

6. What does the man suggest?

    Ⓐ that they ask Betty to move out

    Ⓑ that he move in with his sister

    Ⓒ that they move in with his sister

    Ⓓ that they consider his sister for a roommate

KAPLAN

TOEFL – LISTENING

7. Where does Scott work now?

   (A) in the physics department

   (B) in the philosophy department

   (C) with Steve and Paul

   (D) with the woman

TOEFL – LISTENING

8. What can we assume about Jane?

   (A) She's from the woman's hometown.

   (B) She's from the man's hometown.

   (C) She knows the man who is in the woman's Western Civ. class.

   (D) She's taking Western Civ.

TOEFL – LISTENING

9. What does the man think?

   (A) He can't give his speech today.

   (B) He shouldn't have to give a speech before the class.

   (C) He's before Jack and Susan.

   (D) He should probably give his speech by next week.

TOEFL – LISTENING

10. What does the man say?

Ⓐ They should invite them to join us.

Ⓑ He needs to get a new suit.

Ⓒ They are ill-suited for him.

Ⓓ The woman's idea doesn't suit him.

PRACTICE 5: TIME AND SEQUENCING DISTRACTORS

Listen to Track_5.mov. Then select the correct answer choice for each question.

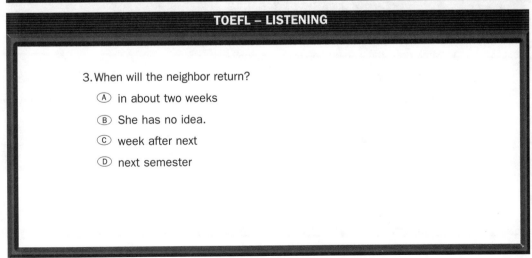

TOEFL – LISTENING

1. Has the woman seen the movie?
   - Ⓐ She plans to go in a couple of days.
   - Ⓑ She saw it yesterday.
   - Ⓒ It left two days ago.
   - Ⓓ She saw it two days ago.

TOEFL – LISTENING

2. When should they turn in their papers?
   - Ⓐ next week
   - Ⓑ They are overdue.
   - Ⓒ day after next
   - Ⓓ in about two weeks

TOEFL – LISTENING

3. When will the neighbor return?
   - Ⓐ in about two weeks
   - Ⓑ She has no idea.
   - Ⓒ week after next
   - Ⓓ next semester

TOEFL – LISTENING

4. What does the woman think of the man's offer?

Ⓐ She's too sleepy to think about it now.

Ⓑ She needs a day to decide.

Ⓒ She can't go with him.

Ⓓ She doesn't like sleeping in Spain.

TOEFL – LISTENING

5. When does the woman plan to go home?

Ⓐ the week after this one

Ⓑ at the end of this weekend

Ⓒ in a couple of days

Ⓓ She won't be able to go home.

TOEFL – LISTENING

6. When does the woman hope to graduate?

Ⓐ this term

Ⓑ She has no idea.

Ⓒ week after next

Ⓓ next semester

TOEFL – LISTENING

7. When does the woman say Thanksgiving is celebrated?
   A every Thursday in November
   B always the last week in November
   C in November on the last Thursday of that month
   D She doesn't know what the man means.

TOEFL – LISTENING

8. About how often does the woman go to the gym?
   A 3 or 4 days a week
   B 5 days a week
   C every 5 days
   D The gym didn't work out.

TOEFL – LISTENING

9. What does the woman say about her research paper?
   A She expects to be finished by the end of the day.
   B She'll be through by 3:00.
   C She's already through with it.
   D She may finish it tomorrow.

TOEFL – LISTENING

10. What can the man do about his class?

Ⓐ drop it and get refunded

Ⓑ pass the deadline

Ⓒ drop it, but it's too late to get his money back

Ⓓ get refunded, then drop the matter

PRACTICE 6: UNREAL SITUATION DISTRACTORS

Listen to Track_6.mov. Then select the correct answer choice for each question.

TOEFL – LISTENING

1. What does the woman think about having class outside?

   Ⓐ She likes the idea.

   Ⓑ She glad that it's stopped raining.

   Ⓒ It would bother her.

   Ⓓ Her allergies aren't bad outside.

TOEFL – LISTENING

2. What does the woman plan to do this Friday?

   Ⓐ go out with the man

   Ⓑ make other plans

   Ⓒ not go out with the man

   Ⓓ make other plans with the man

TOEFL – LISTENING

3. What does the woman say about the man's suggestion?

   Ⓐ It's a good idea, but not possible.

   Ⓑ She'll possibly take him up on it.

   Ⓒ He's full of himself.

   Ⓓ Geometry isn't offered next semester.

TOEFL – LISTENING

4. What does the woman say about the game?

   Ⓐ It's been called off.

   Ⓑ It's uncertain if it will take place today.

   Ⓒ He'd better show up soon.

   Ⓓ It's been changed to a night game.

TOEFL – LISTENING

5. What does the man advise the woman to do?

   Ⓐ She'd better take a crack at tomorrow's lesson.

   Ⓑ She'd better crack up soon.

   Ⓒ She'd better get her act together or she'll be far behind.

   Ⓓ She'd better catch the train soon or she'll be late.

TOEFL – LISTENING

6. What did the man say about the test?

   Ⓐ He wished that he had studied instead of partying.

   Ⓑ Everybody asked about it.

   Ⓒ He wished he had studied more.

   Ⓓ He didn't know that it had been postponed.

TOEFL – LISTENING

7. What does the man imply?
   - Ⓐ He wishes he were taller.
   - Ⓑ He wishes he could play football.
   - Ⓒ He wishes she would try harder.
   - Ⓓ It's too late for the tryouts.

TOEFL – LISTENING

8. What does the woman believe?
   - Ⓐ The evidence is inconclusive.
   - Ⓑ They will be too late for their plane.
   - Ⓒ She will miss him very much.
   - Ⓓ He has gone too far this time.

TOEFL – LISTENING

9. What does the woman imply?
   - Ⓐ She can't go right now.
   - Ⓑ The coffee will be ready in 15 minutes.
   - Ⓒ She needs to be back in 15 minutes.
   - Ⓓ She doesn't want to go with the man.

10. What is the woman's advice?

Ⓐ He should stop jamming.

Ⓑ He should stop getting stuck in a rut.

Ⓒ He shouldn't use the stapler on the machine.

Ⓓ The copier is very old.

KAPLAN

PRACTICE 7: MULTIPLE REFERENT DISTRACTORS

Listen to Track_7.mov. Then select the correct answer choice for each question.

TOEFL – LISTENING

1. What does the man say about the test?
   - Ⓐ About 2/3 passed the test.
   - Ⓑ About 2/3 took it.
   - Ⓒ He could only finish a third of it.
   - Ⓓ Most of the class didn't take it.

TOEFL – LISTENING

2. What does the man say about the test?
   - Ⓐ It's optional.
   - Ⓑ It's mandatory.
   - Ⓒ It will be a take-home.
   - Ⓓ She has to do a research paper as well.

TOEFL – LISTENING

3. How often does the man eat in the cafeteria?
   - Ⓐ as often as he can
   - Ⓑ on rare occasions
   - Ⓒ He's never eaten there.
   - Ⓓ He's there right now and then.

TOEFL – LISTENING

4. How old is John?

  Ⓐ He's the eldest child.

  Ⓑ He's the middle child.

  Ⓒ He's middle-aged.

  Ⓓ He's the youngest child.

TOEFL – LISTENING

5. What does the man say about the Civil War?

  Ⓐ They will finish it before the break.

  Ⓑ It will be discussed before the American Revolution.

  Ⓒ It will be discussed after the break.

  Ⓓ They have to break up the American Revolution first.

TOEFL – LISTENING

6. How many people are living in the suite now?

  Ⓐ three

  Ⓑ four

  Ⓒ one

  Ⓓ five

KAPLAN

TOEFL – LISTENING

7. What does the man say?

   Ⓐ Tim should drop the course soon.

   Ⓑ It's too late for Dr. Kim to drop the course.

   Ⓒ He will say later what he should do.

   Ⓓ Tim is always too late to do anything.

TOEFL – LISTENING

8. What does the man plan to do?

   Ⓐ go over to Sam's house

   Ⓑ mind what he has to do

   Ⓒ go to the gym

   Ⓓ He'll decide later if he likes shooting or not.

TOEFL – LISTENING

9. Where does the man think she should live?

   Ⓐ some place other than Carlin or Monroe

   Ⓑ in either Carlin or Monroe

   Ⓒ He can't say because it isn't up to him.

   Ⓓ Both Carlin and Monroe are good choices.

TOEFL – LISTENING

10.   What does the man imply?

   Ⓐ He doesn't want to go into it.

   Ⓑ He got into the class.

   Ⓒ His overall grade isn't too bad.

   Ⓓ He did much better than before.

LISTENING POWER LESSON ONE SCRIPTS AND ANSWER KEYS

PRACTICE 1: HOMOPHONE DISTRACTORS SCRIPT

(Track_1.mov)

1. **W:** That was quite a scene John made in class yesterday.
   M: Boy, I'll say!
   N: What does the woman mean?

2. **W:** There's a strong smell coming from the chemistry lab.
   M: That's not so strange!
   N: What did the man say?

3. **W:** Let's go the beach today after class.
   M: I don't know—it looks rather gray.
   N: What is the man's response?

4. **W:** How did you do on the psych quiz?
   M: I feel like I didn't do too bad.
   N: What does the man say?

5. **W:** How did Mark plead to the charges against him?
   M: He decided not to fight them.
   N: What did Mark do?

6. **W:** Wow, what was that?
   M: I have no idea—it was quite a noise!
   N: What does the man mean?

7. **W:** I'm glad you switched majors.
   M: Me too. Physics fits me to a T.
   N: How does the man feel about physics?

8. **W:** Is Dr. Lee's class very difficult?

    M: Hard to say—it seems to vary each semester.

    N: What does the man say about Lee's class?

9. **W:** Willy was a very easy-going roommate to have.

    M: Oh, I'm glad to know you two hit it off.

    N: What does the man say about Willy?

10. **W:** Is algebra always this tough?

    M: Not really—it should ease up by mid-term.

    N: What does the man say about the algebra class?

PRACTICE 1 ANSWER KEY

1. C	6. C
2. A	7. D
3. C	8. B
4. B	9. D
5. A	10. A

SCRIPT FOR PRACTICE 2: SYNONYM DISTRACTORS

(**Track_2.mov**)

1. **M:** Do you think you'll be able to go to the football game with us after class?

    W: You bet!

    N: What does the woman mean?

2. **M:** Our T.A. really went out of his way for us.

    W: I'll say!

    N: What does the man say about their T.A.?

3. **M:** When are we going to learn more about 20th century inventors?

    W: We'll take that up next term.

    N: What does the woman mean?

4. **M:** Do you know why Jill dropped out of business school?

    W: I sure do—she made a fortune in the market.

    N: Why did Jill drop out of school?

5. **M:** Excuse me—can I still exchange my books?

    W: Only if you have the receipt.

    N: What does the man want to do?

6. **M:** Is there any decent place to eat near campus?

    W: I don't think so, but let's see what's in our campus guide.

    N: What will the woman do?

7. **M:** Do you want to study together this weekend?

    W: Sorry, I'm going to try to get away from school for a couple of days.

    N: What does the woman want to do?

8. **M:** Mary's been acting kind of strange lately.

    W: She's been in a weird state of mind.

    N: What does the woman say about Mary?

9. **M:** Is it okay if we turn in our papers a week late?

    W: That's out of the question.

    N: What does the teacher say about the man's request?

10. **M:** I wish they would get rid of the math requirement.

    W: I wish they would get rid of all of them!

    N: What does the woman say?

PRACTICE 2 ANSWER KEY

1. C	6. A
2. A	7. D
3. D	8. A
4. A	9. C
5. C	10. B

SCRIPT FOR PRACTICE 3: NEGATIVE DISTRACTORS

(Track_3.mov)

1. **W:** Do you think class will be called off tonight?

    M: Not a chance.

    N: What does the man say about class?

2. **M:** That was a really interesting lecture, don't you think?

    W: Wasn't it, though?

    N: What does the woman say about the lecture?

3. **M:** I couldn't believe we both made the team.

    W: Me neither.

    N: What does the woman respond?

4. **M:** I don't ever want to go through anything like that again.

    W: I'll say.

    N: What does the woman mean?

5. **M:** It's a dismal day.

    W: Isn't it, though?

    N: How does the woman feel about the day?

6. **M:** This test isn't going to be easy.

    W: I couldn't agree with you more.

    N: How does the woman feel about the test?

7. **M:** Are you thinking about going to summer school?

    W: No way.

    N: Will the woman go to summer school?

8. **M:** Can't you lend me a hand?

    W: What do you want me to do?

    N: What does the man need?

9. **M:** Would you like to be part of our study group?

    W: Count me out.

    N: What is the woman's response?

10. **M:** Don't you think it would be a good idea to upgrade your computer?

    W: Well, if you say so.

    N: How does the woman feel about the man's suggestion?

PRACTICE 3 ANSWER KEY

1. D	6. C
2. A	7. D
3. D	8. A
4. C	9. B
5. B	10. A

SCRIPT FOR PRACTICE 4: PRONOUN DISTRACTORS

(Track_4.mov)

1. **W:** Jan wants you and her mom to go the game together.

    M: Who does?

    N: Who wants the man to go to the game?

2. **W:** Who will grade our tests?

    M: Our teacher's T.A. will.

    N: Who will grade the tests?

3. **W:** Should I take Jim up on his offer to find me a tutor?

    M: By all means.

    N: What does the man think?

4. **W:** Grant has asked us to give him our support for student body president.

   M: I've already given mine to Kay.

   N: Who will the man probably vote for?

5. **W:** If you want to get in to Professor Jones' class you should go through preregistration.

   M: I won't be in town then.

   N: What does the man think about the woman's suggestion?

6. **W:** Susan and I are looking for a new roommate since Betty moved out last week.

   M: My sister's looking for a place.

   N: What does the man suggest?

7. **W:** I hope I can get a work-study job like the one Scott has.

   M: I know. He likes working with Paul and Steve a lot better than the job he had in the physics department.

   N: Where does Scott work now?

8. **W:** The man who sits next to me in my Western Civ. class is from my hometown.

   M: Oh, isn't that the same man we met with Jane last week?

   N: What can we assume about Jane?

9. **W:** We'll pick up on our student speeches next week, beginning with Bill, as long as we get through with Jack and Susan's presentation today.

   M: I thought I was supposed to be before Bill.

   N: What does the man think?

10. **W:** Let's see if Tom and Sally can go out with us tonight.

    M: Suits me.

    N: What does the man say?

KAPLAN

PRACTICE 4 ANSWER KEY

1. B	6. D
2. C	7. C
3. D	8. C
4. A	9. D
5. C	10. A

SCRIPT FOR PRACTICE 5: TIME AND SEQUENCING DISTRACTORS

(Track_5.mov)

1. **M:** Have you seen the new movie at the student union?

    W: I did the day before yesterday.

    N: Has the woman seen the movie?

2. **M:** When are our papers due?

    W: He said the week after next.

    N: When should they turn in their papers?

3. **M:** Have you seen our neighbor?

    W: I saw him two days ago and he said he'd be out of town for a couple of weeks.

    N: When will the neighbor return?

4. **M:** Would you like to go to Spain with me on spring break?

    W: I'll see. Let me sleep on it.

    N: What does the woman think of the man's offer?

5. **M:** When will you go home again?

    W: Well, if I can finish this paper in a day or two, maybe I'll leave at the end of next week.

    N: When does the woman plan to go home?

6. **M:** When do you plan to graduate?

    W: If I pass everything this term, I hope to the semester after this.

    N: When does the woman hope to graduate?

7. **M:** Do you know when Thanksgiving is?

    W: I don't know the exact date, but it's always the last Thursday of November.

    N: When does the woman say Thanksgiving is celebrated?

8. **M:** Are you still going to the gym five days a week?

    W: Now I work out every other day.

    N: About how often does the woman go to the gym?

9. **M:** It's almost 3:00—I hope I can finish my research paper by tomorrow.

    W: I should be through with mine in a few hours.

    N: What does the woman say about her research paper?

10. **M:** How late can we drop a class and still get a refund?

    W: I'm afraid it's too late to get your money back.

    N: What can the man do about his class?

PRACTICE 5 ANSWER KEY

1. D	6. D
2. D	7. C
3. A	8. A
4. B	9. A
5. A	10. C

SCRIPT FOR PRACTICE 6: UNREAL SITUATION DISTRACTORS

(Track_6.mov)

1. **M:** If it weren't raining, we could have class outside today.

    W: I'm glad we're not because my allergies are really bad now.

    N: What does the woman think about having class outside?

2. **M:** How would you feel about going out with me this Friday?

    W: I wish I could, but I've already made other plans.

    N: What does the woman plan to do this Friday?

3. **M:** Why don't you take geometry this semester?

    W: I would if I could, but it's full.

    N: What does the woman say about the man's suggestion?

4. **M:** Are the Yankees playing this afternoon?

    W: Not unless these showers let up soon.

    N: What does the woman say about the game?

5. **M:** If I were you, I'd start cracking the books soon, or you'll never catch up.

    W: I'll think about that tomorrow—now I have better things to do.

    N: What does the man advise the woman to do?

6. **M:** Had I known the test was put off last week, I would have gone to the party.

    W: Everybody asked about you.

    N: What did the man say about the test?

7. **M:** If I were taller, I'd have gone out for basketball instead of football.

    W: It's never too late to try.

    N: What does the man imply?

8. **M:** Unless we hurry, we're going to miss our plane.

    W: I think that's a foregone conclusion.

    N: What does the woman believe?

9. **M:** I could really use a cup of coffee.

    W: If you can wait fifteen minutes, I'll join you.

    N: What does the woman imply?

10. **M:** The copier is stuck again.

    W: That's because you used the stapler and it keeps jamming.

    N: What is the woman's advice?

PRACTICE 6 ANSWER KEY

1. C	6. D
2. C	7. A
3. A	8. B
4. B	9. A
5. C	10. C

PRACTICE 7: MULTIPLE REFERENT DISTRACTORS

(Track_7.mov)

1. **W:** Did everybody turn up for the exam?

   M: Only about a third ended up taking it.

   N: What does the man say about the test?

2. **W:** Will we have a final exam?

   M: You have a choice of that or a take-home research paper.

   N: What does the man say about the test?

3. **W:** Do you eat in the school cafeteria often?

   M: Only every now and then if I can help it.

   N: How often does the man eat in the cafeteria?

4. **W:** Who is older? You or your brother John?

   M: My sister Sue is the oldest. I'm in the middle.

   N: How old is John?

5. **W:** When are we going to study the Civil War?

   M: Not until after the break when we've finished with the American Revolution.

   N: What does the man say about the Civil War?

6. **W:** How many suitemates do you have?

    M: I had four until one dropped out last month.

    N: How many people are living in the suite now?

7. **W:** If my grades were as low as Tim's, I'd drop Dr. Kim's course before it was too late to do anything about it.

    M: I'm with you.

    N: What does the man say?

8. **W:** Paul and I are going over to the gym to shoot some baskets with Sam. Want to come along?

    M: Don't mind if I do.

    N: What does the man plan to do?

9. **W:** Which dorm is better: Carlin or Monroe?

    M: Actually, I'd go with something else if I were you.

    N: Where does the man think she should live?

10. **W:** How did you do on your last calculus test?

    M: Not so great, but it's not a big deal—I had a great average going into it.

    N: What does the man imply?

PRACTICE 7 ANSWER KEY

1. D	6. B
2. A	7. A
3. B	8. C
4. D	9. A
5. C	10. C

Listening Power
Lesson Two

FOR LISTENING PART B OF THE TOEFL CBT

At a Glance:

Listening Power Lesson Two will help you with Part B of the Listening Comprehension section of the TOEFL CBT. This part of the test consists of a series of longer conversations and lectures followed by several questions. Between each question there is a pause of about ten seconds. During this pause, the student selects his answer, and then waits for the next question.

It may be tempting for you to take notes while you are listening to the talks, but writing while listening is considered cheating, so don't do it!

Although this Power Lesson is intended to help you get ready for Section B of the Listening Comprehension of the TOEFL CBT, keep in mind that all of the distractors you learned from the first lesson—from homophone distractors to multiple referent distractors—could show up on this part of the test, too.

SESSION A: MAIN TOPIC, MAIN IDEA, AND TONE QUESTIONS

Main Topic

Main topic questions ask you to identify the general topic under discussion. In Part B of the Listening Comprehension Section of the TOEFL CBT, the vast majority of topics will be academic in orientation. When listening to a conversation or talk, you should do the following things in order to catch the topic:

- Try to picture the talk taking place.
- Make assumptions about who is talking.
- Listen to key or repeated vocabulary items.
- Make assumptions about where the people are talking.

It is only by gathering global knowledge of the talk that you will be able to determine the main topic of the talk. Main topic questions are often asked in the following ways:

What is the main topic of the talk?

What are the speakers mainly discussing?

What is the subject of this talk?

Main Idea

Main idea questions ask you to summarize the whole talk. When listening to the talk, you should do the following things in order to catch the main idea.

- Identify the topic under discussion.
- Make assumptions about who is talking.
- Listen to key or repeated vocabulary items.
- Make assumptions about where the people are talking.
- Understand the attitude of each of the speakers while they are talking.
- Understand how each speaker feels about the other speaker's ideas.

It is only by understanding the vocabulary and the attitude of each of the speakers that you will be able to determine the main idea of the talk.

Main idea questions are often asked in the form of:

What is the main idea of the talk?

What best summarizes the talk?

Tone

Tone questions ask you to analyze the attitude of the speakers and the dynamics of their relationship during the conversation or talk. When listening to the talk, you should do the following things in order to catch the tone.

- Identify the topic under discussion.
- Make assumptions about who is talking.
- Listen to key or repeated vocabulary items.
- Understand the position of each of the speakers while they are talking.
- Understand how each speaker feels about the other speaker's ideas.
- Listen carefully to each speaker's intonation pattern.
- Listen carefully for key vocabulary and expressions that will give you the speakers' attitudes.
- Make assumptions about who the audience is, and how they would feel about listening to the talk.

It is only by understanding the vocabulary and the attitude of each of the speakers that you will be able to determine the tone of the talk.

Tone questions are often asked in the form of:

What is the man's/woman's attitude toward the talk?

How does the man/woman feel?

The man's/woman's feeling toward the subject can best be described as:

SESSION B: FACT-BASED AND INFERENCE QUESTIONS

Fact-Based Questions

These questions will require you to recall direct information related in the spoken text. To answer fact-based questions, you should:

- Listen carefully to the details of the talk.
- Try to understand unfamiliar words from context.
- Pay special attention to numbers and proper nouns.

Inference Questions

Inference questions ask you to draw conclusions about specific details in the passage or to make comparisons between details. In order to answer inference questions, you should:

- Listen carefully to the details of the talk.
- Try to understand unfamiliar words from context.
- Use your knowledge about the situation to guess what sort of logical conclusions might occur.

Inference questions are usually asked in the following form:

It can be inferred from the talk that . . .

The man or woman most probably . . .

What will the man or woman probably do next?

Now let's see how all the different types of questions covered in this Power Lesson might come up in a talk.

TOEFL – LISTENING

Example:

MAN: I'd like to tell you about an interesting TV program that'll be shown this coming Thursday. It'll be on from 9 to 10 P.M., on Channel 4. It's part of a series called "Mysteries of Human Biology." The subject of the program is the human brain—how it functions and how it can malfunction. Topics that will be covered are dreams, memories, and depression. These topics are illustrated with outstanding computer animation that makes the explanations easy to follow. Make an effort to see this show. Since we've been studying the nervous system in class, I know you'll find it very helpful.

TOEFL – LISTENING

1. What does the speaker mainly discuss?
    Ⓐ science programs on TV
    Ⓑ dreams, memories, and depression
    Ⓒ requirements for the class
    Ⓓ a television program on the human brain

This is a MAIN TOPIC question. The correct answer is (D). The man is talking about a particular television program whose subject is the human brain.

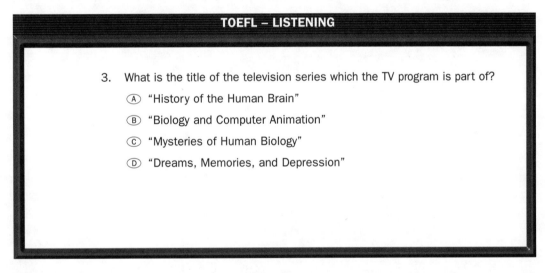

TOEFL – LISTENING

2. How does the speaker feel about the topic?
    Ⓐ enthusiastic
    Ⓑ confused
    Ⓒ inquisitive
    Ⓓ embarrassed

This is a TONE question. The man uses the adjectives *interesting, outstanding,* and *very helpful* to describe the show. Therefore we can describe his feelings about it as (A), enthusiastic.

TOEFL – LISTENING

3. What is the title of the television series which the TV program is part of?
    Ⓐ "History of the Human Brain"
    Ⓑ "Biology and Computer Animation"
    Ⓒ "Mysteries of Human Biology"
    Ⓓ "Dreams, Memories, and Depression"

This is a FACT-BASED question. The correct answer is (C). Don't be fooled by the homophone distractor in (A) and the use of exact words from the talk in (D).

```
                    TOEFL – LISTENING

        4.   What is the main purpose of the program?

             Ⓐ  to demonstrate the latest use of computer graphics

             Ⓑ  to discuss the possibility of an economic depression

             Ⓒ  to explain the workings of the brain

             Ⓓ  to dramatize a famous mystery story
```

This is an INFERENCE question. Answer (C) is correct. The question asks you to infer from the man's statement "The subject of the program is the human brain," and from the subsequent information given, that the purpose of the program is to explain the workings of the brain.

LONG CONVERSATIONS PRACTICE EXERCISES

PRACTICE 1

Look at the picture below and listen to track_8.mov. Then select the correct answer choice or choices for each question.

TOEFL – LISTENING

1. What happened to the man during the test?
   - Ⓐ He knew all the answers.
   - Ⓑ He filled in all the diagrams.
   - Ⓒ He couldn't remember the answers to one of the diagrams.
   - Ⓓ He couldn't answer the fill-in-the-blank section.

TOEFL – LISTENING

2. What can we infer about the woman?

   Select two answers.

   (A) She did well on the test.

   (B) Fill-in-the-blank questions are difficult for her.

   (C) She is a visual learner.

   (D) She likes to draw.

TOEFL – LISTENING

3. What will the speakers do next?

   (A) study separately

   (B) drop the class

   (C) study together

   (D) skip the class

TOEFL – LISTENING

4. Which diagram was difficult for the man?

   (A) the spinal column

   (B) all of them

   (C) the skull

   (D) both A and C

KAPLAN

PRACTICE 2

Look at the picture below and listen to track_9.mov. Then select the correct answer choice or choices for each question.

TOEFL – LISTENING

1. Where does this conversation probably take place?

    Ⓐ the admissions and records office

    Ⓑ the graduate studies office

    Ⓒ the professor's office

    Ⓓ the counselor's office

TOEFL – LISTENING

2. What are the speakers mainly discussing?

Ⓐ the student's work load

Ⓑ the possibility of graduation

Ⓒ the student's transcripts

Ⓓ the classes needed for graduation

TOEFL – LISTENING

3. What advice does the woman give to the man?

Ⓐ to take 18 units this semester

Ⓑ to file papers for graduation in May

Ⓒ to take summer school

Ⓓ to finish school in December

TOEFL – LISTENING

4. Why does the man want to graduate in May?
Select two answers.

Ⓐ He needs a good job.

Ⓑ He wants to get married.

Ⓒ He needs a car.

Ⓓ He needs money for his family.

PRACTICE 3

Look at the picture below and listen to track_10.mov. Then select the correct answer
choice or choices for each question.

TOEFL – LISTENING

1. The woman's attitude toward the conversation can be described as
    - (A) condescending
    - (B) sarcastic
    - (C) hateful
    - (D) bothered

TOEFL – LISTENING

2. How does the man feel?

Ⓐ angry

Ⓑ irritated

Ⓒ defensive

Ⓓ happy

TOEFL – LISTENING

3. The man and woman are probably

Ⓐ friends

Ⓑ a couple

Ⓒ relatives

Ⓓ coworkers

TOEFL – LISTENING

4. What does the woman advise the man to do?

Ⓐ stay at home and watch TV

Ⓑ go to Times Square

Ⓒ go to a New Year's party

Ⓓ make dinner reservations for New Year's Eve

PRACTICE 4

Look at the picture below and listen to track_11.mov. Then select the correct answer choice or choices for each question.

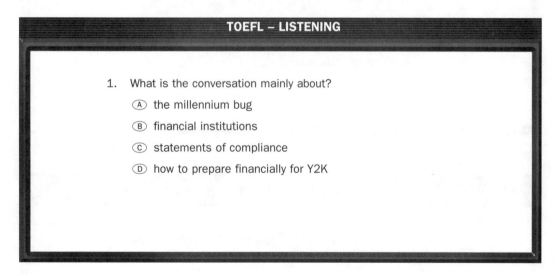

1. What is the conversation mainly about?
   - Ⓐ the millennium bug
   - Ⓑ financial institutions
   - Ⓒ statements of compliance
   - Ⓓ how to prepare financially for Y2K

TOEFL – LISTENING

2. According to the conversation, what is "a statement of compliance"?

   (A) a bank statement

   (B) a statement saying what steps have been taken to ensure a problem-free Y2K

   (C) a statement from the banks proving that they have followed the rules

   (D) a list of appliances that the bank owns

TOEFL – LISTENING

3. What does the man suggest the woman should do?

   Select two answers.

   (A) stockpile food

   (B) cash in savings bonds

   (C) have emergency cash on hand

   (D) avoid worrying too much

TOEFL – LISTENING

4. The woman's feeling toward the subject could best be described as:

   (A) concern

   (B) apathy

   (C) worry

   (D) stress

PRACTICE 5

Look at the picture below and listen to track_12.mov. Then select the correct answer
choice or choices for each question.

TOEFL – LISTENING

1. What is the main topic of the conversation?

   Ⓐ research papers

   Ⓑ the world economy

   Ⓒ It's better to put things off until the last minute.

   Ⓓ procrastination

TOEFL – LISTENING

2. According to the conversation, what does "pull off" mean?

   Ⓐ take off

   Ⓑ peel

   Ⓒ complete

   Ⓓ guess

TOEFL – LISTENING

3. What is the man's attitude toward the subject?

   Ⓐ humorous

   Ⓑ fearful

   Ⓒ confident

   Ⓓ humble

TOEFL – LISTENING

4. What part of the research paper does the woman mention?

   Ⓐ countries

   Ⓑ body

   Ⓒ thesis statement

   Ⓓ bibliography

PRACTICE 6

Look at the picture below and listen to track_13.mov. Then select the correct answer choice or choices for each question.

TOEFL – LISTENING

1. Where does this conversation probably take place?

    Ⓐ in a park

    Ⓑ at a coffee shop

    Ⓒ at someone's home

    Ⓓ in class

TOEFL – LISTENING

2. The man was probably late because

    (A) he lost track of time

    (B) he was working at his internship

    (C) he didn't care about Colleen

    (D) he got lost

TOEFL – LISTENING

3. According to the conversation, what is the topic of the woman's questionnaire?

    (A) women's health

    (B) women's salaries

    (C) women's role in the sciences

    (D) biology

TOEFL – LISTENING

4. We can infer that the man's internship involves

    Select two answers.

    (A) teaching a class

    (B) meeting people for coffee

    (C) working under the supervision of a professor

    (D) tutoring biology

PRACTICE 7

Look at the picture below and listen to track_14.mov. Then select the correct answer choice or choices for each question.

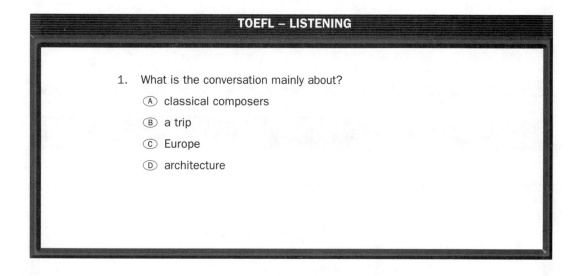

1. What is the conversation mainly about?
   Ⓐ classical composers
   Ⓑ a trip
   Ⓒ Europe
   Ⓓ architecture

TOEFL – LISTENING

2. What can we infer about the speakers?

(A) They like to go on vacation.

(B) They are good musicians.

(C) They sing.

(D) They have the same interest in seeing Europe.

TOEFL – LISTENING

3. Where will the choir tour take place?

(A) Australia

(B) Germany

(C) Norway

(D) France

TOEFL – LISTENING

4. According to the conversation, "check it out" means:

(A) look into it

(B) borrow from a library

(C) look at this

(D) make a check mark next to it

PRACTICE 8

Look at the picture below and listen to track_15.mov. Then select the correct answer choice or choices for each question.

TOEFL – LISTENING

1. Why will the woman miss class?
   - (A) illness
   - (B) because she is going on a trip
   - (C) she wants to go to a party
   - (D) religious reasons

TOEFL – LISTENING

2. Where does this conversation probably take place?
   - Ⓐ in the classroom
   - Ⓑ on the telephone
   - Ⓒ in the park
   - Ⓓ somewhere at the university

TOEFL – LISTENING

3. What does the man advise the woman to do?
   Select two answers.
   - Ⓐ have a good time
   - Ⓑ study chapter 3
   - Ⓒ get notes from a classmate
   - Ⓓ call a classmate

TOEFL – LISTENING

4. What is the man's attitude toward the conversation?
   - Ⓐ helpful
   - Ⓑ disappointed
   - Ⓒ careless
   - Ⓓ angry

KAPLAN

SCRIPT FOR LONG CONVERSATION PRACTICE EXERCISES

PRACTICE 1

(Track_8.mov)

Questions 1–4 refer to the following conversation.

W: Hi, Steve. How did you do on the anatomy test?

M: Not that great. I totally blanked out on one of the diagrams.

W: Which one? The diagram of the skull?

M: No, the spinal column.

W: Really? That one was easy for me. Actually, all of the diagrams were easy for me. It's the fill-in-the-blank section that killed me.

M: I was prepared for that section. Hey, maybe we could study together for the next test. I'll help you with the terms for the fill-ins and you can help me with the diagrams.

W: O.K. That sounds like a plan.

1. What happened to the man during the test?
2. What can we infer about the woman?
3. What will the speakers do next?
4. Which diagram was difficult for the man?

PRACTICE 1 ANSWER KEY

1. C
2. B and C
3. C
4. A

PRACTICE 2

(Track_9.mov)

Questions 1–4 refer to the following conversation.

W: Have a seat. What can I do for you today?

M: I need to talk to you about my schedule. I want to graduate in May, so I'd like permission to take 18 units this semester.

W: I see. How many hours per week are you working?

M: 20, but it's easy work.

W: Well, according to your transcripts, your grades have been OK so far, but even if you take 18 units this semester, you will still have one class to complete. That on top of your work load will make it impossible for you to graduate in May.

M: But I need a better job. I have a family to support.

W: I'm sorry, but the best I can do is suggest that you enroll for summer school and file your papers in order to graduate in August.

1. Where does this conversation probably take place?

2. What are the speakers mainly discussing?

3. What advice does the woman give to the man?

4. Why does the man want to graduate in May?

PRACTICE 2 ANSWER KEY

1. D
2. B
3. C
4. A and D

PRACTICE 3

(**Track_10.mov**)

Questions 1–4 refer to the following conversation.

W: I can't believe the year 2000 is only 100 days away!

M: Do you have millennium plans yet?

W: Yes, my husband is speaking at a conference at Ohio University a few days before New Year's. Then we're planning to drive to New York and celebrate in Times Square.

M: You'd drive all that way so you could stand on a crowded street and barely hear yourself think? You're crazy!

W: Why? What will you do, sit at home watching Dick Clark's *Rockin' Eve*? That's an inventive way to mark the millennium.

M: Hey, don't knock it. Actually, my girlfriend and I will probably go out to a nice restaurant for dinner and then ring in the new century at home.

W: Whatever makes you happy, I guess. You'd better make those dinner reservations now, though. The nice places in town have been accepting reservations since last December.

1. The woman's attitude toward the conversation can be:

2. How does the man feel?

3. The man and woman are probably:

4. What does the woman advise the man to do?

PRACTICE 3 ANSWER KEY

1. A
2. C
3. A
4. D

PRACTICE 4

(Track_11.mov)

Questions 1–4 refer to the following conversation.

M: Susan, is your bank millennium-proof?

W: What does that mean?

M: It means, is your bank prepared for Y2K? You wouldn't want them to lose your money on January 1st just because their computer believes it's suddenly 1900.

W: No, I definitely wouldn't. I want to make sure I don't bounce my tuition check! What can I do to make sure that doesn't happen?

M: Check with your bank to see if they have a statement of compliance. This proves that they have taken steps to avoid Y2K problems.

W: Is there anything else I can do?

M: The only other thing I would suggest is having a little cash on hand in case of an emergency. But don't worry too much. The banks and other financial institutions have been working on this problem for several years now. They'll be ready for it.

1. What is the conversation mainly about?

2. According to the conversation, what is "a statement of compliance"?

3. What does the man suggest the woman should do?

4. The woman's feeling toward the subject could best be described as:

PRACTICE 4 ANSWER KEY

1. D
2. B
3 C and D
4. A

PRACTICE 5

(Track_12.mov)
Questions 1–4 refer to the following conversation.

W: Hi, Mark. Did you finish your research paper yet?

M: Finish it, I haven't even started!

W: Really? But it's due in two days. I've been working on mine for two weeks.

M: I'm not concerned. I'll just go to the library today and then pull an all-nighter tomorrow. I've done it before.

W: Are you sure you can pull off ten pages on the world economy in less than 48 hours?

M: You bet. It's easy—just pick ten countries and write one page per country.

W: I think there's more to it than that. What about your introduction and conclusion? And don't forget your bibliography. Anyway, good luck with it.

M: Thanks.

1. What is the main topic of the conversation?
2. According to the conversation, what does "pull off" mean?
3. What is the man's attitude toward the subject?
4. What part of the research paper does the woman mention?

PRACTICE 5 ANSWER KEY

1. A
2. C
3. C
4. D

PRACTICE 6

(Track_13.mov)
Questions 1–4 refer to the following conversation.

M: Hi, Colleen. Sorry I'm late. This internship is really keeping me busy. Have you ordered yet?

W: Yes. What would you like? It's my treat this time, since you helped me finish that questionnaire.

M: Oh, thanks. I'll just have a coffee.

W: OK. Listen, I wanted to ask you another favor. You're tutoring in a biology class, right?

M: Yeah, Bio 100. Why?

W: Well, I need a place to distribute the questionnaire, and since it's about women's changing role in the sciences, I thought a freshman bio class would be the perfect one.

M: That sounds fine to me, but you'll have to clear it with the professor first.

W: OK, I'll do that. Thanks.

1. Where does this conversation probably take place?

2. The man was probably late because:

3. According to the conversation, what is the topic of the woman's questionnaire?

4. We can infer that the man's internship involves:

PRACTICE 6 ANSWER KEY

1. B
2. B
3. C
4. C and D

PRACTICE 7

(**Track_14.mov**)

Questions 1–4 refer to the following conversation.

M: Laura, are you going on the choir tour to Europe this summer?

W: Oh, I'd love to, but I'm not sure I'll be able to afford it. $2,500 is a lot of money.

M: That's true, but when you consider that the trip is 12 days long and everything is covered but one meal a day and spending money, it's not such a bad deal.

W: I suppose. Plus, we'll be able to perform in Germany and Austria. That area has so much musical history. I mean, Mozart and Beethoven were born there. . .

M: Oh, that doesn't impress me much. I'm more interested in the architecture—and the European women, of course!

W: Maybe if I talk to Professor Sparks, I can get a couple of units of credit for the trip.

M: I bet you can. I know someone in the orchestra who did that when they went to Norway last year. You should check it out.

W: I will, thanks.

1. What is the conversation mainly about?

2. What can we infer about the speakers?

3. Where will the choir tour take place?

4. According to the conversation, "check it out" means:

PRACTICE 7 ANSWER KEY

1. B
2. C
3. B
4. A

PRACTICE 8

(Track_15.mov)

Questions 1–4 refer to the following conversation.

W: Professor Martin, I won't be in class tomorrow or Monday because it's a religious holiday for me. Will I be marked absent?

M: Yes, but you may turn your homework in when you come back to class.

W: OK. What should I do?

M: Study chapter 3 and do the exercises on page 29, and don't forget your lab assignment for the week.

W: I won't. I plan to work on it today after class.

M: You might also want to get notes from someone in the class for the days you miss. That way you won't miss any important material.

W: OK. Thanks a lot.

M: You're welcome. Have a happy holiday.

1. Why will the woman miss class?

2. Where does this conversation probably take place?

3. What does the man advise the woman to do?

4. What is the man's attitude toward the conversation?

PRACTICE 8 ANSWER KEY

1. D
2. D
3. B and C
4. A

LISTENING POWER LESSON TWO: LECTURES

PRACTICE 1

Listen to track_16.mov. Then select the correct answer choice or choices for each question.

TOEFL – LISTENING

1. Who is the speaker?

   ⒜ someone from the IRS

   ⒝ someone from the business department of a college

   ⒞ an accounting student

   ⒟ a recent graduate

TOEFL – LISTENING

2. What is one of the main points that the speaker is trying to make about the field of accounting?

   ⒜ Enrollment in the major has been diminished.

   ⒝ It is still a very worthwhile major.

   ⒞ It's a new field.

   ⒟ It's in the information department.

TOEFL – LISTENING

3. What is one of the main reasons that accounting has stayed popular as a major?

   Ⓐ the diverse options it offers

   Ⓑ low requirements

   Ⓒ high salaries

   Ⓓ a tight market

For question 4, on the actual TOEFL CBT, you would be asked in this question type to click on a profession, then click on the box that contains the correct qualification.

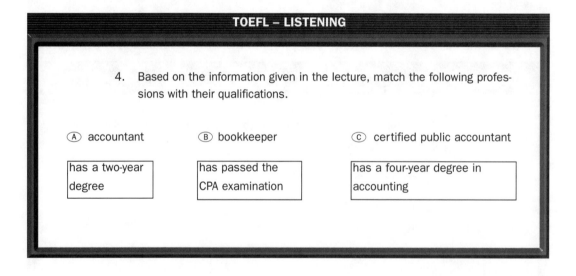

TOEFL – LISTENING

4. Based on the information given in the lecture, match the following professions with their qualifications.

Ⓐ accountant   Ⓑ bookkeeper   Ⓒ certified public accountant

| has a two-year degree | has passed the CPA examination | has a four-year degree in accounting |

TOEFL – LISTENING

5. The speaker implies that the accounting profession is
    Select two answers.

    Ⓐ having a tough time

    Ⓑ being hurt by the computer business

    Ⓒ doing very well

    Ⓓ a good way to move up in the world of business

TOEFL – LISTENING

6. One can infer from the talk that the speaker is

    Ⓐ a corporate recruiter

    Ⓑ an IRS representative

    Ⓒ an accounting professor

    Ⓓ a graduate student

TOEFL – LISTENING

7. One can assume that the majority of accounting students maintain

    Ⓐ B or better average

    Ⓑ straight As

    Ⓒ multiple degrees

    Ⓓ borderline grades

PRACTICE 2

Listen to Track_17.mov. Then select the correct answer choice or choices for each question.

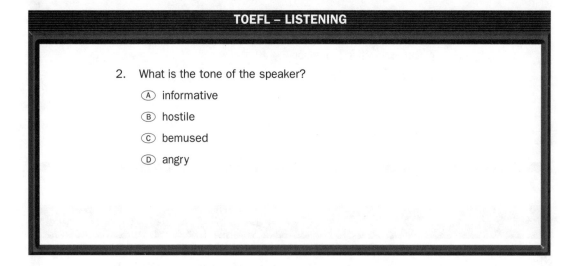

TOEFL – LISTENING

1. What is the speaker doing?
   - Ⓐ giving a lecture
   - Ⓑ giving a campus tour
   - Ⓒ giving an examination
   - Ⓓ giving a slide show

TOEFL – LISTENING

2. What is the tone of the speaker?
   - Ⓐ informative
   - Ⓑ hostile
   - Ⓒ bemused
   - Ⓓ angry

TOEFL – LISTENING

3. What is the main purpose of the speaker?
   - (A) to help with graduation proceedings
   - (B) to orient alumnae
   - (C) to give an overview to new students about the layout of the school
   - (D) to frighten incoming freshman

TOEFL – LISTENING

4. One can assume that this talk is being given to a group of
   - (A) new deans
   - (B) alumni
   - (C) new immigrants
   - (D) new students

TOEFL – LISTENING

5. What is the name of the library?
   - (A) Miller
   - (B) Battson
   - (C) Goldberg
   - (D) Reynolds

For question 6, on the actual TOEFL CBT, you would be asked in this question type to click on a building name, then click on the box that contains its description.

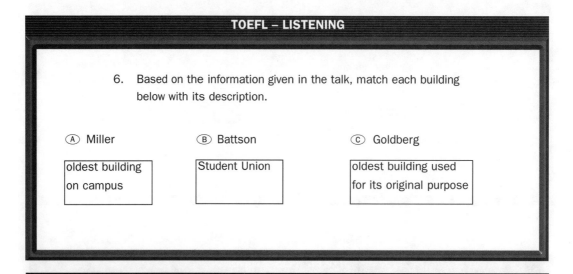

TOEFL – LISTENING

6. Based on the information given in the talk, match each building below with its description.

Ⓐ Miller   Ⓑ Battson   Ⓒ Goldberg

| oldest building on campus | Student Union | oldest building used for its original purpose |

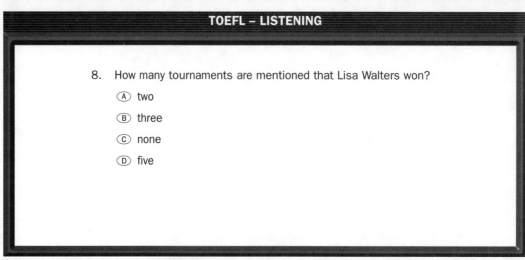

TOEFL – LISTENING

7. What is the name of the man who helped fund the classroom buildings?
    Ⓐ Battson
    Ⓑ Miller
    Ⓒ Reynolds
    Ⓓ Stanley

TOEFL – LISTENING

8. How many tournaments are mentioned that Lisa Walters won?
    Ⓐ two
    Ⓑ three
    Ⓒ none
    Ⓓ five

KAPLAN

PRACTICE 3

Listen to track_18.mov. Then select the correct answer choice or choices for each question.

TOEFL – LISTENING

1. What is the main topic of the lecture?
   - Ⓐ defining creationism
   - Ⓑ defining creativity
   - Ⓒ deciding who is creative or not
   - Ⓓ dispelling the myths of creation

TOEFL – LISTENING

2. The main point of the speaker is to suggest that
   - Ⓐ everyone can be creative
   - Ⓑ no one can be considered creative
   - Ⓒ we should always question psychological definitions
   - Ⓓ no one can define creativity

TOEFL – LISTENING

3. The tone of the speaker is

    Ⓐ silly

    Ⓑ interested

    Ⓒ appalled

    Ⓓ disinterested

TOEFL – LISTENING

4. Creativity is defined as the ability to

    Ⓐ confiscate

    Ⓑ reinvent

    Ⓒ produce

    Ⓓ reproduce

TOEFL – LISTENING

5. In referring to creative people as coming from "almost any walk of life," the speaker implies that a creative person can come

    Ⓐ on foot

    Ⓑ by foot

    Ⓒ from almost any background

    Ⓓ by a long journey

PRACTICE 4

Listen to track_19.mov. Then select the correct answer choice or choices for each question.

TOEFL – LISTENING

1. Who is the speaker?

   Ⓐ a college student

   Ⓑ a new writing professor

   Ⓒ an officer or administrator of the writing program

   Ⓓ a world-famous writer

TOEFL – LISTENING

2. Which of the following is a FALSE statement about what the writing program offers?

   Ⓐ a masters degree

   Ⓑ undergraduate courses

   Ⓒ classes in writing poetry

   Ⓓ a course in business writing

TOEFL – LISTENING

3. One can infer from the speaker's statements that courses

    (A) fill up quickly

    (B) are unpopular

    (C) are located on another campus

    (D) are not offered this semester

TOEFL – LISTENING

4. Before a student can be admitted into one of the classes, the student must

    (A) have published a novel or play

    (B) have important contacts

    (C) turn in writing samples

    (D) meet with the dean

TOEFL – LISTENING

5. Which of the following adjectives do you think the speaker would most likely use to describe the writing program?

Select two answers.

    (A) infamous

    (B) notorious

    (C) prestigious

    (D) popular

PRACTICE 5

Listen to track_20.mov. Then select the correct answer choice or choices for each question.

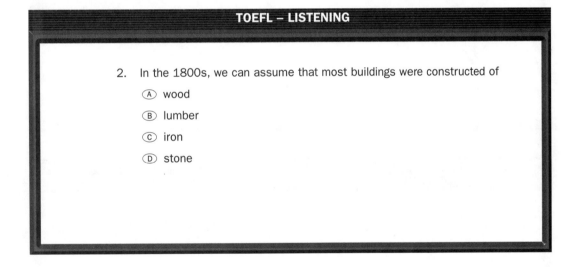

TOEFL – LISTENING

1. This lecture was most likely given in which of these departments?
   - Ⓐ aeronautics
   - Ⓑ astronomy
   - Ⓒ architecture
   - Ⓓ anthropology

TOEFL – LISTENING

2. In the 1800s, we can assume that most buildings were constructed of
   - Ⓐ wood
   - Ⓑ lumber
   - Ⓒ iron
   - Ⓓ stone

TOEFL – LISTENING

3. How many stories does the Empire State Building have?

Ⓐ 1930

Ⓑ 102

Ⓒ 201

Ⓓ 1,001

TOEFL – LISTENING

4. What was the name of the architect behind the Empire State Building?

Ⓐ John Jakob Raskob

Ⓑ Jason Rascal

Ⓒ Jackal Rascal

Ⓓ Jake Reinhart

TOEFL – LISTENING

5. How much money did the architect initially have to borrow to fund this structure?

Ⓐ $5,000

Ⓑ $50,000

Ⓒ $50.00

Ⓓ $50,000,000

PRACTICE 6

Listen to track_21.mov. Then select the correct answer choice or choices for each question.

TOEFL – LISTENING

1. Which of the following is TRUE about the American health care system?

   Select two answers.

   Ⓐ It is nationalized.

   Ⓑ It is socialized.

   Ⓒ It is privatized.

   Ⓓ It is expensive.

TOEFL – LISTENING

2. Who pays for health insurance?

   Ⓐ the government

   Ⓑ individuals or their employers

   Ⓒ individuals' employees

   Ⓓ an individual employer

For question 3, on the actual TOEFL CBT, you would be asked in this question type to click on a name of the fee, then click on the box that contains its definition.

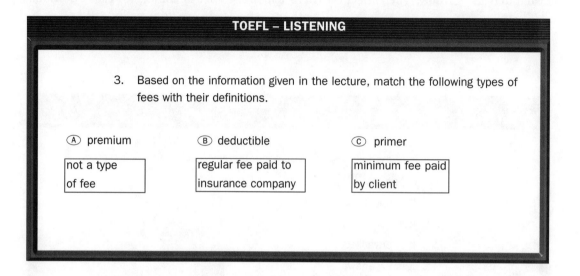

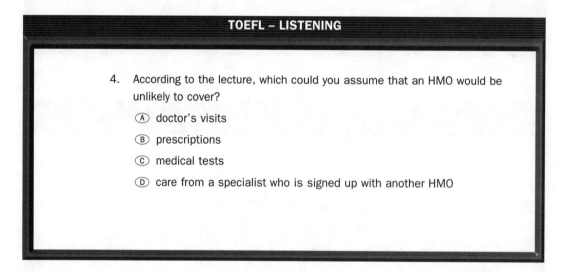

PRACTICE 7

Listen to Track_22.mov. Then select the correct answer choice or choices for each question.

TOEFL – LISTENING

1. The main subject of this talk is
   - Ⓐ The British Invasions
   - Ⓑ Why the French Befriended the Indians
   - Ⓒ The Conspiracy Against Pontiacs
   - Ⓓ The Pontiac Rebellion

TOEFL – LISTENING

2. Which of the following is NOT true about the Pontiac Conspiracy?
   - Ⓐ It was led by a Native American.
   - Ⓑ It had some successes.
   - Ⓒ It was a dismal failure from the start.
   - Ⓓ It received some weapons from the French.

TOEFL – LISTENING

3. The battles described in the passage were fought in which state?
   - Ⓐ Pontiac
   - Ⓑ Ottawa
   - Ⓒ Michigan
   - Ⓓ Detroit

TOEFL – LISTENING

4. The Pontiac Rebellion primarily involved the

Ⓐ Ottawa Indians

Ⓑ Glawdwin's soldiers

Ⓒ British Turncoats

Ⓓ French invaders

TOEFL – LISTENING

5. At the end of the invasion, Pontiac was

Select two answers.

Ⓐ forced to sign a treaty

Ⓑ assassinated

Ⓒ given a pardon

Ⓓ forced to apologize to the British and French

TOEFL – LISTENING

6. One of the reasons given for the failure of the rebellion was that

Ⓐ the Indians were poorly trained

Ⓑ they had overestimated the help they would receive from the French

Ⓒ they had no ammunition

Ⓓ the British and French were working together

SCRIPTS FOR LECTURES PRACTICE EXERCISES 1–7

PRACTICE 1 SCRIPT

(Track_16.mov)

Questions number 1–7 refer to the following talk:

Accounting is one of the oldest business majors in the country. Whereas many new fields, such as those in high-tech areas, have gained a lot of recognition in recent years, here, at Ball State, we have maintained a steady and strong incoming class each new semester. This past year, we graduated our largest number of accounting majors ever.

One of the reasons for the continual popularity of this field is the wide range of job possibilities for someone who holds an accounting degree. What exactly does this field entail? "Accounting" basically refers to the organization, classification, and interpretation of financial activities, which of course covers a whole host of career options. For example, someone could end up working in the public, private, or non-profit sector. Many people first think of the IRS as the place where most accountants end up, but there are scores of other government jobs as well. Additionally, the private sector is full of accounting departments. Accountants may also end up working in all kinds of non-profit organizations, including churches and educational institutions.

An accountant is someone with a degree in accounting from a four-year school. A book-keeper, someone who "keeps the books," generally has less education, perhaps a two-year degree in bookkeeping; he or she may also have simply been trained on the job. A CPA, a cer-tified public accountant, is someone who, in addition to holding an accounting degree, has passed the very difficult CPA examination. Many CPAs have their own practice and clients, rather than work for another person or company.

So, as you can see, getting your accounting degree is still a great way to move up the corpo-rate ladder. Computer skills are not the only expert knowledge in demand in the business world today. And anyone who wishes to get a job in the more service-oriented fields with this degree will be a highly sought-after job candidate in today's competitive market.

We offer not only an undergraduate accounting degree but also degrees at the masters and doctoral levels. And over sixty percent of our undergrads go on to get a Masters in Business Administration or some other degree. To be considered for a higher degree, you should study hard, keep up, and make sure that you maintain at least an overall 3.0 G.P.A., and even high-er in your accounting courses.

1. Who is the speaker?

2. What is one of the main points that the speaker is trying to make about the field of accounting?

3. What is one of the main reasons that accounting has stayed popular as a major?

4. Based on the information given in the lecture, match the following professions with their qualifications.

5. The speaker implies that the accounting profession is:

6. One can infer from the talk that the speaker is a:

7. One can assume that the majority of accounting students maintain:

PRACTICE 1 ANSWER KEY

1. B
2. B
3. A
4. A = has a four-year degree in accounting
   B = has a two-year degree
   C = has passed the CPA examination
5. C and D
6. C
7. A

PRACTICE 2 SCRIPT

(Track_17.mov)

Questions number 1–8 refer to the following talk:

Hi, my name is Robert and I'll be your Miller College tour guide today. We only have 20 minutes before we have to go to the orientation lecture, so I'll be speaking constantly and quickly as we cover as much of the campus grounds as we can. But please, don't be shy—if you have any questions, don't hesitate to interrupt me at any point. Just jump right in. And for those of you who want to see more of the campus, I'll meet you in front of the building after the talk is completed. Okay, let's begin!

First of all, on our left here, you can see Battson Library, the main library on campus. Battson was built in 1874 and is the oldest building on campus that is still used for its original purpose. It's also one of our busiest buildings and is open 7 days a week, from 9 to 9, except on weekends when it closes at 7.

Right behind Battson is the oldest building we have here. This is Miller Hall, used today as a small art gallery that mainly displays student and faculty art shows. Originally, it was used as a health center for students.

On our right are the three main student classroom buildings, adjacent to each other. These are known as the Stanley trio, since they were all funded by large donations from the industrialist Henry Stanley.

Next to the trio, you can see Weiss Gymnasium. The gym was renamed just five years ago, after Miller alumni Lisa Weiss, who, I'm sure you all know, won the U.S. Open tennis tournament three times and Wimbledon twice before retiring eight years ago. Not too surprisingly, she was the star of the tennis team when she was a student here. So if any of you out there play the sport, Miller is a great place to be.

Now, if you follow me over the bridge overlooking 6th Street, you can see Kramer Dormitory, the only dorm we have here, since we only have a little over 700 students. It has been coed since 1989. Before that, all male students had to find off-campus housing. Today about half of our student body resides in the dorm, which is mandatory for all freshmen.

Now, if there aren't any questions, let's move on to Goldberg, the Student Union, where we will hear a brief address by the president of the school, Dr. Wesley Reynolds, before resuming the rest of the tour. Those of you who want to join me should be in front of Goldberg no later than half past four.

1. What is the speaker doing?

2. What is the tone of the speaker?

3. What is the main purpose of the speaker?

4. One can assume that this talk is being given to a group of:

5. What is the name of the library?

6. Based on the information given in the lecture, match each building below with its description.

7. What is the name of the man who helped fund the classroom buildings?

8. How many tournaments are mentioned that Lisa Walters won?

PRACTICE 2 ANSWER KEY

1. B
2. A
3. C
4. D
5. B
6. A = oldest building on campus
   B = oldest building used for its original purpose
   C = student union
7. D
8. D

PRACTICE 3 SCRIPT

(Track_18.mov)

Questions number 1–5 refer to the following talk:

What is creativity? To many people, a creative person is anyone who has great imagination or an inventive mind. To others, it is only someone who is artistically gifted, such as a painter, writer, or architect. The term creativity has been defined as that which brings into existence, causes, or produces new and effective ideas or ways of doing things. According to this definition, a person who is considered creative could include someone from almost any walk of life. However, many people do not often use the term creativity in such a sweeping fashion.

One characteristic many psychologists have agreed upon as being common to creative types is an insatiable curiosity. This endless desire to know more, experience more, and discover more seems to apply to all creative types. That is, the physician who discovered penicillin, or the inventor of a microchip or of a more efficient way to pay bills over the phone, can be thought of as creative, and perhaps just as creative as Picasso or Mozart.

By viewing creativity in its broadest sense, then, do we all have the ability to seen as "creative" people? Many educators believe that creativity not only can be taught, but that teachers need to be doing much more to enhance this skill. One of the most popular areas in U.S. education today is teaching creative thinking skills. But many critics wonder if creativity can in fact be learned, or if it is an inborn trait. These questions have sparked numerous debates between traditional educators and those favoring a more innovative teaching curriculum for our students.

What do you think of when YOU hear the word "creativity"? Perhaps we all need to widen our understanding of this concept. Then, merely by going beyond the more narrow definition in our minds, we can begin to become that more creative person through our visualization. Thus, we are all creative—perhaps, for some of us, this ability to create just remains more untapped, whereas in others it is much more liberated.

1. What is the main topic of the lecture?

2. The main point of the speaker is to suggest that:

3. The tone of the speaker is:

4. Creativity is defined as the ability to:

5. In referring to creative people as coming from "almost any walk of life," the speaker implies that a creative person can come:

PRACTICE 3 ANSWER KEY

1. B
2. A
3. B
4. C
5. C

PRACTICE 4 SCRIPT

(Track_19.mov)

Questions number 1–5 refer to the following talk:

Wesley State has one of the most respected creative writing programs of any college or university in the country. Not only do we have an excellent undergraduate program, we offer both an MFA (Masters in Fine Arts) and a Ph.D. in the field as well.

Students may choose from classes or workshops in a variety of fields, including nonfiction, poetry, short story writing, and film or playwriting. We also offer courses in copyediting and other areas of the publishing business. Additionally, many of our students take some courses in the journalism school, which is considered the best in the nation. And within our own department, we have many well-known authors who teach either on a full or part-time basis, and an outstanding alumni, whose books have no doubt been read and treasured by many of you here today.

Because class size is limited and most courses fill up quickly, you should meet with your adviser as soon as possible. In order to secure a place in the course, you should sign up the first day of early registration, which is next Monday. However, if you wait until regular registration, it is likely that you will not be able to get your first choice. Remember that you must submit two writing samples to the particular professor whose class you have chosen by the end of this week to be considered for any of the credit courses, as well as the non-credit ones.

Now, I will introduce the heads of each of the writing divisions. After introductions, they will give you a brief overview of the individual program they head, and will allow time for a few questions from the audience.

1. Who is the speaker?

2. Which of the following is a FALSE statement about what the writing program offers?

3. One can infer from the speaker's statements that courses:

4. Before a student can be admitted into one of the classes, the student must:

5. Which of the following adjectives do you think the speaker would most likely use to describe the writing program?

PRACTICE 4 ANSWER KEY

1. C
2. D
3. A
4. C
5. C and D

PRACTICE 5 SCRIPT

(Track_20.mov)

Questions number 1–5 refer to the following talk:

Prior to the nineteenth century, most tall buildings throughout the world were made of stone. However, this contributed to many hazardous conditions. Obviously, there was heavy weight involved in the construction of such buildings, and many catastrophes occurred as a result of earthquakes and other natural disasters. So, at the end of the 19th century, an architect in France constructed a great steel tower known as the Eiffel Tower. Soon thereafter in America, several tall steel buildings began to appear. One of the most magnificent of these was the Empire State Building.

The Empire State Building, located in the heart of Manhattan, was constructed in 1930 to 1931. At 102 floors, it was the tallest building in the world for a number of years. It is used primarily as an office building, but the top of the building is also a popular tourist attraction. The observation deck at the top has been featured prominently in several movies, including *King Kong, An Affair to Remember*, and *Sleepless in Seattle*.

The architect behind this great structure was John Jacob Raskob. In order to build his dream, he borrowed $50 million, which of course sounds miniscule by today's standards. His only instructions to those he employed were to build something tall and build it fast. His Fifth Avenue structure is considered to this day to be one of the greatest buildings in the United States. Even though many are taller, its history and the magnificent view from the top have helped its popularity endure throughout the decades.

1. This lecture was most likely given in which of these departments?

2. In the 1800s, we can assume that most buildings were constructed of:

3. How many stories does the Empire State Building have?

4. What was the name of the architect behind the Empire State Building?

5. How much money did the architect initially have to borrow to fund this structure?

PRACTICE 5 ANSWER KEY

1. C
2. D
3. B
4. A
5. D

PRACTICE 6 SCRIPT

(Track_21.mov)

Questions number 1–4 refer to the following talk

Although many countries have a health care system based on socialized medicine, in the United States, it is based on private health insurance. That is, unlike countries where taxes help provide accessible health care for the masses, the U.S. system is privately owned. Thus, it is generally considered to be terribly expensive. So, though many of the most highly acclaimed physicians in the world practice medicine in the United States, these specialists are often inaccessible and unaffordable for much of the public.

To pay for medical services, American health insurance companies charge fees on a regular basis and are generally paid for by individuals or by their employer. These regular fees are known as premiums. In addition to these premiums, most clients must pay additional fees called deductibles. These consist of minimum fees, often a small percentage or a flat fee of one to two hundred dollars, paid by the client (or patient), with the medical facility picking up the bulk of the costs.

Today Health Maintenance Organizations (HMOs) are very common. One advantage of using an HMO is that it often picks up the entire cost for the patient, including prescriptions. However, many patients do not like the fact that their HMO determines which physicians, including specialists, they can use. Most Americans would prefer to have more freedom of choice in determining whom they can go to for their health care.

1. Which of the following is TRUE about the American health care system?

2. Who pays for health insurance?

3. Based on the information given in the lecture, match the following types of fees with their definitions.

4. According to the lecture, which could you assume that an HMO would be unlikely to cover?

PRACTICE 6 ANSWER KEY

1. C and D
2. B
3. A = regular fee paid to insurance company
   B = minimum fee paid by client
   C = not a type of fee
4. D

PRACTICE 7 SCRIPT

(Track_22.mov)

Questions number 1–6 refer to the following talk:

Pontiac's Rebellion symbolized the Ottawa Indians' unwillingness to accept British rule at the end of the French and Indian Wars. Also known as Pontiac's Conspiracy, the movement was named after one of its leaders, Pontiac.

Whereas some of the Indians had formed allegiances with French Jesuit priests who had befriended them, they were far more suspicious of the British soldiers. For instance, many of the Frenchmen had provided all sorts of things, from food to ammunition, to some of the Indians after the war, while the British were not willing to give them anything. Thus, in 1763 a group of Indian leaders met on the shores of the Ecorse River near what is now Detroit, Michigan, to contemplate their next move. They planned to launch a secret attack on the British fort set up nearby; however, this was disclosed to British major Henry Glawdwin, who suppressed the attack.

Over the next two and a half years, Pontiac led his warriors into several battles against the British in the area. Sometimes they were victorious, other times not. In the end, failing to gain as much support from the French as they had assumed that they could count on, Pontiac and his Ottawa Indians were forced to sign a treaty with the opponents, but were subsequently pardoned by the English.

1. The main subject of this talk is:

2. Which of the following is NOT true about the Pontiac Conspiracy?

3. The battles described in the passage were fought in which state?

4. The Pontiac Rebellion primarily involved the:

5. At the end of the invasion, Pontiac was:

6. One of the reasons given for the failure of the rebellion was that:

PRACTICE 7 ANSWER KEY

1. D
2. C
3. C
4. A
5. A and C
6. B

Structure Power

The Structure section of the TOEFL CBT is made up of two types of questions. "Structure" questions consist of a sentence containing a blank that can be completed correctly with only one of four answer choices. "Written expression" questions consist of a complete sentence with four parts underlined; the student must decide which of the four underlined parts contains an error.

This section of the TOEFL essentially tests English grammar. The Structure Power Lessons in the pages that follow include, therefore, a grammar review that will give you the essential terms you need to know to do well in this section. The Grammar Review is followed by seven Structure Power Lessons, which will familiarize you with the most common types of TOEFL Structure questions. They also pinpoint the grammar points you need to know in order to do well on the test, so that you do not lose time by studying grammar points that are not tested.

Before you start to work on the Structure Power Lessons, read through "Structure for the TOEFL CBT" on the following pages. These pages will give you more details on what to expect on the Structure section of the computer-based TOEFL exam.

The Bigger Picture: Grammar Beyond the TOEFL

When American university professors are asked about the academic skills of their international students, the area of greatest concern is often the students' writing skills. Many international students who speak quite well find that their professors cannot understand their written ideas. When you think about it, this makes sense. Students *talk* about things, like cafeteria food and who is doing what over the weekend, but they have to write about complicated subjects, often ideas rather than physical objects. Also, when speaking, an international student can see immediately whether the listener understands. This is not possible in writing.

Therefore, grammar is important, even to students who can communicate well verbally in English. As you go through the Power Lessons, focus on improving your English grammar. If there is something you do not fully understand, refer to a good book on English grammar.

This book concentrates only on the grammar you commonly find on the TOEFL, but don't forget that there is more to English grammar than the TOEFL, and that you will certainly need more than just "TOEFL grammar" when you begin your studies in the United States.

Structure for the TOEFL CBT

Since July, 1998, the TOEFL has been administered by computer. The Structure section on the TOEFL CBT differs from the corresponding section of the paper-based TOEFL both in the way that test takers experience the questions and in the way that they record their answers.

On test day prior to taking the exam, you will have the opportunity to work through a tutorial that will show you, step-by-step, how to use a mouse, how to scroll, and how to use the testing tools. In addition, before each of the four sections, you will be shown how to answer the types of questions that you will encounter in that section. The more comfortable you are with computers, the less you will have to worry about on test day!

This chapter will focus on some unique features of the Structure section of the TOEFL CBT.

COMPUTER ADAPTIVE

The Structure section is "computer adaptive." This means that the difficulty of each question that you see is based on whether or not you answered the previous question correctly. Every computer-adaptive section of the test will begin with a few mid-level difficulty questions. If you answer most of them correctly, then the level of the difficulty of the question that you next receive will increase. If you answer most of the first few questions incorrectly, the questions that follow will become easier. Your goal is to answer as many questions as possible at the highest difficulty level. This is how the test determines your final score.

Because each question that you receive is based on the questions that come before it, you cannot leave any questions unanswered or skip questions to answer later.

TIME

The time you have to take the test will vary from test taker to test taker, but will fall within a range of 15 to 20 minutes, which is a little bit less than on the paper-and-pencil test. The actual amount of time that you are allowed will appear on the screen before you begin.

QUESTION FORMAT

There is actually very little difference in the format of questions between the paper-based test and the computer-based exam. On the computer-based TOEFL, you record your answer directly on the screen rather than transposing your answer to a separate sheet of paper. In this regard, the Structure section is a little easier, and you do not run the risk of making a mistake when transferring your answer from the booklet to the answer grid.

There are two question types in the Structure section of the TOEFL CBT. The question types will be mixed together, unlike on the paper-based test, which segregates the different formats from each other.

Sentence Completion

You are given a sentence with an element missing. Beneath the question there are four choices. You should choose the word or phrase that best completes the sentence from the four choices.

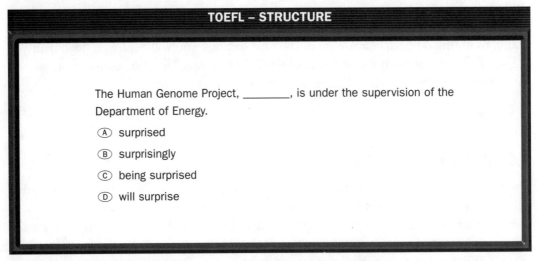

Select your answer by clicking on the oval to the left of your choice.

Error Identification

You are given a sentence that contains four underlined words. One of the four words must be changed in order to make the sentence correct.

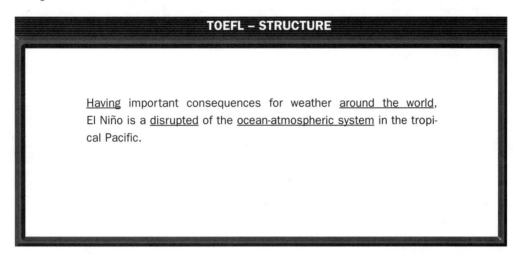

When you select your answer by clicking on the underlined word or phrase it will darken.

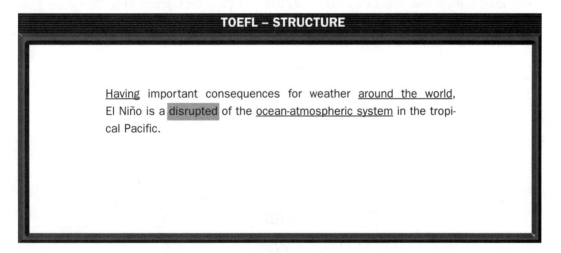

You may change your answer choice as often as you like until you click on **Next** and **Confirm Answer**. Once you have clicked on these boxes, you will receive the next question.

Remember, you will not be permitted to leave any question unanswered, so you cannot come back to it later!

SCORING

The Structure section of the TOEFL CBT is scored on a scale of 0 to 30. This part of the test counts for 50 percent of the final score for the Structure and Writing section. At the end of the computer test, you will see an estimated score range for this section. Your final scaled score is determined after your essay has been scored by readers at ETS.

MAJOR SKILLS TESTED

The following are the major skills tested on the TOEFL CBT:

- Clause identification
- "What is a sentence?" knowledge
- Two subjects avoidance
- Verb tense sequences
- Subject-verb agreement
- Singular and plural noun usage
- Prepositions and prepositional phrase usage
- Articles
- Active and passive voice
- Gerunds and infinitives, and knowing which verbs take each
- Form and meaning of compound participles and infinitives
- Recognition of the difference between *do* and *make*
- Comparatives and superlatives
- *There* and *it* as subjects

You will practice all of these skills as you work through the Structure Power Lessons of this book. Even though the Structure section has been adapted for the computer, the same general skill is being tested as in the paper-based exam—grammar.

STRATEGIES

The following are test-taking strategies that should help you improve your score on the Structure section of the TOEFL CBT.

Fill-In Items

The first thing you should do is read over all of the answer choices. Sometimes you can eliminate choices right away because the grammar within the choice is incorrect. In the sentence completion example above, the fourth choice, "will surprising," is incorrect (to make it correct, you would have to add the word *be*).

The next step is to read through the sentence. Does the correct word automatically pop into your head? Check the answer choices to see if your guess is included in the list. Finally, mentally place each of the remaining alternatives in the blank space. Even though you may think you have immediately identified the correct answer, you must double-check your answer to be sure that none of the other answers are better.

Don't worry: This doesn't take as long to do as it does to read about doing it! And remember, you can't go back and check your answers later, so you have to get it right the first time.

Error Identification Items

The first thing you should do is quickly read over the entire sentence, then reread the choices. If the incorrect element is not clear to you the second time through, try clicking on each of the choices. Imagine that the darkened word or phrase is missing; then try to fill it in with your own word. Does the part of speech, verb tense, or reference fit? If not, then you may have found the incorrect element.

For example:

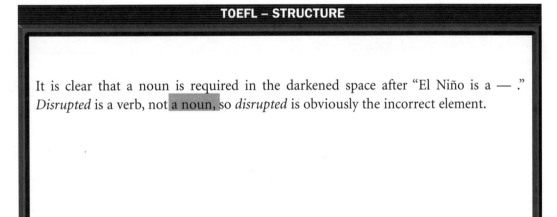

It is clear that a noun is required in the darkened space after "El Niño is a — ." *Disrupted* is a verb, not a noun, so *disrupted* is obviously the incorrect element.

Grammar Review

The following review covers the minimum amount of grammatical concepts and grammatical terms necessary to do the Structure Power Lessons of this book. It is important to note that this grammar review cannot take the place of a solid understanding of English grammar. A comprehensive grammar book will be helpful if you need further information on any of the concepts outlined here.

Noun Groups

- A *noun group* is either a noun, or a noun and a group of words that belong to it.

The kinds of words that "belong to" a noun are usually adjectives, including determiners (see below).

In this example, the underlined words are noun groups.

> John always uses his best French when speaking on the telephone.

Conjunctions

- A *conjunction* is a word that links two equivalent parts of a sentence.

By *equivalent* we mean a noun to a noun, an adjective to an adjective, a prepositional phrase to another prepositional phrase, etcetera.

In this example, the underlined words are conjunctions.

> John always speaks and writes in his best French or German, yet Mary
> doesn't seem to care that she sounds uneducated to other people.

The conjunction *and* links two verbs: speaks and writes.

The conjunction *or* joins two nouns: French or German.

The conjunction *that* links the clause *Mary doesn't seem to care* with the clause *she sounds uneducated to other people.*

The conjunction *yet* joins the first part of the sentence (*John . . . telephone*) to the second (*Mary . . . people*).

Pronouns

Pronouns can be categorized in the following way:

- subject: *I, you, he, she, it, we, they*
- object: *me, your, his, her, it, us, them*
- possessive: *mine, yours, his, hers, its, ours, theirs*
- reflexive: *myself, yourself, himself, herself, oneself, itself, ourselves, yourselves, themselves*
- demonstrative: *this, these, that, those*

Antecedents

- An *antecedent* is a noun that a pronoun can replace.

<u>Sharon</u> has recently accepted a new position. <u>She</u> will not be making a lot of money, but it offers <u>her</u> several career advancement opportunities.

In the above example, the noun *Sharon* is the antecedent for the pronouns *she* and *her*. In other words, *she* represents the noun *Sharon*, and *her* represents the noun *Sharon*.

Here are some more examples.

<u>Karen</u> preferred Kevin's plan because it was more cost efficient than <u>hers</u>.
(*hers = Karen's*)

Mary wasn't satisfied with the restaurant we chose last year, but she will love <u>this</u>!
(*this = the restaurant*)

Very often the demonstrative pronouns—*this, that, these,* and *those*—refer to entire ideas rather than only nouns.

James wants to take two years off from college and tour Asia, but I am sure his parents will never approve of <u>that</u>! (*that = the idea of James's taking two years off from college and touring Europe*)

Possessive adjectives (*my, your, his, her, its, our, their*), like pronouns, have antecedents.

<u>Annette</u> enjoys spending time with <u>her</u> grandmother. (*her = Annette's*)

Usually pronouns and possessive adjectives come after their antecedents. But sometimes they can come before their antecedents.

When <u>she</u> thinks about her family, Annette starts to cry.

Considering <u>her</u> size, <u>Iris</u> is very strong.

See Structure Power Lesson Six, Session B, for further information on pronoun-antecedent agreement.

Possessive Adjectives and Possessive Pronouns

Frequently the TOEFL tests a student's ability to distinguish between possessive adjectives and possessive pronouns. Students frequently confuse the two because they look so much alike.

Possessive Adjectives	Possessive Pronouns
my	mine
your	yours
his	his
her	hers
its	its
our	ours
their	theirs

However, their function in the sentence is entirely different. Possessive adjectives function as adjectives, which means that they must always go before a noun.

my car

your husband

our problem

A possessive pronoun takes the place of another noun.

That's not Wilma's car. Hers is blue. (*hers* = Wilma's car)

She is interested in the culture of the aborigines because theirs is a culture that looks simple on the surface, but in actuality is highly complex. (*theirs* = aboriginal culture)

Types of Nouns

Count Nouns

- *Count nouns* are those that can be counted (for example, *one car, two cars, three cars,* etcetera).

In grammar, count nouns have a singular form and a plural form usually ending in -*s*. Count nouns also take the indefinite article *a/an*.

Noncount Nouns

- *Noncount nouns* are those that are seen as indivisible wholes.

Unlike count nouns, they do not normally have a plural form and do not normally take the indefinite article.

Examples of noncount nouns are:

furniture	relevance	trash
information	freedom	sunlight

To measure noncount nouns, we use quantifying noun expressions.

a piece of furniture	a pile of trash
a period of freedom	a ray of sunlight

Mass Nouns

Mass nouns are a type of noncount noun. They are a little different, however, because sometimes they are used in the plural form. When they have a plural form, they mean "types of."

Cheese

NONCOUNT USAGE:	We need some <u>cheese</u> for the ravioli tonight.
COUNT USAGE:	The store carried more than a dozen <u>cheeses</u> (types of cheese).

Rice

NONCOUNT USAGE:	They ate <u>rice</u> with their beans.
COUNT USAGE:	The region is unique in that many <u>rices</u> (types of rice) can be grown there.

Pasta

NONCOUNT USAGE:	She loves cooking <u>pasta</u>—it's so easy.
COUNT USAGE:	The chef became an expert on the <u>pastas</u> (the types of pasta) of northern Italy.

Some mass nouns can be used in the plural in another way.

Customer:	Give me three <u>coffees</u> and a <u>tea</u>. (COUNT USAGE)
Counter waiter:	Do you want <u>sugar</u> with that? (NONCOUNT USAGE)
Customer:	Yeah. Give me four <u>sugars</u>. (COUNT USAGE)

When the customer says "three coffees and a tea," he does not mean three types of coffee and one type of tea. Instead, he means three cups of coffee and one cup of tea.

In the same way, "four sugars" means four packets of sugar rather than four types of sugar.

Collective Nouns

Collective nouns are groups of individual nouns that are viewed as being a single entity. Usually collective nouns take a singular verb. Examples include *group, herd,* and *committee.*

Collective nouns are discussed in greater depth in Structure Power Lesson Six, Session B.

The difference between count, noncount, and collective nouns is important because the use of words like *much, many,* and other determiners, as well as the use of singular or plural forms of a verb, depend upon the noun in question. The TOEFL often tests a student's ability to make these kinds of judgments.

For more on subject-verb agreement, see Structure Power Lesson Six, Session B.

Transitive versus Intransitive Verbs

Verbs are categorized as *transitive* or *intransitive* depending on whether they take a direct object or not. Intransitive verbs do not take direct objects, while transitive verbs do.

Mary <u>walks</u> for 45 minutes every day. (There is no direct object, so *walks* is intransitive.)

Mary <u>bought a book</u> about the history of the United States. (A *book* is the direct object, so the verb *bought* is transitive.)

A few verbs have both a transitive and an intransitive use. For example:

John <u>read</u> during the entire flight from Los Angeles.

John <u>read a book</u> during the entire flight from Los Angeles.

Some common verbs that are often intransitive are:

come	go	flow
walk	run	travel
occur	happen	

It is important to note that intransitive verbs cannot be passive. Structure Power Lesson Three, Session D, discusses this point further.

Linking Verbs

In addition to transitive and intransitive verbs, there are also linking verbs. Structurally, linking verbs look similar to transitive verbs in that they may be followed by a noun.

John <u>is</u> president of the student organization. (*is* = linking verb)

You can tell a linking verb from a transitive verb because with a linking verb the subject and the noun after the linking verb are the same thing. For example, in the sentence above, *John* and *president* are identical.

However, with a transitive verb, the subject and the noun after the verb are two different things. For example, in the sentence below, *the construction company* and *that house* are two different things.

The construction company <u>built</u> that house. (*built* = transitive verb)

Some common linking verbs are:

be	appear
become	seem

Linking verbs can also be followed by an adjective.

She seems <u>happy</u> today.

It is important to remember that linking verbs, like intransitive verbs, cannot be passive. See Structure Power Lesson Three, Session D.

Determiners

In some of the Grammar Power Lessons, there are rules that involve the concept of determiners. In this grammar, the term *determiner* refers to a specific type of adjective. Determiners are either specific or general.

Specific Determiners

Specific determiners include:

(1) the definite article

the	I didn't like <u>the</u> movie.

(2) demonstrative adjectives

this	*these*	<u>That</u> exercise was very helpful.
that	*those*	

(3) possessive adjectives

my	*our*	
your	*your*	Please give me <u>your</u> homework.
his/her/its	*their*	

General Determiners

General determiners include:

(1) the indefinite articles

a/an	some

(2) quantifiers

all	either	many	neither
another	every	more	no
both	few	most	other
each	little	much	several

<u>All</u> children should have the right to a standard education.

We saw <u>many</u> ships come and go as we sat on the beach.

I wasn't really impressed with <u>either</u> candidate.

To see how determiners are tested on the TOEFL, check Structure Power Lesson Six, Session C.

Structure Power
Lesson One

SESSION A: INDEPENDENT AND DEPENDENT CLAUSES

One of the most important concepts that you need to know for the Structure section of the TOEFL is what a *clause* is.

- A *clause* is a group of related words with a subject and a finite verb.
- A *finite verb* is a verb that, when combined with a subject, makes a complete sentence.

Look at the examples below and compare the finite verbs to the nonfinite verbs.

Finite Verbs	Nonfinite Verbs
walks	to walk
is walking	walking
has given	given

In other words, finite verb forms include the simple present, the present progressive, and the present perfect. Nonfinite verb forms include the infinitive, the present participle, and the past participle.

It is important to understand what a clause is because there are different kinds of clauses. Some combinations of clauses are grammatically correct, while other combinations are not. In English, clauses are divided into two major categories, *dependent clauses* and *independent clauses*.

- An *independent clause* is a clause that can be a grammatical sentence by itself.
- A *dependent clause* is a clause that cannot be a sentence by itself. Therefore, a dependent clause is always connected to an independent clause.

The following sentence contains two clauses.

<u>The president kept none of the promises</u>   <u>that he had made.</u>

The clause *The president kept none of the promises* can form a complete sentence. Therefore, it is the independent clause (also called the *main clause*).

Always make sure that a sentence on the TOEFL has an independent (main) clause.

The clause *that he had made* is not a complete, grammatically correct sentence in English. Therefore, it is a dependent clause.

There are three types of dependent clauses:

(1) Noun clauses, which function grammatically as nouns.

<u>Whether we are going</u> has not yet been decided.

The clause *whether we are going* functions as the subject of the verb in the main clause.

He told me <u>that he would write next week</u>.

The clause *that he would write next week* functions as the direct object of the verb.

(2) Adjective clauses, which function grammatically as adjectives.

Remember that adjectives modify ("give information about") nouns. For example, the adjective *blue* in the phrase *a blue car* tells us something about the noun *car*.

In the same way, an adjective clause gives information about a noun.

Is that the woman <u>whom you told me about</u>?

The clause *whom you told me about* gives additional information about the noun *woman*.

Please give me the letter <u>that he left in his briefcase</u>.

The clause *that he left in his briefcase* modifies the noun *letter*.

(3) Adverb clauses, which function grammatically as adverbs.

Adverbs usually answer questions like "How?," "When?," "Where?," and "Why?," or they give contrastive information. For example, *quickly* in the sentence "He walked quickly" tells us how the man walked. In the sentence "She arrived on time," the adverbial *on time* tells us when she arrived.

Here are some examples of adverb clauses:

<u>As soon as he arrives</u>, tell him to wait in the lobby.

The adverb clause *as soon as he arrives* tells when he will be told to wait.

He will not meet her <u>because she has insulted him</u>.

The adverb clause *because she has insulted him* tells why he will not meet her.

> Although the children had heard the story several times, they always begged their grandfather to repeat it.

The adverb clause *although the children had heard the story several times* gives a contrast to the idea that the children begged their grandfather to repeat a story.

SESSION B: "WHAT IS A SENTENCE?" QUESTIONS

A very common type of question in the fill-in-the-blank section of the Structure section of the TOEFL is the "What is a sentence?" type. In such questions, the test taker must choose an answer that follows the English grammar rules of dependent and independent clauses.

A few examples of this type of question can be found below.

TOEFL – STRUCTURE

Every spring, millions of American children _____ the custom of searching for Easter eggs hidden the night before by their parents.

- (A) enjoying
- (B) enjoys
- (C) who enjoy
- (D) enjoy

In this type of question, you will need to look at the sentence as it stands and ask, "What is missing?" At the same time, keep in mind two points:

(1) Every sentence must contain at least one independent clause.

(2) A clause is a group of words with a subject and a finite verb.

These two points help us realize that the independent clause of the sentence is missing a verb. Now that you know what the sentence is missing, you can begin your search for the correct answer. It is always a good idea also to locate the subject in the sentence before looking at the answer choices. Here the subject is *millions of American children*; it is plural.

Answer choice (A) will not work because the *-ing* form of the verb *alone* is not a finite verb. You are looking for the verb of the main clause.

Answer choice (B) could be a main verb for our sentence, but our subject, *millions of American children*, is plural and *enjoys* is singular.

Answer (C) has the *wh-* word *who*, which would create a noun or adjective clause, two types of dependent clauses. However, you are looking for a verb to serve as the independent clause

Always make sure that the main clause has a finite verb.

verb. The verb of a dependent adjective clause cannot be the verb of an independent clause at the same time.

Answer (D) meets all of the criteria that we have established. It has a plural form and there is no subordinate conjunction like *who* which would not allow it to be the verb of the main, independent clause. (D) is the correct answer.

Here is a second example of a "What is a sentence?" question.

TOEFL – STRUCTURE

_____ of evolution involves the concept of survival of the fittest, often called natural selection.

- Ⓐ That the theory
- Ⓑ Of the theory
- Ⓒ The theory
- Ⓓ Theories

In the above example, we look at the sentence to discover that while we have a verb, *involves*, we do not have a subject for that verb. Notice that the noun *evolution*, which does occur before the verb, cannot be the subject of *involves* because it is the object of the preposition *of*.

A noun can have only one function in a sentence.

This is an important concept.

Because of this rule, it is always safe to say that the object of a preposition can never be the subject of a verb.

Answer (A) cannot be the answer because we are looking for a subject of an independent clause, and the word *that* would create a dependent noun or adjective clause. Answer (B) does not contain a noun that could be the subject. *Theory* in (B) is the object of the preposition *of*, and therefore cannot be the subject for the same reasons discussed above. The noun *theories* in (D) is plural and our verb, *involves*, is singular. Therefore, (D) is not the correct answer.

Only (C) meets all of the requirements. It is a noun that has no function, it is not preceded by a subordinate conjunction, and it is singular. (C) is the correct answer.

Now let's practice some specific skills for this question type. Note that as we talk about independent clauses within the context of a sentence, they will be called main clauses.

PRACTICE 1: MAIN CLAUSE SUBJECT

Circle the correct answer choice for each question.

TOEFL – STRUCTURE

1. _____ , the capital of New York state, is very well known outside of the United States.

   Ⓐ Albany has been

   Ⓑ Albany

   Ⓒ Albany had been

   Ⓓ Albany being

TOEFL – STRUCTURE

2. _____ Pablo Picasso is one of the most famous artists of the 20th century.

   Ⓐ Painter's

   Ⓑ An painter

   Ⓒ Painter

   Ⓓ This painter

TOEFL – STRUCTURE

3. _____ of the students from my class is getting married tomorrow.

   Ⓐ That

   Ⓑ One

   Ⓒ Those

   Ⓓ Some

TOEFL – STRUCTURE

4. Although Mary didn't study much for the exam, _____ still made an "A."

   Ⓐ her

   Ⓑ they

   Ⓒ she'll

   Ⓓ she

TOEFL – STRUCTURE

5. There <u>is</u> several people <u>in</u> our class <u>who</u> are <u>from</u> South America.
    Ⓐ   Ⓑ   Ⓒ   Ⓓ

TOEFL – STRUCTURE

6. When you <u>finish</u> the exam, <u>they</u> can <u>turn</u> it in <u>with</u> your answer key.
    Ⓐ   Ⓑ   Ⓒ   Ⓓ

TOEFL – STRUCTURE

7. The keys to improving your TOEFL score are outlining in this book.

    Ⓐ   Ⓑ   Ⓒ   Ⓓ

TOEFL – STRUCTURE

8. The news are so depressing that I have decided I'll no longer watch it

        Ⓐ   Ⓑ   Ⓒ

on television any more.

   Ⓓ

TOEFL – STRUCTURE

9. <u>Either</u> Mark <u>or me</u> will pick <u>you up</u> in front <u>of</u> the library.

     Ⓐ   Ⓑ   Ⓒ   Ⓓ

TOEFL – STRUCTURE

10. Everybody <u>are</u> here and <u>ready</u> for <u>the</u> examination <u>to begin</u>.

         Ⓐ   Ⓑ   Ⓒ   Ⓓ

KAPLAN

PRACTICE 2: MAIN CLAUSE VERB

Circle the correct answer choice for each question.

TOEFL – STRUCTURE

1. Alexander Graham Bell _____ the telephone.
   - Ⓐ inventing
   - Ⓑ who invented
   - Ⓒ invented
   - Ⓓ in inventing

TOEFL – STRUCTURE

2. Last year, "Furby" _____ toy in the United States.
   - Ⓐ was populated
   - Ⓑ most popular
   - Ⓒ was the most popular
   - Ⓓ most populated

TOEFL – STRUCTURE

3. My professor's criteria for the essay _____ unclear to me.
   - Ⓐ are
   - Ⓑ is
   - Ⓒ was
   - Ⓓ was being

TOEFL – STRUCTURE

4. Both of us _____ waiting for the dean for at least an hour.

   (A) has

   (B) is

   (C) have been

   (D) has been

TOEFL – STRUCTURE

5. Chemistry, being my first choice for a major, _____ long been an interest of mine.

   (A) have

   (B) is

   (C) has

   (D) were

TOEFL – STRUCTURE

6. <u>Neither</u> Tom <u>nor</u> Max <u>are</u> willing to go <u>with us</u> on the trip.

   (A)   (B)   (C)   (D)

TOEFL – STRUCTURE

7. Every student <u>are</u> expected <u>to participate</u> in <u>class</u> discussions <u>in</u> ESL classes.
              Ⓐ   Ⓑ   Ⓒ   Ⓓ

TOEFL – STRUCTURE

8. <u>Most of</u> the classes <u>held</u> here <u>in</u> Butler Hall or <u>on the</u> east campus.
  Ⓐ   Ⓑ   Ⓒ   Ⓓ

TOEFL – STRUCTURE

9. <u>There is</u> a lot <u>of sad</u> experiences she <u>has had</u> to endure <u>this year</u>.
   Ⓐ   Ⓑ   Ⓒ   Ⓓ

TOEFL – STRUCTURE

10. <u>The medium</u> I <u>want to</u> pursue <u>am</u> television <u>reporting</u>.
    Ⓐ   Ⓑ   Ⓒ   Ⓓ

KAPLAN

PRACTICE 3: MAIN CLAUSE SUBJECT AND VERB

Circle the correct answer choice for each question.

TOEFL – STRUCTURE

1. _____ a spice that resembles parsley and is found in Europe.

   Ⓐ Chervil

   Ⓑ Chervil that is

   Ⓒ Chervil is

   Ⓓ Chervil while it is

TOEFL – STRUCTURE

2. Since 1989, Marilyn _____ in New Jersey.

   Ⓐ live

   Ⓑ lived

   Ⓒ has lived

   Ⓓ is living

TOEFL – STRUCTURE

3. There _____ many students waiting to hear the results of the test.

   Ⓐ has

   Ⓑ have

   Ⓒ was

   Ⓓ are

TOEFL – STRUCTURE

4. _____ of us is planning to volunteer to tutor at least two hours a week.

    Ⓐ every

    Ⓑ each

    Ⓒ all

    Ⓓ some

TOEFL – STRUCTURE

5. Although we didn't have much snow, our trip _____ still very enjoyable.

    Ⓐ was

    Ⓑ were

    Ⓒ is being

    Ⓓ was been

TOEFL – STRUCTURE

6. _____ Patric and Dominique are from Belgium.

    Ⓐ each

    Ⓑ all

    Ⓒ both

    Ⓓ we

TOEFL – STRUCTURE

7. Since leaving the presidency years ago, _____
   (A) Ronald Reagan will live in Santa Barbara, California.
   (B) Ronald Reagan to live in Santa Barbara, California.
   (C) Ronald Reagan living in Santa Barbara, California.
   (D) Ronald Reagan has lived in Santa Barbara, California.

TOEFL – STRUCTURE

8. <u>While</u> pursuing the Presidency, <u>many</u> candidates <u>that</u> are affected <u>by</u> serious
   (A)   (B)   (C)   (D)

   invasions of their personal life.

TOEFL – STRUCTURE

9. Before <u>running</u> for President, <u>Bill Clinton</u> <u>to run</u> for governor <u>of Arkansas</u>.
        (A)   (B)   (C)   (D)

TOEFL – STRUCTURE

10. <u>The</u> details of John Kennedy's death <u>continuing to elude</u> the <u>most relentless</u>
     (A)   (B)   (C)

<u>of</u> conspiracy theorists.
(D)

KAPLAN

SESSION C: AVOIDING TWO SUBJECTS

On the Structure section of the TOEFL, a grammar problem that often appears is having too many subjects for a verb. It must be remembered that in English a noun must have one and only one function. For example, a noun cannot be both an object of a preposition and the subject of a verb. Nor can a noun exist in a sentence without any function at all.

INCORRECT: The Empire State Building, <u>it</u> was built in 1933.

In the above example, the subject is the *Empire State Building*. The pronoun *it* in this sentence has no function and therefore does not belong.

This kind of error may be more difficult to spot in a sentence where the subject and verb are separated, as in the example below.

INCORRECT: The Empire State Building, the largest building in New York, <u>it</u> was built in 1933.

Here, the subject is still the *Empire State Building*, but now an appositive (the largest building in New York) separates the subject from its verb.

Always make sure that there is only one subject for each clause.

This brings us to the next main point: A clause can have only one subject per verb. Of course, it is possible for a clause to have two subjects if they are connected by a coordinate conjunction like *and* or *or*. But if a clause has two subjects without a coordinate conjunction, it is wrong.

Here are some more examples of sentences with two subjects. Notice the difference between the correct sentences and the incorrect ones.

INCORRECT: My brothers and all my friends, <u>they</u> threw me a surprise party.

CORRECT: My brothers and all my friends threw me a surprise party.

INCORRECT: Alexander, who lives down the street, <u>he</u> doesn't have many friends.

CORRECT: Alexander, who lives down the street, doesn't have many friends.

PRACTICE 4: AVOIDING TWO SUBJECTS

Circle the correct answer choice for each question.

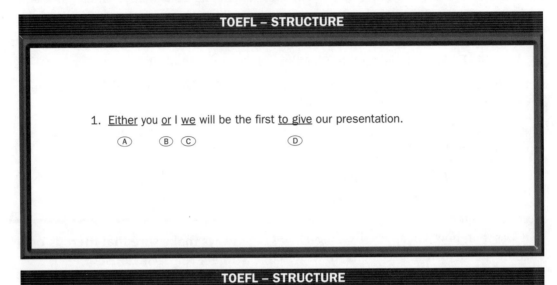

TOEFL – STRUCTURE

1. <u>Either</u> you <u>or</u> I <u>we</u> will be the first <u>to give</u> our presentation.
   Ⓐ　　Ⓑ Ⓒ　　　　　　Ⓓ

TOEFL – STRUCTURE

2. The <u>ultraviolet</u> rays <u>they</u> have <u>had</u> a major impact <u>on</u> the ozone layer.
   　　Ⓐ　　　　　Ⓑ　　　Ⓒ　　　　　　Ⓓ

TOEFL – STRUCTURE

3. <u>Both</u> of them <u>they</u> have offered <u>to help</u> you with <u>your</u> algebra problems.
   　Ⓐ　　　　Ⓑ　　　　　　Ⓒ　　　　　Ⓓ

TOEFL – STRUCTURE

4. <u>Discourse</u> analysis <u>it</u> is one of the <u>subjects offered</u> next semester <u>in</u>
   (A)   (B)   (C)   (D)

   the linguistics department.

TOEFL – STRUCTURE

5. The Clintons, <u>with plans</u> to leave <u>the White House</u> soon, <u>they</u> had to find
   (A)   (B)   (C)

   <u>a new</u> home quickly.
   (D)

PRACTICE FIVE: REVIEW

Circle the correct answer choice for each question.

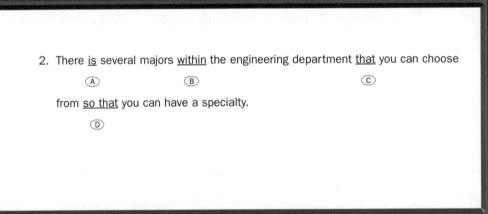

TOEFL – STRUCTURE

1. Neither <u>of us</u> <u>are</u> living <u>off campus</u> this semester because the rents
    Ⓐ   Ⓑ   Ⓒ

    <u>were</u> too high.
    Ⓓ

TOEFL – STRUCTURE

2. There <u>is</u> several majors <u>within</u> the engineering department <u>that</u> you can choose
    Ⓐ   Ⓑ   Ⓒ

    from <u>so that</u> you can have a specialty.
         Ⓓ

TOEFL – STRUCTURE

3. <u>Most</u> of the time, the business classes <u>is</u> taught <u>in the evening</u> so that more
    Ⓐ   Ⓑ   Ⓒ

    people <u>can attend</u> the classes.
           Ⓓ

KAPLAN

TOEFL – STRUCTURE

4. Both professors they are on sabbatical until the end of the next semester,

   Ⓐ   Ⓑ   Ⓒ

   I'm sorry to say.

   Ⓓ

TOEFL – STRUCTURE

5. To vote in the primary, one must resides in the state he wishes to vote in

   Ⓐ   Ⓑ   Ⓒ

   for at least one year prior to the election.

   Ⓓ

TOEFL – STRUCTURE

6. Each of the department heads are going to be present at the

   Ⓐ   Ⓑ   Ⓒ

   graduation ceremony.

   Ⓓ

TOEFL – STRUCTURE

7. <u>When</u> the two ingredients <u>are</u> mixed together, <u>under</u> certain conditions the results
   Ⓐ   Ⓑ   Ⓒ

   <u>they</u> can be deadly.
   Ⓓ

TOEFL – STRUCTURE

8. <u>All</u> of the classes <u>I tried</u> to get <u>was</u> full by the end <u>of the first</u> day of registration.
   Ⓐ   Ⓑ   Ⓒ   Ⓓ

TOEFL – STRUCTURE

9. <u>The</u> polio vaccine <u>it</u> was discovered <u>by</u> a physician <u>named</u> Jonas Salk.
   (A)   (B)   (C)   (D)

TOEFL – STRUCTURE

10. <u>When</u> I saw him <u>in the park</u>, he was smoking <u>at the same</u> time he <u>was jog</u>.
   (A)   (B)   (C)   (D)

STRUCTURE POWER LESSON ONE
ANSWER KEY

Practice 1	**Practice 2**	**Practice 3**
1. B	1. C	1. C
2. C	2. C	2. C
3. B	3. A	3. D
4. D	4. C	4. B
5. A	5. C	5. A
6. B	6. C	6. C
7. C	7. A	7. D
8. A	8. B	8. C
9. B	9. A	9. C
10. A	10. C	10. B

Practice 4	**Practice 5: Review**
1. C	1. D
2. B	2. A
3. B	3. B
4. B	4. B
5. C	5. C
	6. B
	7. D
	8. C
	9. B
	10. D

Structure Power
Lesson Two

At a Glance:

SESSION A: THREE TYPES OF DEPENDENT CLAUSES

As you saw in the last lesson, there are three types of dependent clauses. They are:

- Noun clauses
- Adjective clauses
- Adverb clauses

In this lesson you will learn some more ways in which these clauses are tested on the TOEFL. The most important point to keep in mind is that:

- *A dependent clause cannot form a sentence by itself. In a grammatically correct sentence, the dependent clause is always attached to an independent clause.*

Noun Clauses

Noun clauses are dependent clauses that function as nouns. Therefore, a noun clause can occupy any position that a noun does. Below are examples of noun clause functions that are commonly found on the TOEFL. (For a brief review of grammatical functions, see the Grammar Review.)

As a subject:

> <u>Whether he will come</u> is still uncertain.

As a direct object:

> I don't know <u>whether he will come</u>.

As the subjective complement (predicate nominative):

> The question is <u>whether he will come</u>.

As the object of a preposition:

> We talked all night about <u>whether he would come</u>.

There are, of course, many noun functions that have not been illustrated above. However, for the TOEFL, the above positions are the most common.

SESSION B: THREE TYPES OF NOUN CLAUSES

There are three types of noun clauses.

(1) Some noun clauses come from statements.

> <u>That Dolores plays the piano beautifully</u> is a generally accepted fact.

(2) Some noun clauses come from *wh*- questions.

> I don't know <u>what you need</u>.

(3) Some noun clauses come from yes/no questions.

> <u>Whether she is going to be there</u> is not yet known.

You see from the three noun clauses above that each one is introduced by a different word: *that, what,* or *whether.* In fact, there are many more ways of introducing a noun clause. In order to know how to introduce a noun clause, you first have to know which of the three kinds of noun clauses it is.

We will discuss each of these three types in turn. Then we will consider a special type of noun clause involving the subjunctive.

Noun Clauses Derived from Statements

Sentence #1	Dolores plays the piano beautifully.
Sentence #2	This is generally accepted fact.
Combined:	<u>That Dolores plays the piano beautifully</u> is a generally accepted fact.

This type of sentence can be rephrased thus:

> It is a generally accepted fact that Dolores plays the piano beautifully.

Note that when the noun clause coming from a statement is being used as the object of a verb, the connector *that* can sometimes be omitted.

Sentence #1	I believe something.
Sentence #2	The governor will fight against higher taxes.
Combined:	I believe (that) the governor will fight against higher taxes.

An important exception in this type of noun clause occurs when the noun clause is used as the object of a preposition. In this case, *that is* not used to introduce the noun clause. Instead, *what* is used immediately after the preposition.

Sentence #1	I am against something.
Sentence #2	You have said something.
Combined:	I am against what you have said.

Sentence #1	I don't want to deal with something.
Sentence #2	He deals with something every day.
Combined:	I don't want to deal with what he deals with every day.

The next session of this lesson will discuss another occasion when the word *what* introduces a noun clause—noun clauses derived from *wh-* questions.

> **Make sure that you know when to introduce a noun clause with *what*, and when to introduce one with *that*.**

Noun Clauses Derived from *Wh-* Questions

A noun clause derived from a *wh-* question begins with the same *wh-* word (*who*, *what*, *where*, *when*, *why*, and *how*) that is used to make the question from which it is derived.

Sentence #1	How long is the drive?
Sentence #2	This will decide the time we leave.
Combined:	How long the drive is will decide the time we leave.

It is very important to observe:

Sentence #1	What do you need?
Sentence #2	I don't know this.
Combined:	I don't know what you need.
INCORRECT:	I don't know what do you need.
INCORRECT:	I don't know what you do need.

> **In a noun clause, normal word order is used and the auxiliary *do* is not used.**

Noun Clauses Derived from Yes/No Questions

A noun clause derived from a yes/no question begins with the word *whether* or the word *if*.

Sentence #1	Is the president going to be on television tonight?
Sentence #2	My schedule depends on this.
Combined:	My schedule depends on <u>whether the president will be on television tonight</u>.
Or:	My schedule depends on <u>if the president will be on television tonight</u>.

Note that noun clauses derived from yes/no questions also use normal word order and do not use the auxiliary *do*.

Sentence #1	Is the telephone working?
Sentence #2	I don't know this.
Combined:	I don't know <u>if the telephone is working</u>.
	I don't know <u>whether the telephone is working</u>.
INCORRECT:	I don't know is the telephone working.

A noun clause doesn't use *do, does,* or *did* as auxiliaries, and never has its words ordered in the form of a question.

There is no difference in meaning between the use of *whether* and *if*. However, *if* is not used when the noun clause derived from a yes/no question is the subject or the object of a preposition.

Sentence #1	Did the students already finish the exam?
Sentence #2	This has not yet been reported to me.
Combined:	<u>Whether the students already finished the exam</u> has not yet been reported to me.
INCORRECT:	If the students already finish the exam has not yet been reported to me.

The Subjunctive in Noun Clauses

On the TOEFL you might encounter a fairly unusual type of noun clause in which the noun clause verb is in the simple form. The verb in this type of noun clause is in the subjunctive mode.

After expressions of desire, command, requirement and suggestion, the *that-* noun clause may take its verb in the simple form.

In this type of noun clause, the expression of command, suggestion, etcetera, may be a verb, an adjective, or in some cases, a noun.

Verb:	I <u>recommend</u> that he <u>take</u> the bus. (not *takes*)
Adjective:	It was <u>imperative</u> that John <u>call</u> at just that moment. (not *called*)
Noun:	It is a city <u>ordinance</u> that all pet owners <u>keep</u> their animals on a leash.

Other words and expressions that can introduce this form of the subjunctive are:

Verbs	Adjectives	Nouns
suggest	important	a requirement
demand	vital	a necessity
insist	essential	a law
advise	crucial	a regulation
request	necessary	a stipulation
stipulate		

Note that some of these expressions will be found from time to time without the simple form in the noun clause.

> The police <u>suggested</u> that the criminal was hiding in the abandoned building on Eighth Street.

The reason for not using the simple form in the above sentence is that the subject of the main clause (*police*) is not exercising force onto the subject of the noun clause (*the criminal*).

Don't be fooled into thinking that a sentence like "I insist he stay at home" is incorrect because it is missing the third-person singular -*s* of the simple present tense.

Instead, the police here are simply making a guess about the location of the criminal. All of the cases in which the simple form is used in noun clauses after such expressions must include the idea of force or obligation.

PRACTICE 1: NOUN CLAUSES

Circle the correct answer choice for each question.

TOEFL – STRUCTURE

1. _____ bothers me most is the high cost of the tuition.

   Ⓐ When

   Ⓑ What

   Ⓒ That

   Ⓓ It

TOEFL – STRUCTURE

2. It is essential _____ here on time.

   Ⓐ that you be

   Ⓑ that you are

   Ⓒ that we are

   Ⓓ that is

TOEFL – STRUCTURE

3. _____ is a good time of day to take a walk on the beach.

   Ⓐ If the sun is not too hot

   Ⓑ When the sun is not too hot

   Ⓒ Why the sun is not too hot

   Ⓓ Does the sun not too hot

TOEFL – STRUCTURE

4. <u>Why</u> crime keeps <u>to go</u> down <u>is a</u> mystery <u>to many</u> criminologists.
   (A)   (B)   (C)   (D)

TOEFL – STRUCTURE

5. <u>It is a</u> law that smoking <u>not is</u> allowed in the classrooms or <u>in</u> the
   (A)   (B)   (C)

   <u>corridors</u>.
   (D)

SESSION C: TWO TYPES OF ADJECTIVE CLAUSES

An *adjective clause* is a dependent clause used to give information about a noun in the sentence. Another term for this kind of clause is *relative clause*.

An adjective clause has one of two functions:

(1) A *restrictive adjective* clause limits or restricts the noun so that the reader or listener does not confuse the noun in question with any other noun.

(2) A *nonrestrictive adjective clause* adds extra information to the noun that is not really essential to the message of the whole sentence.

Make sure you know the difference between restrictive and nonrestrictive adjective clauses. The distinction is frequently tested on the TOEFL.

A good rule of thumb is that if the clause describes a proper noun (the name of a person or place), it is nonrestrictive and thus uses commas. The reason for this is that a proper noun refers to a unique person, place, or thing.

Mr. Rogers, who telephoned last night, won't be able to come this afternoon.

Albany, which is the capital of New York State, is a fairly large city in the northern part of the state.

Using Relative Pronouns in Adjective Clauses

Which is used for objects, *who* and *whom* for people, and *that* for objects and people.

Using *Which*

When the noun being described is a thing, the adjective clause begins with *which*.

The table, which you bought at the antique fair, is beautiful.

That secret, which Mary told me last week, has been haunting me ever since.

Using *Who* and *Whom*

When the noun being described is a person, the connector words *who* or *whom* are used.

If the noun being replaced is the subject of the verb in the adjective clause, *who* is used.

The man who marries that woman will be the luckiest man on Earth.

Whom is used if the noun being replaced is the object of the verb or of a preposition.

Sentence #1	The girl has been in a terrible accident.
Sentence #2	We saw the girl in the park yesterday. (The direct object of the verb is *the girl*.)
Combined:	The girl whom we saw in the park yesterday has been in a terrible accident.

Sentence #1   Janet Reno has served in many public offices in her successful career.

Sentence #2   President Clinton appointed Janet Reno as Attorney General. (The direct object of the verb is *Janet Reno*.)

Combined: Janet Reno, <u>whom President Clinton appointed as Attorney General</u>, has served in many public offices in her successful career.

Note that in contemporary English *who* can replace *whom*.

The girl <u>who we saw in the park yesterday</u> has been in a terrible accident.

Using *That*

It is very common for *that* to be used for either objects or people.

> The table <u>that you bought at the antique fair is lovely</u>.
>
> She's with the same man <u>that I saw her with last week</u>.

The relative pronoun *that* never introduces a nonrestrictive adjective clause. For this reason, you can say: If the adjective clause has commas, it can never be introduced with *that*.

However, the relative pronoun *that* can never be used in a nonrestrictive adjective clause.

CORRECT: Virginia, <u>which</u> is said to be quite beautiful, is the home of many senators and representatives.

INCORRECT: Virginia, <u>that</u> is said to be quite beautiful, is the home of many senators and representatives.

Using Prepositions in Adjective Clauses

When the relative pronoun replaces the object of a preposition, there are usually two ways of constructing the sentence. One way is to put the preposition before the relative pronoun; the other is to put the preposition at the end of the adjective clause.

Sentence #1   The man is leaving.

Sentence #2   You spoke to the man. (*The man* is the object of the preposition *to*.)

Combined: The man <u>to whom you spoke</u> is leaving.

Or: The man <u>whom you spoke to</u> is leaving.

For the TOEFL you should know both constructions. The test will often ask you to supply a missing preposition for a relative pronoun. The example below illustrates this.

TOEFL – STRUCTURE

The method _____ products are recycled requires a strict separation of white and colored paper.

(A) which most paper

(B) by which most paper

(C) that most paper

(D) most paper

Examination of the sentence tells us that it consists of two finite verbs. For this reason it must contain two clauses. We can see that the sentence can be divided into two parts:

> The method requires a strict separation of white and colored paper. Products are recycled _____ a method.

A preposition must be inserted into the space to make the second sentence complete. Possible prepositions are *through, by,* or *in.* Looking at the choice of answers, we see that only one offers a preposition, and that this preposition fits grammatically into the original sentence of the question. (B) is the correct answer.

Omission of the Relative Pronoun

If the relative pronoun is the object of its clause, the relative pronoun can be omitted in restrictive clauses.

Sentence #1	I suggest that you read the book.
Sentence #2	I bought the book at the book fair. (*The book* is the direct object of the verb.)
Combined:	I suggest that you read the book <u>that I bought at the book fair</u>.
Or:	I suggest that you read the book <u>I bought at the book fair</u>.

If the relative pronoun is the subject of its clause, it cannot be omitted.

CORRECT:	I suggest that you read the book <u>that</u> won the Pulitzer Prize.
INCORRECT:	I suggest that you read the book won the Pulitzer Prize.

A good way to remember this point is to keep in mind that a clause is a group of related words with a subject and a finite verb. Without the word *which*, the adjective clause in the sentence above has no subject.

Using *Where* and *When* in Adjective Clauses

Occasionally *where* and *when* are used to build adjective clauses. *Where* is used to describe a location noun and *when* is used to describe a time noun. In this case, *when* and *where* are called relative adverbs.

> **Keep in mind that you cannot omit a relative pronoun when it functions as the subject of the clause.**

> The city <u>where I grew up</u> is now famous for an extremely high crime rate.

> She would never forget the day <u>when Sam arrived</u>.

It is very important to remember that when the relative adverbs, *where* or *when*, are used, prepositions are not necessary. Compare:

> The city <u>that</u> I grew up in is now famous for a high crime rate.

> The city <u>where</u> I grew up is now famous for an extremely high crime rate.

Showing Possession in Adjective Clauses

Sometimes it is necessary to show possession in an adjective clause. The word *whose* can be used to introduce an adjective clause. It is usually used when the possessor is a person, but it can also be used for objects.

> **Do not use prepositions with *where* or *when* in an adjective clause.**

> The chairperson, <u>whose committee was so successful last year</u>, has been reelected for another term.

> The table <u>whose leg is broken</u> cannot be fixed.

A prepositional *of* phrase can also be used when the possessor is a thing. The formula for such constructions takes the form: *noun + of + which*.

Such relative constructions are usually separated by commas.

> The table, <u>the leg of which is broken</u>, cannot be fixed.

> We used the red book, <u>the title of which I cannot remember</u>.

PRACTICE 2: ADJECTIVE CLAUSES

Circle the correct answer choice for each question.

TOEFL – STRUCTURE

1. Charlie Chaplin, _____ , is considered one of the greatest comics of all time.

   Ⓐ who was born in England

   Ⓑ which was born in England

   Ⓒ who were born in England

   Ⓓ that was born in England

TOEFL – STRUCTURE

2. The *International Herald Tribune*, _____ is co-owned by the *Washington Post* and *The New York Times*, is headquartered in Paris.

   Ⓐ that

   Ⓑ which

   Ⓒ who

   Ⓓ where

TOEFL – STRUCTURE

3. The dean of the architecture school, _____ is from Japan, is world famous.

   Ⓐ whom

   Ⓑ where

   Ⓒ that

   Ⓓ who

KAPLAN

TOEFL – STRUCTURE

4. Museums, _____ art of various kinds, have become increasingly popular in recent years.

    (A) to feature

    (B) feature

    (C) which featuring

    (D) which feature

TOEFL – STRUCTURE

5. The University of Texas, _____ has several branches, is one of the most heavily endowed schools in the country.

    (A) which

    (B) who

    (C) that

    (D) where

SESSION D: TYPES OF ADVERB CLAUSES

An *adverb clause is* a dependent clause that gives information about time, place, contrast, cause, result, purpose, condition, manner, or degree.

Below is a list of common words that begin an adverb clause. The list is not complete. To get a fuller view of all of the possibilities, you should consult a good grammar of American English.

Some Common Words that Begin Adverb Clauses:

where(ever)	now that
because	as . . . as
since	in that
before	so
after	so that
until	if
although	in order that
even though	unless
whereas	in case
while	as if
as though	

Make sure you know the meanings of the subordinate conjunctions that introduce adverb clauses.

The difficult task with adverb clauses on the TOEFL is choosing the correct introductory word for the meaning of the sentence. Therefore, it is essential to know the exact meaning of each of the words in the above list and to know exactly how they are used.

Here are examples of some adverb clauses introduced with words that frequently give students trouble:

Boys follow her <u>wherever she goes</u>.

He has a good job <u>in that he likes the work enormously</u>.

<u>Now that the kids have left for college</u>, I can go out and look for a job.

In an adverbial time clause, neither the future *will* nor the future *to be going to* is used. Instead, the present tenses are used.

> <u>After the guests arrive</u>, we will have dinner.

> They are going to have to work <u>until the project is finished</u>.

> You should bring an umbrella <u>in case it rains tonight</u>.

Note that in standard English punctuation, a comma is used after the adverb clause when it is before the main clause. When the adverb clause follows the main clause, a comma is usually not used.

> The forms will be given out <u>when the plane is in flight</u>.

> <u>When the plane is in flight</u>, the forms will be given out.

PRACTICE 3: ADVERB CLAUSES

Circle the correct answer choice for each question.

TOEFL – STRUCTURE

1. _____ the polar icecaps melt, many coastal cities and small islands could be completely submerged.

   Ⓐ For

   Ⓑ However

   Ⓒ If

   Ⓓ Although

TOEFL – STRUCTURE

2. _____ the Chinese calendar is based on the lunar cycle, the Chinese New Year falls on a different date in the Western calendar each year.

   Ⓐ For the reason

   Ⓑ Because

   Ⓒ Consequently

   Ⓓ Due to

TOEFL – STRUCTURE

3. My brother only cares about earning as much money _____ he can.

   Ⓐ is

   Ⓑ how

   Ⓒ as

   Ⓓ that

Structure Power Lesson Two

TOEFL – STRUCTURE

4. <u>If accep</u>t to the University <u>of</u> Chicago, I will <u>definitely</u> accept because <u>it's</u> my
    Ⓐ   Ⓑ   Ⓒ   Ⓓ

first choice.

TOEFL – STRUCTURE

5. <u>As soon</u> as we <u>receive</u> your transcripts, we <u>begin</u> your application <u>process</u>.
   Ⓐ   Ⓑ   Ⓒ   Ⓓ

SESSION E: REDUCED DEPENDENT CLAUSES AND APPOSITIVES

Dependent clauses can often be reduced into phrases. Here we will discuss *reduced adjective clauses*, *reduced adverb clauses*, and a related structure called *appositives*.

Reduced Adjective Clauses

In an adjective clause, if the subject of the adjective clause is the same as the noun being modified, it can be reduced to a phrase.

A *phrase* is a group of related words that do not contain either a subject or a finite verb.

An adjective clause can be reduced only if the subject of the adverb clause is the same as the subject of the main clause.

The building <u>that is being destroyed</u> is located on Fifth Avenue. (ADJECTIVE CLAUSE)

The building <u>being destroyed</u> is located on Fifth Avenue. (ADJECTIVE CLAUSE)

If the subject of the adjective clause is not the same as the noun being modified, then no reduction can take place:

> **CORRECT:** The building that they are destroying is located on Fifth Avenue. (ADJECTIVE CLAUSE)
>
> **INCORRECT:** The building destroying is located on Fifth Avenue.

Adjective Clauses with Forms of the Verb *Be*

How you reduce an adjective clause to a phrase depends upon whether the verb in the adjective clause contains a form of *be*. To reduce the clause to a phrase:

(1) Delete the relative pronoun (that is, the subject of the adjective clause);

(2) Delete the form of *be*.

> The man <u>who is standing near the tree</u> looks like a wanted criminal.
>
> The man <u>standing near the tree</u> looks like a wanted criminal.

Adjective Clause without a Form of the Verb *Be*

The adjective clause is constructed according to the following principle:

(1) Delete the relative pronoun;

(2) Change the verb to the present participle.

> The Smiths, <u>who live in the southernmost suburb</u>, must drive more than an hour to get to work. (ADJECTIVE CLAUSE)

The Smiths, <u>living in the southernmost suburb</u>, must drive more than an hour to get to work. (ADJECTIVE PHRASE)

That cat <u>that made so much noise every night</u> was probably a stray. (ADJECTIVE CLAUSE)

That cat <u>making so much noise every night</u> was probably a stray. (ADJECTIVE PHRASE)

Note that the restrictive versus nonrestrictive distinction exists also in the adjectival phrases, and the use of commas is the same as in the clauses:

Bill Clinton, <u>who was reelected president in 1996</u>, was formerly the governor of Arkansas. (NONRESTRICTIVE ADJECTIVE CLAUSE)

Bill Clinton, <u>reelected president in 1996</u>, was formerly the governor of Arkansas. (NONRESTRICTIVE ADJECTIVE PHRASE)

> **Remember that the distinction between restrictive and nonrestrictive clauses is true of phrases as well.**

Reduced Adverb Clauses

Like an adjective clause, an adverb clause can be reduced only if the subject of the adverb clause is the same as the subject of the main clause.

<u>While I was walking in the park</u>, I saw my old roommate. (ADVERB CLAUSE)

<u>While walking in the park</u>, I saw my old roommate. (ADVERB PHRASE)

<u>After Bill moved to Mexico</u>, he began speaking Spanish wonderfully. (ADVERB CLAUSE)

<u>After moving to Mexico</u>, Bill began speaking Spanish wonderfully. (ADVERB PHRASE)

The candidates went on to California <u>after they had finished the campaign in Vermont</u>. (ADVERB CLAUSE)

The candidates went on to California, <u>after having finished the campaign in Vermont</u>. (ADVERB PHRASE)

Many times the adverb phrase can be reduced even more if it is located at the beginning of the sentence. In such cases the subordinate conjunction is deleted. Note that in these cases, the implied subject of the *-ing* participle must be the same as the subject of the main clause.

<u>Walking in the park</u>, I saw my old roommate. (*I* did the walking.)

<u>Having finished the campaign in Vermont</u>, the candidates went on to California. (The *candidates* finished the campaign in Vermont.)

Learn to recognize a dangling modifier. This kind of error appears frequently on the TOEFL.

If the implied subject of the *-ing* participle is not the same as the subject of the main clause, you have the grammar error frequently called a *dangling modifier*.

INCORRECT: Making all kinds of noise, I watched the trucks go down the highway.

This sentence says that *I* made the noise—not *the trucks*.

An adverb clause with *because* can be reduced in a similar way.

<u>Because the program is not receiving good ratings</u>, it has been moved to another time. (ADVERB CLAUSE)

<u>Not receiving good ratings</u>, the program has been moved to another time. (ADVERB PHRASE)

Appositives

The *appositive* is an often-found structure on the TOEFL. In many ways, it is similar to the reduced adjective clause.

- An *appositive* is a noun used to give some extra information about another noun in the sentence.

An appositive may be used after any noun in a sentence, but most commonly it is found after the subject. The appositive may be a single noun, or it may be a noun group that includes articles, adjectives, and so forth.

George Washington, <u>the first president of the United States</u>, was born on a farm in the state of Virginia.

The big tree in front of the house, <u>a 100-year-old oak</u>, presents a danger since it is nearly dead.

Note that it may also be possible to have the appositive first and the subject after it.

<u>The hottest planet in the solar system</u>, Mercury is a mere 36,000,000 miles away from the Sun.

In the above example, *the hottest planet in the solar system* is the appositive and *Mercury* is the subject. As always, special attention should be paid to comma usage in such sentences, because the placement of the comma is often the clue that will help you find the best answer on the TOEFL.

You are very likely to find some appositives on the TOEFL. Learn to use commas to quickly identify them.

PRACTICE 4: REDUCED CLAUSES AND APPOSITIVES

Circle the correct answer choice for each question.

TOEFL – STRUCTURE

1. MIT, _____ father's alma mater, is high on my list of favorite schools.
   Ⓐ who is my
   Ⓑ my
   Ⓒ that my
   Ⓓ was

TOEFL – STRUCTURE

2. The dish _____ as grits is rarely eaten in the northern part of the country.
   Ⓐ is known
   Ⓑ knowing
   Ⓒ known
   Ⓓ was known

TOEFL – STRUCTURE

3. <u>My</u> dormitory, <u>building</u> in the <u>last century</u>, is certainly <u>in need</u> of major repairs.
      Ⓐ   Ⓑ   Ⓒ   Ⓓ

TOEFL – STRUCTURE

4. Dr. Wells, <u>action</u> chairman <u>of</u> our department, will be <u>sorely</u> missed when
     (A)   (B)   (C)
   <u>he has to</u> step down next term.
     (D)

TOEFL – STRUCTURE

5. <u>The</u> 1980s <u>were</u> a time of prosperity <u>for</u> many investors, several of
    (A)   (B)   (C)
   <u>which have since retired</u>.
      (D)

PRACTICE 5: REVIEW

Circle the correct answer choice for each question.

TOEFL – STRUCTURE

1. The concept that free enterprise is good for all citizens _____ a controversial notion.
   - (A) are
   - (B) is
   - (C) is being
   - (D) have been

TOEFL – STRUCTURE

2. _____ annoys me most about the city are the rude manners of so many strangers you encounter on the street.
   - (A) Where
   - (B) Why
   - (C) When
   - (D) What

TOEFL – STRUCTURE

3. It is essential that all teachers _____ a minimum of a masters degree.
   - (A) have
   - (B) be
   - (C) are
   - (D) is

KAPLAN

TOEFL – STRUCTURE

4. New Orleans, _____ has many great restaurants, is one of my favorite cities.

Ⓐ that

Ⓑ who

Ⓒ where

Ⓓ which

TOEFL – STRUCTURE

5. Some people _____ claim to be vegetarians actually allow themselves to eat fish and chicken.

Ⓐ which

Ⓑ whom

Ⓒ who

Ⓓ why

TOEFL – STRUCTURE

6. Chopsticks, often <u>offer</u> to customers <u>in</u> Chinese restaurants here, <u>take</u> some
   　　　　　　　Ⓐ　　　　　　　　Ⓑ　　　　　　　　　　　　Ⓒ

Americans a while <u>to learn</u> how to use.
   　　　　　　　　Ⓓ

TOEFL – STRUCTURE

7. The professor <u>who</u> class you <u>wanted</u> to take will <u>be teaching</u> three
      Ⓐ   Ⓑ   Ⓒ

courses <u>this</u> semester.
    Ⓓ

TOEFL – STRUCTURE

8. <u>As soon</u> we can <u>visit</u> your hometown, I <u>promise</u> we will go there <u>with you</u>.
  Ⓐ   Ⓑ   Ⓒ   Ⓓ

TOEFL – STRUCTURE

9. <u>What computer science</u> has been <u>one</u> of the fastest growing major <u>over</u> the
    (A)   (B)   (C)

last decade <u>is a</u> fact that few could deny.
      (D)

TOEFL – STRUCTURE

10. <u>Medieval</u> British history, <u>he</u> specialty, is only <u>offered</u> in the spring
     (A)   (B)   (C)

<u>and</u> summer terms.
 (D)

STRUCTURE POWER LESSON TWO
ANSWER KEY

Practice 1

1. B
2. A
3. B
4. B
5. B

Practice 2

1. A
2. B
3. D
4. D
5. A

Practice 3

1. C
2. B
3. C
4. A
5. C

Practice 4

1. B
2. C
3. B
4. A
5. D

Practice 5: Review

1. B
2. D
3. A
4. D
5. C
6. A
7. A
8. A
9. A
10. B

Structure Power
Lesson Three

At a Glance:

SESSION A: VERB TENSE SEQUENCES

Though the TOEFL often tests verb forms, it generally does not test verb tenses. Occasionally, however, it will test the *past perfect* or the sequencing of tenses between two verbs in a sentence.

The Past Perfect and the Simple Past

The past perfect should only be used when the action expressed in the past perfect verb happens before another past event in the sentence. This other past event may be expressed by another verb in the sentence, as the example below shows:

> Before we <u>ate</u>,   we <u>had finished</u> all of our work.
>   2ND EVENT   1ST EVENT

Or the other past event may be expressed by an adverbial expression in the sentence.

> Before <u>1929</u>,   no one <u>had believed</u> that the economy could ever crash.
>   2ND EVENT   1ST EVENT

The word *ago* is never used with the past perfect. It can be used only with the simple past.

> I last went to Thailand three years <u>ago</u>.

If you want to speak about an event that took place before a more recent second event, use the word *before* and the past perfect.

> He remembered that he had last been to Thailand <u>three years before</u>.

Other Troublesome Verb Sequences

The term *verb sequences* means the use of different verb tenses together. Sometimes mixing verb tenses is perfectly grammatical, but it can lead to problems at other times. When a sentence has two verbs, make sure that the relationship between the two verbs is correct.

I <u>live</u> in New York now,   but I <u>lived in</u> Chicago before.
CURRENT EVENT   FORMER EVENT

In the above example, the first verb has a present time reference, while the second verb has a past time reference. Since the two verbs logically refer to separate points in time, the mix of tenses is correct. But look at the sentence below.

INCORRECT: While she <u>has been addressing the committee</u>, she kept repeating the main points of her speech.

This sentence is ungrammatical because the two actions in the sentence occur at the same time. The first verb, in the present perfect progressive, refers to a present time frame, whereas the second verb, in the simple past, refers to the past. To express this idea correctly, we would use the past progressive:

While she <u>was addressing</u> the committee, she <u>kept</u> repeating the main points of her speech.

In the error identification part of the Structure section, the TOEFL will often give you sentences in which the sequence of tense is wrong. Here is an example:

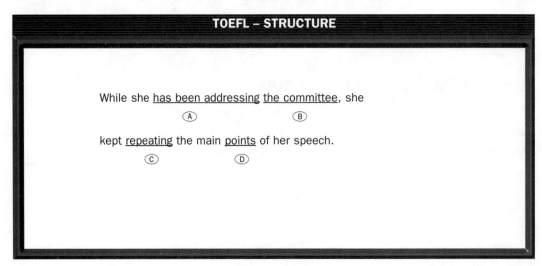

TOEFL – STRUCTURE

While she <u>has been addressing</u> <u>the committee</u>, she
        Ⓐ   Ⓑ

kept <u>repeating</u> the main <u>points</u> of her speech.
   Ⓒ   Ⓓ

For such a question the student would choose (A), since it is the element in the sentence that needs to be changed in order to form a correct sentence.

PRACTICE 1: VERB TENSES

Circle the correct answer choice for each question.

TOEFL – STRUCTURE

1. The TOEFL CBT _____ in effect since July 1998 in many countries.

   (A) is

   (B) was

   (C) has been

   (D) had been

TOEFL – STRUCTURE

2. If I _____ you, I would take the introductory course first before trying to tackle the more advanced ones.

   (A) am

   (B) be

   (C) was

   (D) were

TOEFL – STRUCTURE

3. The <u>Wall Street Crash</u> of 1929 <u>leads</u> to <u>years of</u> economic <u>depression in</u>
             (A)   (B)   (C)   (D)

   the United States.

TOEFL – STRUCTURE

4. We _____ to jog at least three or four times a week.

Ⓐ try

Ⓑ will be tried

Ⓒ trying

Ⓓ have been tried

TOEFL – STRUCTURE

5. Whether we go to the baseball game or not depends on who the team
_____ that night.

Ⓐ are playing

Ⓑ will be played

Ⓒ is playing

Ⓓ did play

KAPLAN

SESSION B: INCORRECT VERB FORMS

Here is a list of rules that you should learn to avoid some impossible compound verb forms.

The auxiliary verb *have* is followed by the past participle, whether it is used as:

(1) Part of a finite verb

We <u>have seen</u> that movie three times.

(2) A participle

<u>Having seen</u> the movie three times, we really didn't want to see it again.

(3) An infinitive

He was glad to <u>have seen</u> the movie so that he could follow the discussion on it.

The verb *be* is followed by:

(1) A present participle in the progressive tenses

Kate has <u>been writing</u> her book for the last five years.

John will <u>be joining</u> us for lunch tomorrow.

(2) A past participle in the passive

The books <u>were given</u> to the students on the first day of class.

All accidents must <u>be reported</u> to the medical offices immediately.

(3) An infinitive with the meaning of *must*, or the meaning of an unreal present conditional (See Session C):

Students <u>are to report</u> to the foreign student advisor as soon as they arrive in the country.

If we <u>were to leave</u> at five, we would get there on time.

> **Remember that the auxiliary *have* is always followed by a past participle.**

A modal verb is always followed by the simple form of the verb without the word *to*.

Citizens <u>should play</u> an active role in the election of their political leaders.

We <u>might have</u> been living in that house at the time, but I honestly don't remember.

An apparent exception to this is the modal *ought to*.

You <u>ought to pay</u> more attention to pedestrians when you drive.

PRACTICE 2: INCORRECT VERB FORMS

Circle the correct answer choice for each question.

TOEFL – STRUCTURE

1. Archaeologists believe that the calendar _____ by the Aztecs centuries before it appeared in Europe or the Middle East.

   Ⓐ were inventing

   Ⓑ have been invented

   Ⓒ had been invented

   Ⓓ being invented

TOEFL – STRUCTURE

2. Your exams _____ by a computer, rather than by hand.

   Ⓐ will grade

   Ⓑ will be graded

   Ⓒ grade

   Ⓓ are grade

TOEFL – STRUCTURE

3. Many Southerners have an ancestry _____ of German, African, or Scotch-Irish origins.

   Ⓐ make

   Ⓑ made up

   Ⓒ been made

   Ⓓ makes up

TOEFL – STRUCTURE

4. The <u>researcher's</u> discovery <u>based</u> on <u>over</u> thirty years <u>of</u> perseverance and
     Ⓐ   Ⓑ   Ⓒ   Ⓓ

sweat.

TOEFL – STRUCTURE

5. Gwyneth Paltrow <u>was award</u> an Oscar <u>for her</u> <u>performance</u> in the
              Ⓐ   Ⓑ   Ⓒ

<u>popular</u> movie *Shakespeare in Love.*
 Ⓓ

SESSION C: CONDITIONALS

Conditional verb forms present special problems for TOEFL takers because of the complexity of the verbs and because of the contrary-to-fact information often contained in the sentences.

There are four types of conditional sentences:

- Real present
- Real future
- Unreal present/future
- Unreal past

In referring to conditional sentences, we will refer to the *if* clause and the result clause, that is the main clause of the sentence.

I <u>would have met you at the airport</u>	<u>if I had known you were coming</u>.
RESULT CLAUSE	*IF* CLAUSE

The order of the *if* clause and the result clause is interchangeable. If the result clause is first, there is no comma between the clauses; but if the *if* clause is first, a comma comes before the result clause.

<u>If I had known you were coming</u>,	<u>I would have met you at the airport</u>.
IF CLAUSE	RESULT CLAUSE

Real Conditionals

Real conditionals are used when the *if* clause expresses an idea that is probably true, or at least very possible.

Real Present Conditional Sentences

A *real present* condition is one in which the situation is true in the habitual present time. This form is usually used to express general truths.

If it <u>rains</u>, we <u>carry</u> our umbrellas.

Water <u>boils</u> if it <u>is heated</u> to 212 degrees Fahrenheit.

In the real present condition (like in the examples above), a present tense is used in the *if* clause and a present tense is used in the result clause. In these examples, the simple present is used, but, depending on the intended meaning, we could also see the present progressive, a present modal, or even the present perfect, as the following examples illustrate.

If it <u>is raining</u>, we <u>may carry</u> our umbrellas.

Water <u>boils</u> if it <u>has been heated</u> to 212 degrees Fahrenheit.

Real Future Conditional Sentences

A *real future* condition is one in which the situation will most probably be true in the future.

> If it <u>rains</u> tomorrow, we *will carry* our umbrellas.

In a real future condition, we use present tense (any present tense) in the *if* clause, and a future tense (any future tense) in the result clause. Imperative verb forms are also possible in the result clause.

> If the sun <u>is shining</u> tomorrow, he <u>will have already gone</u> to the beach by the time we get to his house.

> <u>Tell</u> me if you <u>see</u> anything strange.

Real future conditions can also be formed with the modal *should*. This conveys the impression that the action in the *if* clause is a little less likely (though still far more likely than it would be if the unreal present or future were used). It is also fairly formal.

> If I <u>see</u> her, I will tell her. (It is very likely that I will see her.)

> If I <u>should see</u> her, I will tell her. (It is a little less likely that I will see her.)

Note that the modal *will* is almost never used in an *if* clause.

Unreal Conditions

We use unreal conditions when the idea expressed in the *if* clause is impossible or unlikely.

Unreal Present/Future Conditional Sentences

The *unreal present/future condition* is one in which the action is impossible or highly doubtful in the opinion of the speaker.

> If I <u>called</u> the president, he probably <u>wouldn't speak</u> to me. (But I'm not going to call the president.)

> If the United States <u>won</u> the next World Cup Games, the entire world would be ˋshocked. (But it is unlikely that the United States will win the Games.)

The time reference in this type of conditional is either to a repeated, habitual event in the present:

> If you <u>studied</u> harder, I'm sure you <u>would do</u> better in school.

Or to a specific point in the future:

> If I <u>called</u> the president, he probably <u>wouldn't speak</u> to me.

Note that the verb in the *if* clause is identical in form to the past and the verb form in the result clause begins with the modal *would* plus the simple form of the main verb. In reality, either the simple past or the past progressive could all be used in the *if* clause. And *would*, *could*, or *might* could be used in the result clause.

The following formula summarizes these different possibilities:

***IF* + simple past/past progressive, subject + *would/could/might* + simple form of the verb**

The formula is illustrated in these examples.

> If the United States <u>won</u> the next World Cup Games, the entire world <u>would be</u> shocked. (It is unlikely that the United States will win the games.)

> If they <u>were playing</u> instead of sleeping, their mother <u>might be</u> very angry. (But they aren't playing. They are sleeping.)

A past tense verb in an *if* clause refers to the unreal present and not the past.

Progressive forms are possible in the result clause:

If their mother <u>were working</u> now, the children <u>would probably be playing</u>. (But their mother isn't working now.)

Pay attention to the verb *be*. In the unreal present/future, it always appears in the form *were* in the *if* clause. Although in colloquial English native speakers often use *was* in the unreal present/future unreal with the first and third person, it is not considered standard for the TOEFL.

> **FORMAL/TOEFL:** If he <u>were</u> here, I would tell him exactly how I feel.
>
> **FORMAL/TOEFL:** I hate to think what John <u>would do</u> if he <u>were</u> president of the company.
>
> **INFORMAL:** If I <u>was</u> rich, I would buy a new car.

Were + infinitive can replace an unreal present verb.

> If I <u>were to call</u> the president, he probably wouldn't speak to me.

Unreal Past Conditional Sentences

An *unreal past condition* is one in which the situation did not occur in the past. In such sentences, the speaker is imagining the past as different from the way it happened. The speaker is talking about "the way things could have been" under a different set of conditions.

> If there <u>had been</u> more time, we <u>would have finished</u> the project. (But, in reality, we didn't have more time, and we didn't finish the project.)

> My sister <u>would never have seen</u> South America if she hadn't met that young man from Bolivia. (But she did meet that man from Bolivia, so she has seen South America.)

In the unreal past, the verb in the *if* clause is identical in form to the past perfect (or past perfect progressive) and the verb in the result clause contains the modal *would*, *might*, or *could* plus the perfect auxiliary *have* plus the past participle of the main verb.

The following formula might be helpful:

***IF* + past perfect/past perfect progressive, subject + *WOULD/MIGHT/COULD* + *HAVE* + past participle**

If she <u>hadn't been dancing</u>, she <u>would never have broken</u> her leg.

If we <u>had seen</u> you at the party, we <u>might have stayed</u> longer.

As with the unreal present, the result clause may contain a progressive form:

If I <u>had taken</u> that job with so little money, I <u>would have been watching</u> every penny I spent.

Mixed Conditionals

It is possible to mix certain conditions. It is quite common, for example, to mix an unreal past *if* clause and an unreal present result clause.

If you <u>had been born</u> in Japan, you <u>would speak</u> Japanese.

If I <u>hadn't gotten</u> into that car accident last week, I <u>would be swimming</u> in the Caribbean right now.

Omitting the Word *If*

Sometimes the word *if* can be omitted from a conditional sentence. *If* can be omitted:

- In an unreal past condition
- In an unreal present condition if the main verb or auxiliary verb is *be* (*were*)
- In a real future condition that contains the modal *should*

If the word *if* is omitted, the subject and the auxiliary are reversed, and the sentence begins with a verb.

If <u>he had called</u> me, I would not have been so angry.
<u>Had he called</u> me, I would not have been so angry.

If <u>it were</u> sunny today, I would gladly volunteer to go.
<u>Were it</u> sunny today, I would gladly volunteer to go.

If <u>you should need</u> help, don't hesitate to call.
<u>Should you need</u> help, don't hesitate to call.

If the word *if* is omitted from a clause in the negative, the word *not* is separated from the auxiliary and placed before the main verb. In this case, it cannot be contracted.

If <u>she hadn't called</u> me, I would never have heard the news.
<u>Had she not called</u> me, I would never have heard the news.

If <u>it weren't</u> such a long drive, I would have gone.
<u>Were it not</u> such a long drive, I would have gone.

If <u>you shouldn't manage</u> to find her, please let me know.
<u>Should you not manage</u> to find her, please let me know.

PRACTICE 3: CONDITIONALS

Circle the correct answer choice for each question.

TOEFL – STRUCTURE

1. If you _____ more, you might have had a higher score on the exam.

   Ⓐ study

   Ⓑ had studied

   Ⓒ will study

   Ⓓ studies

TOEFL – STRUCTURE

2. We plan on taking Professor Jones's class unless he _____ on sabbatical next term.

   Ⓐ is

   Ⓑ be

   Ⓒ were

   Ⓓ has been

TOEFL – STRUCTURE

3. The rent will go up even more if you _____ not sign a two-year lease.

   Ⓐ did

   Ⓑ had

   Ⓒ has

   Ⓓ do

TOEFL – STRUCTURE

4. <u>Had you asked</u> me earlier, I <u>will</u> certainly <u>have gone</u> to the movies

       Ⓐ   Ⓑ   Ⓒ

<u>with</u> you tonight.

Ⓓ

TOEFL – STRUCTURE

5. Many <u>of</u> the writing instructors <u>does</u> not <u>accept</u> late assignments

       Ⓐ   Ⓑ   Ⓒ

<u>from</u> their students.

Ⓓ

SESSION D: ACTIVE AND PASSIVE VOICE

In an active sentence the subject is the doer of the action and the direct object is the receiver of the action. In a passive sentence, the subject is the receiver of the action. You can get a strong idea of the structure and meaning of the passive by comparing it to an active counterpart.

ACTIVE:	*doer*	*action*	*receiver*
	John	bought	the book.
	subject	*verb*	*direct object*

PASSIVE:	*receiver*	*action*	*doer*
	The book	was bought	by John.
	subject	*verb*	*prepositional byphrase*

In this way you can see that in an active sentence, the direct object of the active counterpart has become the subject. This leads to one of the most important points to remember when dealing with the TOEFL:

- *A passive verb cannot have a direct object.*

There is an exception to this rule. Some active verbs that take a direct object (DO) and an indirect object (IO), like *give* and *send*, may actually keep a direct object if the indirect object becomes the subject of the passive.

ACTIVE:	Mary gave <u>John</u> <u>the book</u>.
	(IO) (DO)

PASSIVE:	John was given <u>the book</u>.
	(DO)

But this is rare on the TOEFL, and the best advice to follow is the above assertion that a passive verb does not have a direct object.

The following is a list of passive forms for the various English verb tenses. The tenses in which the passive is not possible are not included.

Tense	Passive Verb Form
past perfect	had been loved
simple past	was loved
past progressive	was being loved
present progressive	has been loved
simple present	is loved
present progressive	is being loved
future perfect (will)	will have been loved
simple future (will)	will be loved
future perfect (to be going to)	is going to have been loved
simple future (to be going to)	is going to be loved

Not all verbs can be in the passive voice. Only transitive verbs (verbs that take a direct object) can be passive. Therefore, an intransitive verb must be in the active voice. (See the Grammar Review for a discussion of transitive and intransitive verbs).

There are several verbs that often cause trouble for the student learning English. *Happen, occur, seem,* and *appear* present special problems for students and can cost points on the TOEFL. It should be remembered that these verbs are never passive in form, and that some verbs are always passive, like *be born*.

> **The verbs *happen, occur, seem,* and *appear* are always in the active voice.**

An accident <u>occurred</u> on Main Street early this morning.

That man <u>appears</u> to be quite ill.

She <u>was born</u> on a cold night in January, 1889.

PRACTICE 4: ACTIVE AND PASSIVE VOICE

Circle the correct answer choice for each question.

TOEFL – STRUCTURE

1. Two of the best speeches _____ by former students of the program.

   Ⓐ was given

   Ⓑ were given

   Ⓒ gave

   Ⓓ to be given

TOEFL – STRUCTURE

2. How memory is viewed in terms of intelligence _____ a matter of much debate in educational circles.

   Ⓐ is

   Ⓑ has

   Ⓒ are

   Ⓓ is being

TOEFL – STRUCTURE

3. The settlement _____ between the two attorneys.

   Ⓐ work out

   Ⓑ working out

   Ⓒ was worked out

   Ⓓ be worked out

TOEFL – STRUCTURE

4. I <u>wish</u> I had <u>gave</u> his generous <u>offer</u> much more consideration

   Ⓐ   Ⓑ   Ⓒ

before making <u>a final decision</u>.

          Ⓓ

TOEFL – STRUCTURE

5. <u>In</u> France, wine <u>often drinking</u> <u>during</u> lunch <u>or</u> dinner.

  Ⓐ   Ⓑ   Ⓒ   Ⓓ

PRACTICE 5: REVIEW

Circle the correct answer choice for each question.

TOEFL – STRUCTURE

1. If you _____ time, may I meet with you this afternoon?

   Ⓐ have

   Ⓑ had

   Ⓒ are

   Ⓓ be

TOEFL – STRUCTURE

2. The general consensus _____ to be that it is better to live on campus.

   Ⓐ seeming

   Ⓑ had seem

   Ⓒ seems

   Ⓓ is seemed

TOEFL – STRUCTURE

3. Whenever he _____ tired, he loses his temper.

   Ⓐ is

   Ⓑ will be

   Ⓒ were

   Ⓓ was

KAPLAN

TOEFL – STRUCTURE

4. If we take the subway, we _____ there much faster.

   Ⓐ gets

   Ⓑ will get

   Ⓒ have gotten

   Ⓓ had got

TOEFL – STRUCTURE

5. The roof of our dormitory always leaks when it _____.

   Ⓐ rains

   Ⓑ was rained

   Ⓒ raining

   Ⓓ has been rained

TOEFL – STRUCTURE

6. <u>The</u> tornado <u>seen</u> by all <u>of us</u> while we <u>were on</u> the soccer field.

   Ⓐ   Ⓑ   Ⓒ   Ⓓ

TOEFL – STRUCTURE

7. If I <u>was</u> you, I <u>would try</u> to save more money <u>by eating</u> out less
       (A)   (B)   (C)

   and not <u>going</u> to so many plays and concerts.
           (D)

TOEFL – STRUCTURE

8. <u>The</u> rainbow was <u>admiring from</u> all of us <u>as we sat</u> on the terrace
   (A)   (B)   (C)

   after <u>the</u> rainstorm.
       (D)

TOEFL – STRUCTURE

9. Steven <u>had</u> to <u>get</u> a tetanus shot after he <u>biting</u> the <u>neighbor's dog</u>.
        (A)   (B)   (C)   (D)

KAPLAN

TOEFL – STRUCTURE

10. <u>The</u> ten amendments <u>to</u> the constitution <u>knowing</u> as <u>the</u> Bill of Rights.
   Ⓐ   Ⓑ   Ⓒ   Ⓓ

STRUCTURE POWER LESSON THREE
ANSWER KEY

Practice 1	Practice 2	Practice 3
1. C	1. C	1. B
2. D	2. B	2. A
3. B	3. B	3. D
4. A	4. B	4. B
5. C	5. A	5. B

Practice 4	Practice 5: Review
1. B	1. A
2. A	2. C
3. C	3. A
4. B	4. B
5. B	5. A
	6. B
	7. A
	8. B
	9. C
	10. C

Structure Power
Lesson Four

At a Glance:

SESSION A: USING GERUNDS AND INFINITIVES IN SENTENCES

- A *gerund* is an *-ing* participle that is used as a noun.

  <u>Skydiving</u> is dangerous, but fun.

- An *infinitive* consists of *to* followed by the simple form of the verb.

  But, Mom, I don't want <u>to visit</u> Uncle Clark!

The topic of gerunds and infinitives is very important in the study of English grammar. Listed below are some quick facts about gerunds and infinitives that will help you on the TOEFL.

Gerunds

Indicating the "Subject" of a Gerund

The gerund is formed from a verb, so very often there is a subject, or doer, of the action.

You can indicate the doer of the action with a possessive adjective or with the possessive form of a noun.

> I understand <u>your</u> wanting to leave us for a better-paying job elsewhere.

> <u>My brother's</u> losing his job meant that the family now had no source of regular income.

> Mr. Thomas justified <u>his client's</u> breaking the law to the jury.

With intransitive verbs, the subject may be expressed after the gerund in an *of* phrase. This usually happens when the definite article precedes the gerund. Therefore, you may see both forms:

> <u>The children's screaming</u> was heard by everyone.

> <u>The screaming of the children</u> was heard by everyone.

Indicating the "Object" of a Gerund

The object, or receiver, of a gerund's action can follow the gerund like a direct object:

> <u>Posting notices</u> on the street is strictly forbidden.

You can also indicate the receiver of an an action with the structure *A/the* + gerund + *of* + noun.

> <u>The posting of notices</u> on the street is strictly forbidden.

> We saw Westminster Abbey and <u>the changing of the guards</u> at Buckingham Palace when we were in London last year.

Therefore, we may see both of the following sentence structures:

> <u>Signing a contract</u> is a big step for someone as young as you.

> <u>The signing of a contract</u> legally requires the presence of a witness.

You will not be tested on the difference in meaning among the various ways of expressing subjects and objects of gerunds on the TOEFL. What is important is that you be familiar with the different ways of expressing subjects and objects of gerunds, and be able to recognize correct and incorrect combinations.

Infinitives

Indicating the "Subject" of Infinitives

To show the subject, or doer, of an infinitive, we use the preposition *for* and the object case of the noun or pronoun before the infinitive.

> It will be necessary <u>for him</u> to sign these papers.

> I am going to pay <u>for Martha</u> to go to college.

The infinitive after certain verbs, however, does not need to be preceded by *for*. Many of these verbs are provided in List 3 of Session B of this lesson. An example of the use of such a verb is:

> I asked <u>him to meet me</u> there at noon.

Indicating the "Object" of Infinitives

Objects, or receivers, of the action of an infinitive are generally expressed by placing the noun or pronoun directly after the infinitive.

> I don't intend to study <u>economics</u> beyond the required 3 credits.

> I challenge you to find <u>anything wrong</u> with my thesis statement.

Problems with Gerunds and Infinitives on the TOEFL

The following is a discussion of troublesome areas on the TOEFL regarding gerunds and infinitives.

Using Infinitives to Express Purpose

The TOEFL often tests the use of infinitives to express purpose. A typical question might look like the following:

TOEFL – STRUCTURE

We came here _____ the beautiful beaches.

(A) for visit

(B) visiting

(C) to visit

(D) for visiting

The correct answer is (C), which completes the sentence with the meaning of "in order to visit." Be careful not to fall for the distractors in (A) and (D).

You can recognize an infinitive of purpose by placing *in order* in front of the word *to*. If the new sentence still "sounds good," it is an infinitive of purpose.

Melissa hurried <u>to get</u> there on time.

Melissa hurried <u>in order to get</u> there on time.

Other examples of the use of an infinitive to express purpose can be found in the sentences below.

He stayed up all night <u>to study</u> for his exams.

We worked hard <u>to finish</u> by midnight.

Using Gerunds after Prepositions

An infinitive never follows a preposition, while a gerund may.

Try to leave quietly, <u>without waking</u> everybody in the house up.

CORRECT: I am <u>against your going</u> to Florida for spring break.

INCORRECT: I am against you to go to Florida for spring break.

See Structure Power Lesson Seven, Session A for more on prepositions.

To + Gerund

Do not be fooled by sentences where a gerund follows the preposition *to*. Many students avoid sentences such as:

He is addicted <u>to gambling</u>.

because they are more accustomed to using the simple form of a verb after the word *to*.

You should be aware that in a sentence like:

He is used <u>to living</u> in a small town.

the word *to* is a preposition, while in a sentence like:

He used <u>to live</u> in a small town.

the word *to* is part of the infinitive *to live*.

The most difficult point about gerunds and infinitives for the TOEFL is knowing which verbs take a gerund object and which verbs take an infinitive object. Session B on the following pages is dedicated to this topic.

SESSION B: LEARNING WHICH VERBS TAKE GERUND OBJECTS AND WHICH VERBS TAKE INFINITIVE OBJECTS

Deciding whether a verb requires a gerund object or an infinitive object is a special problem for students. Although it is possible to acquire native-speakerlike intuition on this grammar point, the fastest and most direct method of mastering it for the TOEFL is simply through memorization. The following lists classify many verbs according to whether they take a gerund or an infinitive. The most common verbs are boldfaced.

The lists classify verbs in four ways:

- Verbs that take a gerund
- Verbs that are followed directly by an infinitive
- Verbs that are followed by a direct object + infinitive
- Verbs whose meaning changes depending on whether a gerund or an infinitive is used

> **Learning when to use an infinitive and when to use a gerund is hard work. If you have little time before you take the TOEFL, study the boldfaced verbs in these lists instead of trying to memorize them all.**

Some verbs take either a gerund or an infinitive, but without a significant change in meaning. These verbs are listed twice.

List 1: Verbs That Take a Gerund

abhor	defer	**finish**	**postpone**	**risk**
acknowledge	**delay**	**give up**	**practice**	sanction
admit	**delay**	**imagine**	**prevent**	**suggest**
advocate	detest	**involve**	**put off**	tolerate
anticipate	dread	justify	**quit**	understand
appreciate	**enjoy**	**keep**	**recommend**	urge
avoid	entail	**keep on**	relish	withhold
cannot help	escape	leave off	renounce	
commence	evade	mention	report	
consider	facilitate	**miss**	**resent**	
contemplate	fancy	necessitate	**resist**	

Here are some examples of the verbs in List 1. Note the use of the possessive adjective to indicate the subject of the gerund.

After years of marriage, <u>I've given up trying</u> to understand my husband.

The defendant <u>admitted being</u> at the scene of the crime.

The professor <u>resented his students' wearing</u> baseball caps in the classroom.

She <u>recommended our visiting</u> the campus before we enrolled there.

List 2: Verbs That Are Followed Directly by an Infinitive

arrange	condescend	**hate**	prepare	swear
ask	consent	hesitate	pretend	**tend**
attempt	**continue**	**hope**	proceed	threaten
beg	**decide**	**intend**	profess	undertake
begin	decline	**learn**	**promise**	venture
bother	**deserve**	**like**	propose	volunteer
cannot afford	desire	**love**	**refuse**	**want**
cannot bear	determine	**manage**	resolve	wish
cannot stand	dislike	**mean**	seek	
care	endeavor	neglect	**start**	
choose	**expect**	**plan**	strive	
claim	fail	**prefer**	struggle	

Here are some examples of the verbs in List 2:

> She <u>can't afford to buy</u> a new car.

> I <u>didn't mean to hurt</u> him!

> We <u>managed not to wake</u> the baby up.

Compare these examples to the verbs below from List 3, which require a direct object to come between the main verb and the infinitive.

> I <u>caution</u> you to <u>listen</u> carefully.

> We <u>got</u> John <u>to do</u> the dishes.

> The Great Depression <u>caused</u> the nation <u>to reevaluate</u> its treatment of its least fortunate citizens.

List 3: Verbs That Are Followed by a Noun + Infinitive

advise	**convince**	forbid	oblige	**tell**
allow	**dare**	**force**	**order**	tempt
ask	defy	**get**	permit	urge
beg	desire	impel	**persuade**	**want**
cause	direct	implore	prepare	warn
caution	empower	incite	**promise**	wish
challenge	enable	induce	provoke	would like
coerce	**encourage**	instruct	**remind**	would love
command	entitle	**invite**	request	
compel	entreat	motivate	**require**	
condemn	**expect**	obligate	**teach**	

List 4: Verbs Whose Meaning Changes Depending on Whether a Gerund or an Infinitive Is Used

forget   regret   remember   stop   try

Let's deal with these five on a verb-by-verb basis.

Forget

Forget + infinitive is used when we fail to do something.

> John <u>forgot to call</u> his mother on her birthday. (John did not call his mother.)

Forget + gerund is used when we can no longer remember something that happened. This structure is not very common and is almost always in a negative or question form.

> I'll never <u>forget reading</u> *For Whom the Bell Tolls* for the first time.

Regret

Regret + infinitive is usually used with a reporting verb in the infinitive position.

> I <u>regret to inform</u> you that your son has passed away.

> He is, <u>I regret to say</u>, one of the most disobedient students I have ever encountered.

The material in this session is important. You are almost certainly going to see some exercises testing the use of gerunds and infinitives on the TOEFL.

Regret + gerund is used when we wish something in the past hadn't happened.

> Now, of course, I <u>regret not inviting</u> Larry to the party.

> Even in jail, she <u>did not regret having</u> told Mary the truth.

Remember

Remember + infinitive can be said to be the opposite of *forget* + infinitive.

> John forgot to call his mother on her fifty-third birthday, but he <u>remembered to</u> call her on her fifty-fourth birthday.

Remember + gerund is used when we recall something that happened in the past.

> As the car pulled out of the driveway, she looked back and <u>remembered arriving</u> at the house for the very first time.

Stop

Stop + infinitive expresses purpose.

> On the way home, he <u>stopped to get</u> some groceries.

Stop + gerund is used when an action ends.

> The traffic light changed and the cars temporarily <u>stopped making</u> so much noise.

> Jimmy, <u>stop hitting</u> your sister!

Try

Try + infinitive is used when our ultimate goal is to perform the action in the infinitive position.

> I <u>tried to exercise</u> more frequently, but I just didn't have the time.

> I'll <u>try to do</u> better in the future.

Try + gerund is used when the action in the infinitive position is one way of reaching a different goal.

> Melanie <u>is trying to find</u> the right career for herself. She <u>has tried working</u> in an office, she'<u>s tried teaching</u>, and she'<u>s even tried managing</u> a pizza parlor. She's thinking about <u>trying to get</u> an M.B.A.

In the example above, Melanie's goal is to find a suitable career, so *try* + infinitive is used. On the other hand, she hoped to accomplish this goal by working in an office, by teaching, and by managing a pizza parlor. She is considering an M.B.A. as another way of reaching her goal. Since these actions are ways of reaching her goal, and not the goal itself, *try* + gerund is used.

PRACTICE 1: GERUNDS AND INFINITIVES

Circle the correct answer choice for each question.

TOEFL – STRUCTURE

1. Dr. Jenkins advised _____ calculus next semester.
   - Ⓐ me taking
   - Ⓑ me to take
   - Ⓒ me take
   - Ⓓ to taking for me

TOEFL – STRUCTURE

2. I'd like to defer _____ your question until I have more information.
   - Ⓐ answering
   - Ⓑ to answer
   - Ⓒ has answered
   - Ⓓ being answered

TOEFL – STRUCTURE

3. They will keep on _____ English until they have 550 or better on the TOEFL.
   - Ⓐ to study
   - Ⓑ study
   - Ⓒ studying
   - Ⓓ have been studied

TOEFL – STRUCTURE

4. <u>Even</u> though I <u>didn't like</u> it, I know <u>that</u> my teacher was justified
   Ⓐ   Ⓑ   Ⓒ

   <u>in given</u> me such a low grade.
   Ⓓ

TOEFL – STRUCTURE

5. She intended <u>majoring</u> in speech, but <u>changed</u> to drama <u>after</u> she
             Ⓐ   Ⓑ   Ⓒ

   fell <u>in love with</u> acting.
        Ⓓ

KAPLAN

SESSION C: THE FORM AND MEANING OF COMPOUND PARTICIPLES AND INFINITIVES

Students are most familiar with simple infinitives and simple participles.

>   He loves <u>to watch</u> a good baseball game.

>   He loves <u>eating</u> popcorn when he watches a baseball game.

However, in written and formal forms of English you will frequently find several compound forms of the infinitive and the participle. These forms often appear on the TOEFL.

Here is a list of all the forms of the infinitive and participle in English. A discussion of the meaning of the forms follows.

Forms of the Infinitive:

	Active	Passive
(simple)	to give	to be given
(progressive)	to be giving	—
(perfect)	to have given	to have been given
(perf. progressive)	to have been giving	—

Forms of the Participle:

	Active	Passive
(simple)	writing	written
(progressive)	—	being written
(perfect)	having written	having been written
(perf. progressive)	having been writing	—

Notice that there are several "missing" forms in the above lists. This is an indication that the forms do not exist, or are so extremely rare that they never appear on the TOEFL.

Compound Participles

(1) Progressive participles and infinitives indicate a continuous action.

>   Mario seems <u>to be sleeping</u>, so I don't want to disturb him.

The action of the progressive infinitive, *sleeping*, is happening at the same time as the action of the main verb.

(2) Passive participles and infinitives indicate a passive meaning.

>   <u>Being told</u> that he would no longer receive government money, the researcher had to look for another source of support. (The researcher was told that he would no longer receive government money.)

He loves <u>to be watched</u> when he plays baseball. (He loves it when he is watched by other people.)

<table>
<tr><td>

You don't need to know the names of all the possible participles and infinitives, but you should be familiar with how they are formed and what they mean.

</td><td>

(3) Perfect participles and infinitives indicate a completed action.

<u>Having finished</u> my homework, I met my friends downtown. (First I finished my homework, then I met my friends.)

</td></tr>
</table>

I want <u>to have completed</u> this project when the conference begins. (I want to complete the project before the conference begins.)

Participles and Infinitives at the Beginning of a Sentence

It is important to note that when a participle or infinitive occurs at the beginning of a sentence, it must modify the subject of the sentence.

<u>Being used daily</u>, the telephone book next to the dictionary began to look rather old and torn up. (The telephone book—not the dictionary—was being used daily, because the telephone book is the subject of the verb *began*.)

We have already seen in Structure Power Lesson Two, Session E, that this kind of mistake is called a *dangling modifier*.

Participles or infinitives that aren't at the beginning of a sentence come after the nouns they modify.

You should give this book to the boy <u>sitting over there</u>. (The participle phrase *sitting over there* refers to the noun *boy*.)

Of course, a participle that is not part of a phrase usually comes before the noun it modifies.

I looked at the <u>dancing</u> couples.

The <u>bored</u> cat stretched himself out on the carpet and yawned.

PRACTICE 2: COMPOUND PARTICIPLES AND INFINITIVES

Circle the correct answer choice for each question.

TOEFL – STRUCTURE

1. _____ for over six hours, I began to lose feeling in my right hand.

   (A) Have written

   (B) Having written

   (C) Had written

   (D) Has written

TOEFL – STRUCTURE

2. You seem _____ great progress in your Spanish lessons.

   (A) to make

   (B) to be making

   (C) to be made

   (D) made

TOEFL – STRUCTURE

3. He <u>appears</u> to have <u>fall asleep</u> while driving and <u>ran off</u> the road
        (A)   (B)   (C)

   and <u>hit</u> a tree.
       (D)

TOEFL – STRUCTURE

4. <u>Having gotten</u> over twelve hours <u>of sleep</u> last night, I <u>feel</u> that
   Ⓐ   Ⓑ   Ⓒ

   I may now be <u>get over</u> my jet lag.
                    Ⓓ

TOEFL – STRUCTURE

5. <u>Have</u> said that, I <u>want</u> to emphasize that <u>this is</u> just a
   Ⓐ   Ⓑ   Ⓒ

   minor detail and <u>should not</u> be taken too seriously.
                         Ⓓ

SESSION D: THE DIFFERENCE BETWEEN *DO* AND *MAKE*

Do and *make* must be carefully distinguished for the TOEFL.

Generally speaking, *make* means to create something new:

> The chef <u>made</u> a wonderful salad from romaine lettuce.

Do generally means to manipulate something that is already created:

> The children <u>did</u> the exercise with little difficulty.

Usually, this distinction is quite subtle and difficult for the nonnative speaker to grasp. There are also several obvious exceptions. For these reasons, it may be best to learn phrases with *do* or *make* individually.

Some of the most common phrasal verbs and expressions with *do* or *make* can be found in the following lists. A good dictionary will give you still more examples of these usages, as well as provide you with even more phrasal verbs and expressions that are not included on these lists.

Phrasal Verbs with *Make*:

Example	Meaning
He <u>made for</u> the door.	He went to the door in a hurry.
What do you <u>make of</u> her story?	What is your opinion of her story?
The tall man <u>made off with</u> the diamonds.	The tall man stole the diamonds and took them with him.
I couldn't <u>make out</u> what they were saying.	I couldn't understand what they were saying.
She looked, but in the darkness she couldn't <u>make out</u> where her brother was hiding.	She looked, but in the darkness she couldn't see where her brother was hiding.
Women <u>make up</u> only 13 percent of the executive staff.	Only 13 percent of the executive staff are women.
He <u>made</u> that story <u>up</u>.	He invented that story.
Can we <u>make up</u> for lost time?	Can we do something to regain the time that we have lost?
We finally <u>made up</u> after three years.	We finally became friends again after the quarrel we had three years ago.
I promise I will <u>make it up to you</u> somehow.	I promise I will repay you for the favor you have done for me (OR repay you for the problem I have caused you).
<u>Make up your mind!</u>	Make a decision!

Idiomatic Expressions with *Make*:

Example	**Meaning**
Her story <u>made me</u> sad.	I felt sad after I heard her story.
He always <u>makes us</u> laugh.	We always laugh when we are with him.
He promised to <u>make her</u> a star.	He promised that she would become a movie star because of his effort.
Am I <u>making myself understood</u>?	Am I speaking clearly (OR understandably)?
Bob <u>made $100,000</u> last year.	Bob earned over $100,000 last year.
I need to <u>make some money</u>.	I need to earn some money.
He <u>makes friends</u> very easily.	He finds new friends easily.
This house <u>is made of</u> brick.	This house was built with brick.
Do you want me to <u>make some coffee</u>?	Do you want me to prepare some coffee?
Don't <u>make a mistake</u> by acting too quickly.	It might be a mistake if you act too quickly.
He'll <u>make a good</u> father someday.	He will be a good father someday.
Can you <u>make it to</u> the party?	Can you come to the party?
<u>I finally made it!</u>	It wasn't easy (OR there was some problem), but I've arrived!
<u>Make believe that</u> you are alone on a desert island.	Imagine that you are alone on a desert island.
We'll just have to <u>make do with</u> what we have.	We'll have to manage (OR live our lives) with the few things that we have.

Phrasal Verbs with *Do*:

Example	**Meaning**
We must <u>do away with</u> racism.	We must eliminate racism.
She <u>did away with</u> her husband.	She killed her husband.
His work was so bad that I had to ask him to to <u>do it over</u>.	His work was so bad that I had to ask him redo it (OR ask him to do it again).
If I had the chance to <u>do it over</u>, I never would have taken that job in the first place.	If I could relive that moment (OR live that moment again), I never would have taken that job in the first place.

You'll just have to <u>do without</u> a brand new computer. — You will have to manage (OR survive) with out a brand new computer.

What does this <u>have to do with</u> you? — How does this concern (OR relate to) you?

But what you're saying <u>has nothing to do with</u> the issue. — But what you're saying is not related to the issue.

Idiomatic Expressions with *Do*:

Example	Meaning
I couldn't <u>get</u> any work <u>done</u> today.	I didn't complete much work today.
They refused to <u>do anything about</u> his problem.	They refused to help him with his problem.
It'll <u>do you a lot of good</u> to rest.	You badly need to rest.
You don't realize what liquor <u>does to</u> you.	You don't realize how badly you behave when you drink. (OR: You don't realize how much liquor is hurting you.)
<u>What do you do</u>?	What's your job?
<u>How do you do</u>?	It's nice to meet you. (A formal way of saying "hello" when you meet someone for the first time.)
What did you <u>do with</u> my book?	I can't find my book, and I think you put it someplace.
Okay, <u>that will do</u>!	That's enough!
She <u>did well for herself</u>.	Her life was (OR is) very successful.
<u>What do you think you're doing</u>?	I don't like what you are doing.
He has to have a Porsche. No other car <u>will do</u>.	He has to have a Porsche. No other car will satisfy him.
<u>That won't do</u>.	That is not satisfactory.
<u>Just do it</u>!	Don't hesitate, don't think—take action!

PRACTICE 3: *DO* VS. *MAKE*

Circle the correct answer choice for each question.

TOEFL – STRUCTURE

1. <u>So</u> that you won't <u>fall behind</u>, you should <u>make</u> your homework
   (A)   (B)   (C)

   <u>every</u> night.
   (D)

TOEFL – STRUCTURE

2. We <u>share</u> the chores; I <u>make</u> the dishes and <u>my</u> husband <u>makes</u>
   (A)   (B)   (C)   (D)

   the beds.

TOEFL – STRUCTURE

3. John <u>did</u> a <u>big</u> decision <u>last night</u> about <u>his future</u>.
   (A)   (B)   (C)   (D)

TOEFL – STRUCTURE

4. I'm afraid I can't do out what you're trying to say here.
    Ⓐ   Ⓑ   Ⓒ   Ⓓ

TOEFL – STRUCTURE

5. You need to make sure that you speak clear so that people at the
    Ⓐ   Ⓑ   Ⓒ

    back of the room can hear you.
                  Ⓓ

STRUCTURE POWER LESSON FOUR
ANSWER KEY

Practice 1	Practice 2	Practice 3
1. B	1. B	1. C
2. A	2. B	2. B
3. C	3. B	3. A
4. D	4. D	4. B
5. A	5. A	5. C

KAPLAN

Structure Power
Lesson Five

SESSION A: INVERSION AFTER INITIAL NEGATIVES AND OTHER STRUCTURES

Normally the words in an English sentence appear in subject-verb-object order. Beginning learners of English quickly learn that this pattern changes to verb-subject-object for most questions. More advanced learners must learn that there are other times when the usual word order changes to verb-subject-object or even object-verb-subject. This change of word order is called *inversion*. In addition to questions, inversion can take place when a sentence begins with any of the following:

- Some negative expressions
- Some near-negative expressions
- *Only, such,* and *so*
- *Here* and *there*
- Some other expressions of location

Inversion after Negatives and Near-Negatives

In formal or written English, a negative or a near-negative expression may be placed at the beginning of a sentence. Doing this requires subject-auxiliary inversion.

Negative expressions include:

no	not
never	none

Near-negative expressions include:

barely	hardly	seldom
rarely	little	scarcely

almost never

Look at the following examples. The first sentence of each pair has the negative expression in its normal position in the sentence. The second sentence shows the negative expression moved to the first or initial position of the sentence.

He had never gone there alone before.
Never had he gone there alone before.

They could not see a single ship.
Not a single ship could they see.

Note that in the first pair the subject *he* and the auxiliary *had* have changed positions, while the main verb *gone* does not move. In the second pair the subject *they* and the auxiliary *could* (a modal verb) reverse positions.

The example below shows that forms of the verb *be* change in exactly the same way.

They were scarcely able to hear the music.

Scarcely were they able to hear the music.

If there is no auxiliary verb, then *do, does,* or *did* is placed before the subject and the verb is used in the simple form. This resembles the way a question is constructed in English.

The enemy had no chance of winning the battle.
No chance did the enemy have of winning the battle.

They know little about their son's affairs.
Little do they know about their son's affairs.

It is important to remember that inversion is used only when the negative or near-negative refers to a part of the sentence other than the subject.

Not a single ship did they see. (A *single ship* is the direct object.)

Never had he gone there alone before. (*Never* is an adverb.)

Little do they know about their son's affairs. (Here, *little* functions as an adverb.)

Compare these sentences to the following sentences, in which the negative or near-negative refers to the subject of the sentence, so that no inversion is used.

Little water can be found in the desert.

Not a single ship was found.

No human being can learn in that kind of situation.

Inversion after *Only, Such,* and *So*

When an expression containing *only, such,* or *so* is placed at the beginning of a clause, the normal subject-verb order is changed in exactly the same way as in sentences beginning with negatives and near-negatives.

I have been to Argentina only once.
Only once have I been to Argentina.

He was so hungry that he ate nonstop for three whole hours.
So hungry was he that he ate nonstop for three whole hours.

The falling pots made such a clamor that the noise woke the sleeping baby.
Such a clamor did the falling pots make that the noise woke the sleeping baby.

Note that, again, when the expression refers to the subject of the sentence, no inversion takes place.

Only John was awake.

So many people came to the party that we ran out of food.

Inversion after *Here* and *There*

In both formal and informal English, if a sentence begins with *here* or *there*, the subject and object are inverted. The rules of this type of inversion are different from those of the type of inversion you have seen so far, however. After *here* and *there*, the entire verb—not just the auxiliary—changes positions with the subject.

Usually this kind of structure is limited to the verbs *be, go,* and *come.* In literary English, other verbs are possible.

There are your books.
Here comes Mary.

There goes Thomas.
Here lies Wilfred B. Owen (an expression used on gravestones).

If a pronoun is used instead of a noun, no inversion occurs.

There they are.

Here she comes.

There he goes.

Inversion after Other Expressions of Location

Inversion can also take place after prepositional phrases which express location. There are two cases: when inversion is optional, and when inversion is necessary.

When Inversion Is Optional

The verbs usually used in this type of structure are: *be located, be situated, hang, lie* (in the sense of "to lie in bed"), *rise,* and *stand.* In this case, the entire verb—not simply the auxiliary—changes position with the subject.

> Over the top of the hill <u>stands the oldest house</u> in the entire area.

> On the top of the mountain <u>is located the cabin</u> where my father was born.

> In the closet <u>hung a number of dresses</u> from the 1920s.

> Across the front yard <u>lay the old oak tree</u>.

Unlike the other structures that use inversion, this structure is usually optional. That is, inversion is usually not necessary.

> In the closet <u>a number of dresses</u> were hung.

> Across the front yard <u>the old oak tree lay</u>.

When Inversion Is Necessary

Sometimes inversion is necessary with the verb *be.* Inversion is necessary when the prepositional phrase is needed to make the sentence complete.

> A golden pen was on his desk.

In this sentence, the prepositional phrase *on his desk* is needed. In other words, *a golden pen was* is not a complete sentence. Therefore, if you want to begin the sentence with the prepositional phrase, you must use inversion.

> On his desk <u>was a golden pen</u>.

In the next sentence, however, the prepositional phrase is not needed.

> The grass is always greener on the other side of the fence.

The grass is always greener forms a complete sentence by itself. In this case, inversion cannot be used if the sentence starts with the prepositional phrase.

> **CORRECT:** On the other side of the fence, <u>the grass is</u> always greener.

> **INCORRECT:** On the other side of the fence is the grass always greener.

PRACTICE 1: INITIAL NEGATIVES/NEAR NEGATIVES INVERSION

Circle the correct answer choice for each question.

TOEFL – STRUCTURE

1. Seldom _____ such an outstanding class at the introductory level.

   Ⓐ we have

   Ⓑ do have we

   Ⓒ do we have

   Ⓓ has we

TOEFL – STRUCTURE

2. Only one bad grade _____ not hurt your overall GPA.

   Ⓐ should

   Ⓑ have

   Ⓒ is

   Ⓓ do

TOEFL – STRUCTURE

3. Not until <u>I moved</u> to the United States <u>I became</u> a <u>fluent</u> speaker
                Ⓐ   Ⓑ   Ⓒ

   <u>of</u> English.
   Ⓓ

TOEFL – STRUCTURE

4. <u>Such</u> a move <u>were</u> necessary for me to <u>fully learn</u> the idiomatic
   Ⓐ   Ⓑ   Ⓒ

   phrases that I had such difficulty with before I <u>came here</u>.
                                              Ⓓ

TOEFL – STRUCTURE

5. Never <u>before</u> had I <u>saw</u> such a beautiful sunset as the one we
           Ⓐ   Ⓑ

   <u>spotted</u> last night while we <u>were walking</u> home from the game.
    Ⓒ   Ⓓ

SESSION B: WORD ORDER IN DEPENDENT CLAUSES BEGINNING WITH *WH-* WORDS

Dependent clauses that begin with a *wh-* word (*who, what, where, when, how, why*) present a special problem. These clauses begin with question words, but they do not have the question word order. They also differ from questions in that they do not use the auxiliaries *do, does,* and *did*.

The examples below illustrate this fundamental difference between *wh-* clauses and questions.

QUESTION:	What	<u>is</u> VERB	<u>your name</u>? SUBJECT
DEPENDENT CLAUSE:	I asked you what	<u>your name</u> SUBJECT	<u>is</u>. VERB
QUESTION:	Whom	<u>did</u> AUX. VERB	<u>you</u> <u>speak</u> to at the party? SUBJECT MAIN VERB
DEPENDENT CLAUSE:	He insisted on knowing whom	<u>you</u> <u>spoke</u> to. SUBJECT VERB	
QUESTION:	Whom	<u>did</u> AUX. VERB	<u>you</u> <u>see</u>? SUBJECT MAIN VERB
DEPENDENT CLAUSE:	The man whom	<u>you</u> <u>saw</u> is my father. SUBJECT VERB	

- The presence or absence of a question mark can tell you whether a sentence is a true question or whether it is really a dependent clause beginning with a question word.

PRACTICE 2: WORD ORDER/DEPENDENT CLAUSES

Circle the correct answer choice for each question.

TOEFL – STRUCTURE

1. The number of foreign students who _____ in our college has doubled in ten years.

   Ⓐ enrolling

   Ⓑ has enrolled

   Ⓒ have enrolled

   Ⓓ will enroll

TOEFL – STRUCTURE

2. What _____ on my nerves is when people are constantly late.

   Ⓐ is get

   Ⓑ gets

   Ⓒ will be gotten

   Ⓓ be gotten

TOEFL – STRUCTURE

3. That <u>your</u> score <u>25 points</u> higher this time <u>should make</u> you very
   　　　　Ⓐ　　　　　　Ⓑ　　　　　　　　　　　Ⓒ

   proud <u>of</u> yourself.
   　　　Ⓓ

TOEFL – STRUCTURE

4. You <u>can</u> call <u>whomever</u> you want to; just <u>make sure</u> it's a local <u>calling</u>.
   (A)   (B)   (C)   (D)

TOEFL – STRUCTURE

5. President Kennedy, <u>who</u> greatly <u>admired</u> by <u>many Americans</u>, grew
                       (A)   (B)   (C)

   up <u>in</u> Massachusetts.
      (D)

SESSION C: PARALLEL STRUCTURE

Parallel structure is probably one of the most easily recognized and therefore most easily avoided mistakes on the TOEFL. The rule of parallel structure states that coordinate conjunctions must join structures of the same type.

Using Coordinate Conjunctions (*and, but, or,* and *yet*)

Look at the following example:

The issue is too <u>large</u> and <u>complicated</u> to be solved in one meeting.

In the example above, you can see that the adjective *large* is on one side of the conjunction *and*. Another adjective, *complicated*, is on the other side. The adjectives are therefore parallel structures.

INCORRECT:	On the weekend, I like playing tennis, hiking, and to take my dog for walks.

This sentence is not considered grammatically correct because the three structures linked by the word and are not of the same type: *playing* and *hiking* are gerunds, whereas *to take* is an infinitive. To make the sentence correct, change either the gerunds to infinitives, or the infinitive to a gerund.

The coordinate conjunctions that involve parallel structure are: *and, but* and *or*. These conjunctions can link any part of speech as well as phrases and even entire clauses. See the examples below.

VERBS LINKED:	I would like to <u>visit</u> but not <u>live in</u> New York City.

Notice that the word *to* precedes both *visit* and *live in*, so they are parallel structures. The following sentence is also correct:

I would like <u>to visit</u> but not <u>to live in</u> New York City.

ADVERBS LINKED:	You can travel <u>comfortably</u>, <u>quickly</u>, or <u>safely</u>, but never all three at the same time.
PREPOSITIONAL PHRASES LINKED:	You can get there by driving <u>around the tunnel</u> or <u>over the mountain</u>.
NOUN CLAUSES LINKED:	I know that <u>he loves her</u> but <u>she doesn't love him</u>.

Using Correlative Conjunctions

English also has a set of paired conjunctions that are called *correlative conjunctions*. They are *either . . . or, neither . . . nor,* and *both . . . and.* Correlative conjunctions add emphasis when they are used.

Like coordinate conjunctions, structures linked by correlative conjunctions must be in parallel structure.

NOUNS LINKED:	Both <u>mother</u> and <u>daughter</u> have beautiful black hair.
VERBS LINKED:	One can either <u>see</u> or <u>hear</u> if there is a problem with the car.
ADJECTIVES LINKED:	The speech is neither <u>too long</u> nor <u>too boring</u>.

In the last example above, the word *too* comes before both adjectives. If only one *too* were used, the structures would no longer be parallel, and therefore the sentence would be incorrect.

Using *Than* and *Not*

Note also that *than* and sometimes *not* also follow the rule of parallel structure:

VERBS LINKED:	I would rather <u>die</u> than <u>hurt</u> a single hair on her head.
NOUNS LINKED:	It was the <u>roller coaster</u>, not <u>the popcorn</u>, that made me sick!

The TOEFL often tests parallel structure in the following way:

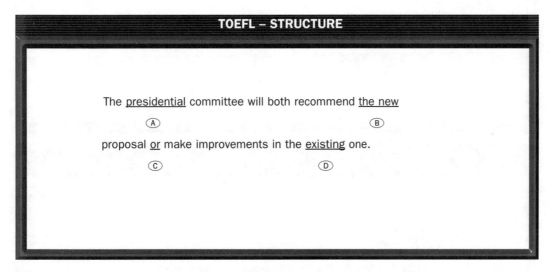

TOEFL – STRUCTURE

The <u>presidential</u> committee will both recommend <u>the new</u>
    Ⓐ   Ⓑ

proposal <u>or</u> make improvements in the <u>existing</u> one.
    Ⓒ   Ⓓ

Naturally, (C) is the correct choice here because the correlative conjunction is made up of *both . . . and,* never *both . . . or.* The correlatives, in the pairs given above, are the only possible combinations.

PRACTICE 3: PARALLEL STRUCTURE

Circle the correct answer choice for each question.

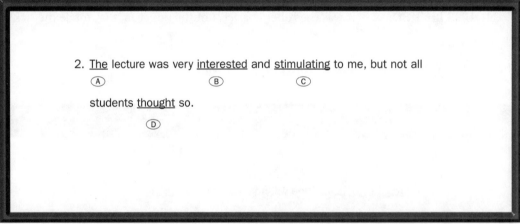

TOEFL – STRUCTURE

1. Neither <u>smoking</u> nor <u>to eat</u> are <u>allowed</u> in the classroom <u>at</u> Ball
   Ⓐ   Ⓑ   Ⓒ   Ⓓ

   State College.

TOEFL – STRUCTURE

2. <u>The</u> lecture was very <u>interested</u> and <u>stimulating</u> to me, but not all
   Ⓐ   Ⓑ   Ⓒ

   students <u>thought</u> so.
       Ⓓ

TOEFL – STRUCTURE

3. <u>It's</u> hard <u>to know</u> who our waiter <u>is</u> because we were served
   Ⓐ   Ⓑ   Ⓒ

   drinks by one person and our food <u>brought</u> by another one.
               Ⓓ

TOEFL – STRUCTURE

4. Whenever you <u>go</u> to the gym, I <u>could have used</u> <u>the</u> computer while
             Ⓐ   Ⓑ   Ⓒ

   you <u>are out</u>.
       Ⓓ

TOEFL – STRUCTURE

5. Jackson <u>plans</u> to major <u>in</u> business and <u>minoring</u> in international
           Ⓐ   Ⓑ   Ⓒ

   <u>affairs</u>.
   Ⓓ

SESSION D: COMPARATIVE AND SUPERLATIVE ADVERBS AND ADJECTIVES

Comparatives and superlatives are tested on the TOEFL in two ways: first, according to whether the form is correct, and, second, according to whether the comparative or the superlative is used correctly.

When a comparison is made between two things, the adjective or adverb takes an *-er* ending or has the word *more* preceding it.

For this reason, Session D concentrates on the form and usage of comparatives and superlatives. Remember, an adjective is used to describe a noun, while an adverb is used to describe a verb, an adjective, or another adverb.

Forms of the Comparative

-*Er* is used for:

(1) adjectives of one syllable (that are not past participles—see below):

big	bigger	white	whiter

(2) one-syllable adverbs that do not end in *-ly*:

hard	harder	fast	faster

(3) two-syllable adjectives ending in *-y*, *-ple*, or *-le*:

sunny	sunnier	simple	simpler
little	littler		

Either *-er* or *more* is used for:

(1) two-syllable adjectives ending in *-ly*, *-er*, or *-ow*:

friendly	friendlier/more friendly
clever	cleverer/more clever
narrow	narrower/more narrow

***More* is used for:**

(1) other adjectives that have two or more syllables:

useful	more useful
loathsome	more loathsome
interesting	more interesting

(2) a few other common adjectives:

stupid	more stupid
quiet	more quiet
handsome	more handsome

(3) participles used as adjectives:

bored	more bored
tired	more tired

(4) adverbs ending in -*ly*:

quickly	more quickly
happily	more happily
softly	more softly

Irregular comparative forms:

good	better (adjective)
well	better (adverb)
far	farther (adjective and adverb)
bad	worse (adjective and adverb)

Usage of the Comparative

The comparative form is used to compare two things. It is often followed by the word *than*.

Allen writes <u>faster than</u> I write.

He has seen that movie <u>more often than</u> they have seen it.

Note that after the word *than*, a clause is used. If the verb and complement are the same in both clauses of the sentence, the *than* clause can be reduced in two ways.

> **The rules for forming the comparative are the same as the rules for forming the superlative. Therefore, making the effort to learn them will pay off in two ways.**

(1) The verb and complement can be reduced to an auxiliary.

Allen writes faster than I <u>do</u>.

He has seen that movie more often than they <u>have</u>.

(2) The verb can be completely omitted so that only the subject is used. In this case, one should be sure to use the subject form of the pronoun.

Allen writes faster than <u>I</u>.

He has seen that movie more times than <u>they</u>.

Forms of the Superlative

When a comparison is made of three or more things, the adjective or adverb takes an *-est* ending or has the word *most* preceding it.

Generally, *-est* is used in the superlative wherever *-er* is used in the comparative.

big	bigger	biggest
sunny	sunnier	sunniest
fast	faster	fastest
clever	cleverer	cleverest

The word *most* precedes the adjective wherever *more* is used in the comparative.

interesting	more interesting	most interesting
quickly	more quickly	most quickly
bored	more bored	most bored

Adjectives and adverbs that are irregular in the comparative are also irregular in the superlative.

good	better	best
well	better	best
far	farther	farthest
bad	worse	worst

Usage of the Superlative

The superlative is used to compare three or more things. It is almost always preceded by the definite article *the*.

The Cadillac <u>is the biggest</u> car that we have.

He was talking to <u>the most gorgeous</u> woman I have ever seen.

Equal Comparisons

To say that things are equal in terms of a certain adjectival or adverbial quality, English uses the formula *as* + **adjective/adverb** + *as*.

ADJECTIVE: Marcia is <u>as</u> lucky <u>as</u> I am lucky.

ADVERB: Few authors today write <u>as</u> well <u>as</u> Graham Greene did.

Note that after the second *as*, a clause is used. If the verb and complement are the same after the word *as*, this clause can be reduced in two ways.

(1) The verb can be reduced to an auxiliary.

Marcia is as lucky as I <u>am</u>.

Bill Rogers drives as fast as his wife <u>does</u>.

My family has visited that area as often as yours <u>has</u>.

(2) The verb can be completely omitted so that only the subject is used. In this case, one should be sure to use the subject form of the pronoun.

Marcia is as lucky as <u>I</u>.

Bill Rogers drives as fast as <u>his wife</u>.

My family has visited that area as often as <u>yours</u>.

PRACTICE 4: COMPARATIVES, SUPERLATIVE ADVERBS, AND ADJECTIVES

Circle the correct answer choice for each question.

TOEFL – STRUCTURE

1. Two hamburgers contain _____ the same number of chicken drumsticks.

   (A) more than fat as

   (B) more fat than

   (C) more fat as

   (D) as fat protein

TOEFL – STRUCTURE

2. The weight of the fat man is _____ everyone else in his family.

   (A) greater than that of

   (B) as large as

   (C) more greater

   (D) broader than the one of

TOEFL – STRUCTURE

3. Mercury being the closest, Venus is _____ planet to the sun in our solar system.

   (A) the second of the

   (B) of the second closest

   (C) the second closest of the level

   (D) the second closest

TOEFL – STRUCTURE

4. Though they swim _____ the Bering Straights, the whales always return to the coast of California.

    (A) far away as

    (B) far as away

    (C) as far away as

    (D) away as far

TOEFL – STRUCTURE

5. New York City has _____ population of any city in the United States.

    (A) larger

    (B) the larger

    (C) the largest

    (D) as large as

SESSION E: THE PARTS OF SPEECH

The TOEFL often requires you to identify an incorrect form of the word in a sentence. The mistake will often be based on the fact that the word in question is in the wrong part of speech for its grammatical use in the sentence.

To answer this type of question correctly, you need to know:

(1) What part of speech should be used in various grammatical functions

(2) What sorts of expressions are used in English

The second type of knowledge is more difficult to acquire than the first, as this example may show:

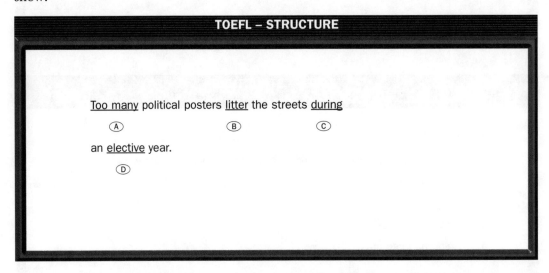

TOEFL – STRUCTURE

<u>Too many</u> political posters <u>litter</u> the streets <u>during</u>

Ⓐ   Ⓑ   Ⓒ

an <u>elective</u> year.

Ⓓ

A student who has only the first type of knowledge listed above might think that the word *elective* is correct because he or she might believe that the adjectival form of the word *election* is needed to modify the noun *year*. Sometimes this kind of reasoning will be sufficient to identify the incorrect part of the sentence.

Unfortunately, such reasoning doesn't work in this case. In English, the compound noun *election year* is always used to refer to the year in which an election is held. The expression *elective year* does not exist in this sense. Therefore, (D) is the answer.

The only way to learn fixed expressions is one at a time.

Remember to be flexible about learning grammar. Fixed expressions, like idioms and collocations such as *election year*, are often tested on the TOEFL, but they don't always seem to follow the rules of grammar.

PRACTICE 5: PARTS OF SPEECH

Circle the correct answer choice for each question.

TOEFL – STRUCTURE

1. The _____ was written in iambic pentameter.
   - (A) poet
   - (B) poem
   - (C) poetry's
   - (D) poetic

TOEFL – STRUCTURE

2. San Francisco, _____ of as one of America's most beautiful cities, is located in northern California.
   - (A) thinking
   - (B) thought
   - (C) was thought
   - (D) thoughtfully

TOEFL – STRUCTURE

3. The <u>opposing</u> counsel <u>presented</u> an enormous amount of <u>evident</u>

        (A)   (B)   (C)

   to support <u>their claim</u>.

              (D)

TOEFL – STRUCTURE

4. Rarely <u>do</u> we have such <u>heat</u> temperatures <u>this late</u> in <u>the season</u>.
     Ⓐ   Ⓑ   Ⓒ   Ⓓ

TOEFL – STRUCTURE

5. We <u>thought</u> it <u>was</u> one of the most <u>bored</u> movies we had ever
     Ⓐ   Ⓑ   Ⓒ

<u>had ever</u> seen.
  Ⓓ

KAPLAN

SESSION F: *THERE* AND *IT* AS SUBJECTS

Often in English, *there* and *it* occupy the subject position of a sentence while the real subject appears elsewhere in the sentence after the verb.

Using *There*

There is used when a noun is being introduced for the first time.

> Waiter, <u>there</u> is a fly in my soup.

In this case, the waiter does not know yet that a fly is in the customer's soup. The customer is pointing out the fly to the waiter. The sentence could be rephrased in this way: "A fly exists in my soup."

It is important to remember that the word *there*, as used in this example, does not mean the same as the word *there* when used to indicate a place.

Finally, remember that the noun following the *there is/there are* construction determines whether the verb is singular or plural in form.

> There <u>are five bottles</u> on the table.

> There <u>has</u> been <u>a problem</u> with this car since we first bought it.

Using *It*

It is used as the subject when the subject is a long clause or phrase.

> It is important <u>that all students report to the main office</u>.

In this example, the real subject is the *that* clause. In such a sentence the *it* has no meaning by itself, but simply fills in the subject spot for the real subject. The form of the verb in such sentences is always singular. Sometimes the real subject is an infinitive phrase, as in the example below:

> It seems foolish <u>to complain about such things</u>.

Not just the verb *be*, but also *seem, appear,* and *take* are often used with it.

> It seems obvious <u>that we will be late</u>.

> It appears <u>that you have missed the point</u>.

> It takes <u>two hours to get there</u>.

PRACTICE 6: *THERE* AND *IT*

Circle the correct answer choice for each question.

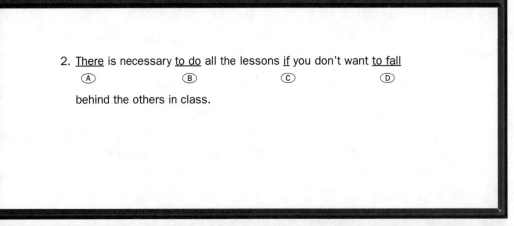

TOEFL – STRUCTURE

1. <u>There</u> is essential <u>that</u> you <u>call home</u> tonight because <u>your family</u>
   Ⓐ   Ⓑ   Ⓒ   Ⓓ

   is very concerned about you.

TOEFL – STRUCTURE

2. <u>There</u> is necessary <u>to do</u> all the lessons <u>if</u> you don't want <u>to fall</u>
   Ⓐ   Ⓑ   Ⓒ   Ⓓ

   behind the others in class.

TOEFL – STRUCTURE

3. <u>There are</u> so many <u>new</u> students <u>in</u> our class that <u>there will be</u>
   Ⓐ   Ⓑ   Ⓒ   Ⓓ

   difficult to memorize all the names.

TOEFL – STRUCTURE

4. <u>Boston</u> is <u>a place</u> where <u>it is</u> very <u>many</u> college students.
   (A)   (B)   (C)   (D)

TOEFL – STRUCTURE

5. I <u>hope</u> it will <u>be a</u> good play that we <u>were going</u> to <u>see tomorrow</u>
   (A)   (B)   (C)   (D)

   evening.

STRUCTURE POWER LESSON FIVE
ANSWER KEY

Practice 1	**Practice 2**	**Practice 3**
1. C	1. C	1. B
2. A	2. B	2. B
3. B	3. B	3. D
4. B	4. D	4. B
5. B	5. A	5. C

Practice 4	**Practice 5**	**Practice 6**
1. B	1. B	1. A
2. A	2. B	2. A
3. D	3. C	3. D
4. C	4. B	4. C
5. C	5. C	5. C

Structure Power
Lesson Six

At a Glance:

SESSION A: SUBJECT-VERB AGREEMENT

Singular/plural or "number" agreement is an important aspect of the English language. English is often said to be a very "redundant" language for this reason.

The <u>two</u> smartest girls in the class <u>were</u> chosen to win the award.

In this example sentence, there are three ways in which the subject (*girls*) is shown to be plural: (1) the adjective *two*; (2) the plural marker *-s* at the end of the noun; and (3) the verb *to be* in its plural form (*were*). In English grammar, the adjective, subject, and verb *agree* if they all indicate either a singular or plural number.

A common type of TOEFL question tests your ability to recognize agreement errors. Below is a list of some of the confusing areas in subject-verb agreement that occur on the TOEFL.

When a Subject Is Separated from the Verb by a Prepositional Phrase

When trying to determine whether a verb should be in the singular or plural form, find the subject and ignore all other words coming after it in the sentence. If the subject is singular, then the verb is singular. If the subject is plural, then the verb is plural.

The <u>problems</u> with the student have not yet been resolved.

The <u>cat</u> lying in the midst of hundreds of papers <u>is</u> content to doze in the afternoon sun.

The word *problems* is the subject of the first sentence, so the verb is in the plural form; the subject of the second sentence is *cat*, so the verb is in the singular form.

Using *All, Most, Some,* and *Any* + a Plural Count Noun

When these words are followed by a plural count noun, the verb is plural. This rule does not change if *of the* comes between the word and the noun.

All men	are created equal.
Most of the notebooks	were completed last week.
Some of the students	have finished.
Any members of that group	are permitted to enter the museum for free.

Using *All, Most, Some,* and *Any* + a Noncount Noun

When these words are followed by a noncount noun, the verb is singular. This rule does not change if *of the* comes between the word and the noun.

All of the cake	has been eaten.
Some fat	is good for you.
Most car exhaust	contains pollutants that threaten all living things.
If any of the sugar	is lost, you will be responsible.

For more information on noncount nouns, see the "Types of Nouns" section in the Grammar Review.

Using *None* and *Neither*

In "TOEFL English," *none* and *neither* always take a singular verb, whether followed by a plural or a noncount noun.

None of the dogs belongs to me.

Neither of the women is the one who spoke to me yesterday.

None of the boys wants to go on the field trip with the girls.

In "TOEFL English," *none* and *neither* always take singular verbs.

Neither computer has enough memory to run this software.

None of the tea in this store is fresh.

Note that the rule for *neither* alone is not the same for *neither . . . nor*, as the next grammar point makes clear.

Using *Either . . . Or* and *Neither . . . Nor*

With these expressions, the noun that is closest to the verb determines whether the verb is singular or plural.

Neither the children nor their mother	wants to leave.
Either you or I	am going to call an end to this charade.

In the first sentence above, *their mother* is closer to the verb than *the children*, so the verb takes the third-person singular form, *wants*. In the second sentence, *I* is closer to the verb than *you*, so the verb takes the first-person singular form, *am*.

Notice the same logic in the sentences below:

Neither Eve nor <u>her children</u>	<u>want</u> to leave.
Either I or <u>you</u>	<u>are</u> going to call the police.

Note that *both . . . and* is always plural.

<u>Both my brother and I</u>	are interested in joining the team.

Using *Every*

Although it does not seem logical, nouns following *every* are singular, and they take singular verbs. This includes the nouns *everyone*, *everybody*, and *everything*.

<u>Everybody</u>	<u>is</u> going to be there!
<u>Every man</u>, <u>woman</u>, and <u>child</u>	<u>has</u> been rescued.
<u>Every watch</u> in the store	<u>is</u> on sale.

- Remember: *every* is always followed by a singular noun and a singular verb.

Using Singular Nouns that End in *-s*

There are a few nouns that end in *-s* that take a singular verb. These nouns often refer to countries, fields of study, activities, and diseases.

Countries: *the United States, the Philippines, the Netherlands, Wales*

<u>The United States</u>	<u>doesn't</u> have a centralized governing body for educational affairs.

Fields of study: *mathematics, classics, economics, genetics, linguistics, physics, electronics, statistics* (*Statistics*, when not referring to a field of study, is plural.)

> **Make sure you learn the singular nouns ending in *-s* that are listed in this session. It is easy to lose points on the TOEFL because of this grammar point.**

<u>Mathematics</u>	<u>was</u> not my favorite subject in school.
The <u>statistics</u>	<u>do</u> not seem correct.

Activities: *aerobics, politics, athletics*

The <u>politics</u> of even a small town	is often very complicated.

Diseases: *measles, mumps, diabetes, rabies*

<u>Measles</u>	<u>is</u> a serious childhood disease if not treated properly.

Other common nouns ending in -s taking singular verbs: *news, series*

The <u>news</u>	<u>was</u> interesting.
That television <u>series</u>	<u>is</u> broadcast on Thursday nights.

Using Collective Nouns

A noun is considered collective when it refers to a group of individuals. Most collective nouns take the singular form of the verb because the group is seen as a united whole.

The <u>committee</u>	<u>doesn't</u> have to come up with a solution until next week.
The <u>crowd</u>	<u>has</u> been standing in front of the building for almost two hours already.

Some common collective nouns are: *army, military, audience, committee, press, public, team, jury, government,* and *family.*

Remember, however, that the nouns *people* and *police* are considered plural, so they take plural verbs.

The <u>people</u>	<u>were</u> happy to see the return of their king.
The <u>police</u>	<u>are</u> here to serve and protect.

Using Expressions of Time, Distance, and Money in the Plural Form

Expressions of time, distance, and money are often seen as collective items and so take a singular verb.

<u>Two miles</u>	<u>is</u> too far to walk in this blistering sun.
<u>Sixty dollars</u>	<u>is</u> a fair price for such an old painting.
<u>Five hours</u>	<u>has</u> already passed since his surgery ended.
<u>Three days</u>	<u>is</u> too long for them to wait.

Using *the* + an Adjective as a Subject

The + an adjective takes a plural verb because it refers to a whole group of people.

<u>The rich</u>	<u>are</u> not respected by the blue-collar constituency of this area.
<u>The educated</u>	<u>are</u> at an advantage when looking for a job.
<u>The sick</u>	<u>were</u> be taken to the hospital immediately.
<u>The unemployed</u>	<u>do</u> not have to work on the weekends.

Using Adjective Clauses

The verb inside a relative clause agrees with the subject of the clause. If the subject is a relative pronoun (*who, which,* or *that*), the verb agrees with the antecedent of the pronoun.

The <u>woman</u> who <u>lives</u> there is my mother.

The subject of the verb *lives* is *who. Who* is singular because its antecedent—*woman*—is singular.

If the antecedent for a relative pronoun is plural, then the verb form in the adjective clause is also plural:

The <u>women</u> who <u>live</u> there are my aunts.

PRACTICE 1: SUBJECT/VERB AGREEMENT

Circle the correct answer choice for each question.

TOEFL – STRUCTURE

1. The traffic laws of each <u>state</u> <u>varies</u> with regards to speed <u>limit</u> and
   Ⓐ   Ⓑ   Ⓒ

   <u>minimum</u> driving age.
   Ⓓ

TOEFL – STRUCTURE

2. Several <u>breeds</u> of dog <u>is trained</u> specifically <u>for</u> <u>police work</u>.
   Ⓐ   Ⓑ   Ⓒ   Ⓓ

TOEFL – STRUCTURE

3. The Iowa Caucus, the first primary <u>election</u> in the race for the
   Ⓐ

   American presidency, has traditionally been an <u>accurate</u> <u>forecasts</u>
   Ⓑ   Ⓒ

   of who will be the major <u>parties</u>' nominees.
   Ⓓ

KAPLAN

TOEFL – STRUCTURE

4. Every one <u>of</u> the students <u>are</u> present today <u>for</u> our
   Ⓐ   Ⓑ   Ⓒ

   <u>final exam</u>.
   Ⓓ

TOEFL – STRUCTURE

5. Much <u>of</u> the strikers' <u>anger</u> <u>have to</u> do <u>with money</u>.
   Ⓐ   Ⓑ   Ⓒ   Ⓓ

SESSION B: PRONOUN-ANTECEDENT AGREEMENT

The *antecedent* of a pronoun is the noun to which the pronoun refers. Possessive adjectives also have antecedents.

Here are some examples of pronouns and possessive adjectives and their antecedents.

> Christopher Columbus first sailed to the new world in 1492, when he was trying to find a new route to India.

> All citizens have the responsibility of voting in order to preserve their freedom through the democratic process.

For more information on pronouns, possessive adjectives, and antecedents, see the Grammar Review.

Pronouns and possessive adjectives must agree with their antecedents. This means making sure that all pronouns are correctly singular or plural depending on their antecedents. Pronouns must also agree with the gender (the sex) of their antecedents.

As mentioned in Session A, collective nouns (*family, committee,* etcetera) are considered singular in American English. *People* and *police* are generally plural. Pronouns and possessive adjectives referring to these nouns should agree with them according to number and gender.

> A family will always feel a duty to protect its members.

> The committee worked late into the night reviewing its policy and procedure manual.

> The police are eager to improve their image in the eyes of the public.

Certain pronouns, while commonly used in the plural in informal speech, are considered singular in the more formal style of English which the TOEFL tests. For example, *everybody, everyone,* and the like are often referred to with the possessive adjective *their.* While this is acceptable for speaking, it should be avoided in more formal English and therefore, avoided on the TOEFL.

> **FORMAL/TOEFL:** Everybody has to live his own life.

> **INFORMAL:** Everybody has to live their own life.

Although usually the antecedent of a pronoun is introduced first and the pronoun second, in adverb clauses and phrases that occur at the beginning of a sentence, the pronoun is given before the noun to which it refers.

> During his eight years as president, Ronald Reagan held the admiration of the American people.

PRACTICE 2: PRONOUN/ANTECEDENT AGREEMENT

Circle the correct answer choice for each question.

TOEFL – STRUCTURE

1. Every man who was assigned to Carlton Hall must check in with ____ resident adviser today.

   Ⓐ their

   Ⓑ his

   Ⓒ her

   Ⓓ your

TOEFL – STRUCTURE

2. All of us should do ____ best to keep an eye out for each other.

   Ⓐ their

   Ⓑ his

   Ⓒ your

   Ⓓ our

TOEFL – STRUCTURE

3. If the professor's class is full, you should ask him if he can let you get into ____ next term.

   Ⓐ it

   Ⓑ them

   Ⓒ him

   Ⓓ his

TOEFL – STRUCTURE

4. Everybody <u>should</u> just mind <u>their</u> own business <u>and</u> we would
            (A)   (B)   (C)

   all be <u>better off</u>.
         (D)

TOEFL – STRUCTURE

5. <u>Whatever</u> your opinion <u>of</u> Mr. Jelks <u>is</u>, you must admit that <u>him</u>
     (A)   (B)   (C)   (D)

   has very impressive credentials.

KAPLAN

SESSION C: SINGULAR AND PLURAL NOUN USAGE

The TOEFL often tests a student's ability to recognize whether a noun should be in singular or plural form. The following rules will help you avoid some of the most common mistakes on the TOEFL.

Using *Another*

The word *another* is always followed by a singular count noun.

> <u>Another topic</u> that we will cover is the forced migration of the Cherokee from the East toward Oklahoma.

> We don't need <u>another boss</u>; we need someone who will do the work.

Keep in mind that *another* can never be preceded by a determiner (*the, a/an, this, that, my, your, his,* etcetera). See the Grammar Review for a more complete list of determiners.

Using *Few* and *a Few*

Few and *a few* are always followed by a plural.

> <u>Few people</u> have seen the Northern Lights.

> The army is looking for <u>a few</u> good <u>men</u>.

Using *Less, Much, Fewer,* and *Many*

Less and *much* are used before noncount nouns while *fewer* and *many* are used before plural-count nouns.

> There is <u>less food</u> than I thought there would be.

> We don't have <u>much work</u>, so I can meet you at 5:00.

> How <u>much gasoline</u> can I get for a dollar?

> I wish you would make <u>fewer mistakes</u>.

> There are <u>many ways</u> to deal with this challenge.

> How <u>many amoebas</u> can fit on a microscope slide?

Note also that *a lot of* can be followed by either a plural-count or a noncount noun.

> <u>A lot of people say</u> he would make a great politician.

> I take <u>a lot of sugar</u> in my tea.

Using *Some* and *Most*

Some and *most* are always followed by a noncount noun or a plural count noun.

> Some children never learn to read.
>
> If you're thirsty, drink some water.
>
> Most people are nice, once you get to know them.
>
> Nowadays, most petroleum is found deep beneath the surface of the earth.

Some of and *most of* are always followed by *the* + a noncount noun or *the* + a plural-count noun.

> Most of the men have received their orders.
>
> Some of the food has been eaten.

Using *the Majority Of*

The majority of is usually followed by a plural noun, but is sometimes found preceding a non-count noun.

> The majority of the pens were blue.
>
> The majority of oxygen molecules consist of two atoms combined.
>
> The pesticides destroyed the majority of the groundwater.

Using *Every*

Every is always followed by a singular-count noun.

> Every book was too old to read easily.
>
> We looked at every house for sale in the area.

Using Numbers

The words *hundred, thousand, million,* etcetera do not have a plural *-s* when preceded by numbers greater than one (a definite number).

These words do take an *-s* when they refer to an indefinite number. In such cases the number is always followed by an *of* phrase with a plural noun.

> I have three hundred CDs at home. (= exactly 300)
>
> The university had thousands of international students. (indefinite—between a thousand and ten thousand)

Using *Both*

Both, used as an adjective or a pronoun, always refers to exactly two things, so *both* is always followed by a plural noun.

> Both men were happy to be rescued.

Using *Between* and *Among*

Between always refers to two things. *Among* always refers to three or more things. Therefore, they always have plural nouns as their objects.

> Between the trees, there are many beautiful flowers. (two trees)

> Among the trees, there are many beautiful flowers. (three or more trees)

Every singular noncount noun must be modified by a determiner (that is, a word like the, *a/an, my, his, this, that,* and *another*). Note that this rule may be broken in certain idiomatic expressions.

PRACTICE 3: SINGULAR AND PLURAL NOUNS

Circle the correct answer choice for each question.

TOEFL – STRUCTURE

1. Each _____ is responsible for finding his/her own living accommodations.
   Ⓐ students
   Ⓑ student
   Ⓒ of all student
   Ⓓ of students

TOEFL – STRUCTURE

2. _____ may be bought used for half the price of new ones.
   Ⓐ Many textbooks
   Ⓑ Many textbook
   Ⓒ Much textbook
   Ⓓ Much of the textbook

TOEFL – STRUCTURE

3. My brother and <u>other</u> friend <u>of his</u> are going <u>to Europe</u> for spring <u>break</u>.
                   Ⓐ   Ⓑ   Ⓒ   Ⓓ

TOEFL – STRUCTURE

4. Each student <u>is</u> required <u>to make</u> a <u>speeches</u> at the <u>end</u>
          (A)   (B)   (C)   (D)

of the term.

TOEFL – STRUCTURE

5. <u>Much</u> money <u>can be</u> saved <u>if</u> you don't spend <u>them</u> so carelessly.
    (A)   (B)   (C)   (D)

PRACTICE 4: REVIEW

Circle the correct answer choice for each question.

TOEFL – STRUCTURE

1. None of them _____ their homework assignment.

   (A) done

   (B) had done

   (C) doing

   (D) be done

TOEFL – STRUCTURE

2. _____ a relief it was to hear that your father's going to be all right.

   (A) That

   (B) Why

   (C) What

   (D) If

TOEFL – STRUCTURE

3. All the schools he applied to accepted _____.

   (A) him

   (B) them

   (C) he

   (D) his

TOEFL – STRUCTURE

4. Everything _____ to be in its place or Jane gets very upset.
   - Ⓐ needing
   - Ⓑ need
   - Ⓒ needs
   - Ⓓ will be needing

TOEFL – STRUCTURE

5. Many <u>of</u> the teachers I <u>had</u> last year still <u>haven't</u> turned in

        Ⓐ   Ⓑ   Ⓒ

   <u>your</u> grades for the finals.

  Ⓓ

TOEFL – STRUCTURE

6. <u>Never</u> before <u>I have had</u> such a delicious dinner <u>as</u> the one we

    Ⓐ   Ⓑ   Ⓒ

   <u>had last</u> night in Chinatown.

  Ⓓ

TOEFL – STRUCTURE

7. WXYN News <u>are located</u> on <u>the</u> top floor <u>of</u> the Betters Building,
   (A)   (B)   (C)

   just <u>outside of</u> town.
        (D)

TOEFL – STRUCTURE

8. Rarely <u>can</u> we <u>be seen</u> such a movie <u>in</u> my country
          (A)   (B)   (C)

   <u>due to</u> censorship by the government.
   (D)

KAPLAN

TOEFL – STRUCTURE

9. My paper <u>written</u> last night, but I <u>was</u> so tired <u>that</u> I don't
        Ⓐ   Ⓑ   Ⓒ

   think my teacher will understand <u>much</u> of it.
                                            Ⓓ

TOEFL – STRUCTURE

10. Each of us <u>are</u> ready <u>whenever</u> your team <u>feels</u> prepared
                Ⓐ   Ⓑ   Ⓒ

    <u>to begin</u>.
     Ⓓ

STRUCTURE POWER LESSON SIX
ANSWER KEY

Practice 1

1. B
2. B
3. C
4. B
5. C

Practice 2

1. B
2. D
3. A
4. B
5. D

Practice 3

1. B
2. A
3. A
4. C
5. D

Practice 4: Review

1. B
2. C
3. A
4. C
5. D
6. B
7. A
8. B
9. A
10. A

Structure Power
Lesson Seven

SESSION A: PREPOSITIONS

Correct use of English prepositions can be very difficult for nonnative speakers of English. One reason for this is that, although there are sometimes rules for the use of prepositions, many prepositional phrases fall under the category of idiomatic expressions. This means that there is often no easily identifiable reason why one preposition is correct while another preposition is wrong.

Native speakers usually learn prepositions in association with other words (often a verb or an adjective). We recommend that you learn these in the same way—in *verb + preposition* or *adjective + preposition* combinations.

In this session, you will first review some rules for the use of prepositions with expressions of time. Then you will learn some verb + preposition and adjective + preposition combinations. Finally, you will learn a list of adverb clause conjunctions and prepositions that are similar in meaning but used in different ways.

Prepositions Used with Expressions of Time

Use *at* for specific times of the day:

> Sheila got up at 6:30. She ate lunch <u>at</u> noon.

Use *on* for days:

> He'll arrive <u>on</u> June 4th.

His job forces him to travel all the time. <u>On</u> Christmas Day he was in Houston, and <u>on</u> New Year's Eve he traveled to Phoenix.

Use *in* for weeks, months, seasons, years, and centuries:

I hope to have it finished <u>in</u> the second week of September.

She was born and died <u>in</u> the same month.

What do farmers do <u>in</u> the winter?

We moved to Portugal <u>in</u> 1986.

<u>In</u> the 1700s, the horse offered the fastest means of transportation.

In English, people say *in the morning, in the afternoon,* and *in the evening,* but for the words *day* and *night, by day* and *at night* are used.

I work <u>in the morning</u> and study <u>in the afternoon</u>. <u>In the evening</u> I watch TV.

A nocturnal animal is one that does most of its activity <u>at night</u>. An animal that does most of its activity <u>by day</u> is said to be diurnal.

Some Verb + Preposition Combinations

Some verbs can take more than one preposition, but with a change in meaning. For example, *speak* and *talk* can be followed by *to* or *with* + the person being addressed, and *about* + the topic being discussed.

He spoke <u>to</u> Marilyn. He spoke about literature.

Sally talked <u>with</u> Howard <u>about</u> what movie they would watch.

The verbs *argue* and *quarrel* take *with* + the person being disagreed with, and *about* or *over* + the issue causing the disagreement.

My sister argued <u>with</u> my brother. She argued <u>with</u> him <u>about</u> (or over) politics.

The left and right wings of the party quarreled <u>with</u> each other over (or <u>about</u>) which side would get the most cabinet positions.

The verb *agree* takes *with* + a person, and *on* + the topic of agreement.

Terri agreed <u>with</u> Lawrence <u>on</u> where they should look for a house.

Almost all other verbs take only one preposition. A few may take more than one preposition, but have the same meaning with either one. Here are some of the verb + preposition combinations you might find on the TOEFL. As you study the list, note that some of the verbs are transitive (that is, they take a direct object), whereas others are intransitive (they have no direct object). For example:

As you learn verbs other than the verbs in this list, learn the preposition or prepositions that usually go with them. That will make your learning easier. You will find a good English dictionary indispensible for this task.

TRANSITIVE: I <u>thanked Alfred</u> for his help.

INTRANSITIVE: Lori <u>prayed for</u> a major snowstorm on the day of the exam.

For more on transitive and intransitive verbs, see the Grammar Review.

Verb + Preposition Combinations

against

react against

at

stare at
hint at

for

apologize for
blame for
excuse for
fight for
hope for
pay for
pray for
substitute for
thank for
vote for

from

distinguish from
emerge from
escape from
hide from
obtain from
prevent from
prohibit from
recover from
rescue from
stop from
suffer from

in

believe in
excel in
invest in
participate in
result in
succeed in

of

accuse of
think of

on

bet on
insist on

to

belong to
contribute to
lead to
object to
respond to

with

associate with
cover with
provide with
sympathize with

Verbs That Can Take More Than One Preposition Without a Change in Meaning:

care about/care for
compare to/compare with
complain of/complain about
contribute to/contribute towards
count on/count upon
decide on/decide upon

depend on/depend upon
dream of/dream about
end in/end with
improve on/improve upon
insist on/insist upon
rely on/rely upon

Some Adjective + Preposition Combinations

Like some verbs, many adjectives are usually followed by a single preposition. Here are some adjective + preposition combinations you might find on the TOEFL.

There is no complete list of TOEFL verb + preposition or adjective + preposition combinations. As you read in English, or listen to English-language movies or television, you can improve your TOEFL score by making your own lists of combinations that are not in this session.

about

concerned about
confused about
excited about
worried about

against

discriminated against

for

known for
prepared for
qualified for
remembered for
responsible for

from

absent from
different from

in

dressed in
interested in
involved in

of

afraid of
aware of
capable of
composed of
conscious of
envious of
fond of
guilty of
innocent of
jealous of
proud of
scared of
terrified of
tired of

to

able to
accustomed to
addicted to
committed to
connected to
confined to
dedicated to
engaged to
equal to
exposed to
faithful to

inferior to
limited to
opposed to
polite to
related to
similar to
superior to
unrelated to
used to

with

acquainted with
annoyed with
associated with
bored with
content with
displeased with
dissatisfied with
done with
familiar with
filled with
finished with
furnished with
patient with
pleased with
satisfied with
upset with

Adjectives That Can Take More Than One Preposition Without a Change in Meaning:

angry at/angry with
based on/based upon
disappointed in/disappointed with
friendly to/friendly with

made of/made from
puzzled at/puzzled by
surprised by/surprised at

As discussed in Structure Power Lesson Four, Session B, if a verb comes after a preposition, it must be in the form of a gerund. Thus:

We're afraid of an airplane crash.
We're afraid of <u>dying</u> in an airplane crash.

I am annoyed with Peter.
I am annoyed with Peter's <u>leaving</u> early.

Prepositions that Resemble Adverb Clause Subordinate Conjunctions

A few prepositions resemble or are identical in form and meaning to subordinate conjunctions that introduce adverb clauses. These deserve special attention. The first column consists of a list of subordinate adverb clause conjunctions, while the second column consists of a list of prepositions. This means that the words in the first column should be followed by a clause (subject and verb) and the words in the second column should be followed by a noun.

Subordinate Conjunctions	Prepositions
because	because of
while	during
despite the fact that	despite
in spite of the fact that	in spite of
until	until
since	since
after	after
before	before

Examples:

Because it rained, the game was cancelled.
Because of rain, the game was cancelled.

While he was in class, he fell asleep.
During class, he fell asleep.

Despite the fact that they lost money, they still have hope for the future.
Despite losing money, they still have hope for the future.

Since he arrived yesterday, he has done nothing but complain.
Since yesterday, he has done nothing but complain.

PRACTICE 1: PREPOSITIONS

Circle the correct answer choice for each question.

TOEFL – STRUCTURE

1. Vitamin C is _____ citrus fruits.

   Ⓐ obtained by

   Ⓑ obtained from

   Ⓒ obtained in

   Ⓓ obtained of

TOEFL – STRUCTURE

2. <u>Every year</u> <u>on</u> November, we <u>celebrate</u> Thanksgiving,
      Ⓐ   Ⓑ   Ⓒ

   often <u>with</u> a big meal <u>with</u> family and friends.
        Ⓒ   Ⓓ

TOEFL – STRUCTURE

3. Broadway <u>is known</u> <u>throughout</u> the world <u>of</u> the center
           Ⓐ   Ⓑ   Ⓒ

   for many famous <u>plays and musicals</u>.
                   Ⓓ

TOEFL – STRUCTURE

4. <u>Although</u> some teachers are superior <u>in quality</u> <u>from</u> others,
   Ⓐ   Ⓒ   Ⓑ

   the success of a class depends <u>to</u> a great
                                   Ⓓ

   extent on what the students do.

TOEFL – STRUCTURE

5. <u>Most</u> Americans <u>polled</u> said <u>that</u> they <u>believe on</u> God.
   Ⓐ   Ⓑ   Ⓒ   Ⓓ

SESSION B: PATTERNS WITH *LIKE* AND *ALIKE*

Most of the questions that test *like, alike, unlike,* and *not alike* on the TOEFL are based on the ability to recognize patterns in which these words appear. Although the word pairs have very similar meanings, they are used in different and very specific sentence patterns.

Like (Preposition) and *Alike* (Adjective/Adverb)

Like and *alike* both convey the idea of "the same." The difference is that *like* is a preposition, so is always followed by a noun. On the other hand, *alike* is either a predicate adjective or an adverb, which means that it always comes after the verb of the clause it is in.

Like is used in the first four sentence patterns below, and *alike* is used only in the fourth.

Like X, Y . . .

Like Kate, Vicky stays out all night.

Like oranges and grapefruits, lemons contain vitamin C.

X, like Y, . . .

Kate, like Vicky, stays out all night.

X . . . like Y

I don't stay out all night like Kate and Vicky.

Kate is like Vicky.

X and Y are like each other

Kate and Vicky are like each other in that both stay out all night.

X and Y . . . alike

Kate and Vicky talk very much alike.

Insofar as they both contain vitamin C, lemons and oranges are alike.

Unlike (Preposition) and *Not Alike/Unalike* (Adjective/Adverb)

In a way similar to *like* and *alike*, *unlike* and *not alike* convey similar meanings but use different patterns.

Unlike X, Y . . .

Unlike Millie, Vicky stays out all night.

Unlike oranges and grapefruits, apples contain no vitamin C.

X, unlike Y, . . .

Vicky, <u>unlike</u> Millie, stays out all night.

X . . . unlike Y

I prefer to read at home on Friday nights, <u>unlike</u> Kate and Vicky.

Oranges and grapefruits are very much <u>unlike</u> broccoli.

Oranges and broccoli are <u>unlike</u> each other.

X and Y . . . not . . . alike/
X and Y . . . unalike

Kate and Vicky do not look much <u>alike</u>.

Lemons and broccoli are <u>not</u> at all <u>alike</u>.

Kate and Vicky look very much <u>unalike</u>.

Lemons and broccoli are completely <u>unalike</u>.

Like and *alike* are related in exactly the same way that *unlike* and *not alike/unalike* are related. If you understand the difference between the first pair, you understand the difference between the second.

PRACTICE 2: PATTERNS WITH *LIKE* AND *ALIKE*

Circle the correct answer choice for each question.

TOEFL – STRUCTURE

1. Although John and Jim are twins, they don't look that much _____ .
   - (A) like
   - (B) unlike
   - (C) alike
   - (D) liking

TOEFL – STRUCTURE

2. _____ my mother, I prefer to watch old movies instead of most of the new ones.
   - (A) As
   - (B) Not alike
   - (C) Like
   - (D) Alike

TOEFL – STRUCTURE

3. My roommate and I didn't get along very well because we were not much _____ in tastes or lifestyle.
   - (A) alike
   - (B) unalike
   - (C) like
   - (D) not alike

TOEFL – STRUCTURE

4. The plums in my country and the American plum are not alike
   (A)   (B)   (C)   (D)

   each other in taste or texture.

TOEFL – STRUCTURE

5. If you like mystery novels, I think this one is alike the last one
            (A)   (B)   (C)

   you read, so I can recommend it to you.
                                (D)

SESSION C: IDENTIFYING THE MISSING WORD

On the error identification part of the TOEFL Structure Section, a word that is necessary for the grammatical correctness of a sentence is often left out.

This type of error actually requires you to use your knowledge of many other grammar points learned in this book. For example, a missing word could affect whether an adjective clause has been constructed correctly or not.

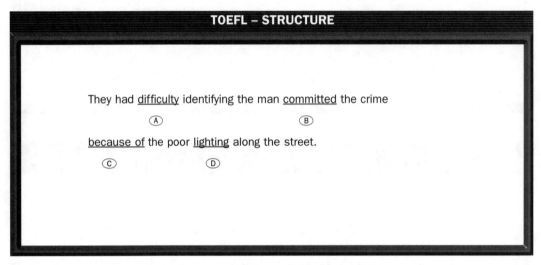

In the above sentence, (B) is the incorrect part of the sentence because the relative pronoun *who* is missing after *the man*, which would serve as the subject for the verb *committed*. It is your knowledge of adjective clauses that will tell you whether this is correct or not. Specifically, you will need to be able to recognize that the relative pronoun cannot be omitted in an adjective clause if it is the subject of that clause. (See Structure Power Lesson Two, Session C, where adjective clauses are discussed.)

Look at another example:

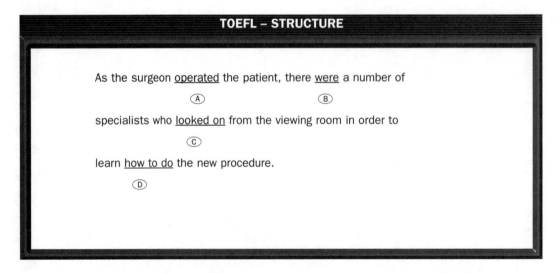

In the above example, (A) is the incorrect part of the sentence. Your being able to recognize this really comes from your knowledge about which verbs are transitive and therefore take a direct object, and which verbs are intransitive and therefore require a preposition. (See Session A of this lesson).

On the error-identification part of the TOEFL, remember to look not just for a word or expression that is wrong—you must also look for underlined parts of the sentence that might be missing a word.

Specifically, *operate* is an intransitive verb and therefore cannot take a direct object; we need the preposition *on* between the verb *operate* and the noun *the patient*. Therefore, the answer is (A).

PRACTICE 3: DISCOVERING MISSING WORDS

Circle the correct answer choice for each question.

TOEFL – STRUCTURE

1. The <u>Heart</u> is a Lonely Hunter was <u>name</u> of both <u>a</u> popular
   Ⓐ   Ⓑ   Ⓒ

   book and <u>play</u>.
         Ⓓ

TOEFL – STRUCTURE

2. <u>One</u> of <u>main reasons</u> I <u>moved</u> to Dallas is because <u>I really</u>
   Ⓐ   Ⓑ   Ⓒ   Ⓓ

   don't care for long winters.

TOEFL – STRUCTURE

3. <u>In spite</u> rain, we <u>finished</u> the marathon <u>in</u> our best
   Ⓐ   Ⓑ   Ⓒ

   <u>recorded</u> time yet.
     Ⓓ

TOEFL – STRUCTURE

4. <u>Most</u> of our class <u>going</u> to the lecture <u>in</u> Dodge Hall this afternoon
    Ⓐ   Ⓑ   Ⓒ

<u>even though</u> it is not required.
    Ⓓ

TOEFL – STRUCTURE

5. <u>Quite lot</u> of students in our class <u>were born</u> in Japan, but many
     Ⓐ   Ⓑ

<u>of</u> them <u>grew up</u> in the United States.
 Ⓒ   Ⓓ

SESSION D: ARTICLES

The rules for the correct use of articles (*a, an, the*) in English are difficult to master, but very interesting to learn. The reason that the article system (and there really is a system) is so hard for a nonnative speaker of English to understand fully is that the correct use of articles is very closely connected to subtle differences in meaning that English speakers are trying to convey.

Fortunately, the TOEFL usually does not try to test these subtle differences in meaning. Usually the TOEFL tests articles in only a few ways. The rules in this section will help you avoid the common mistakes in article usage that the TOEFL tests.

Rule 1: All singular count nouns must be modified by a determiner.

The articles *a, an,* and *the* are determiners. Other determiners are words like *this, that, my, your, his,* and *her*. For more information on determiners, see the Grammar Review.

What this rule tells you is that a singular count word—for example, *pen*—cannot be used in a sentence without a determiner.

> <u>This pen</u> is red.
>
> Where is <u>the pen</u>?
>
> That's a strange <u>pen</u>.
>
> Someone has chewed on <u>my</u> favorite <u>pen</u>.

Keep Rule 1 in mind as you take the TOEFL—it can save you a lot of easy points.

Rule 2: *A* and *an* are used only with singular nouns.

Rule 3: An expression of a definite quantity in the singular is usually preceded by *a/an*.

Expressions of a definite quantity include *a mile, a quart, a pound, a dozen,* and *a ton*.

Rule 4: No article is used in English with noncount nouns when they refer to general concepts of the noun.

> <u>Freedom</u> is our most important possession.
>
> <u>Gold</u> makes a wonderful gift for a person you love.
>
> <u>Sugar</u> costs 50 cents a pound.

If the noncount noun is followed by a descriptive adjective clause or phrase, we use the article *the*.

> <u>The freedom that Thomas Jefferson envisioned</u> is very different from the kind of freedom we have today.
>
> He could buy a car with all <u>the gold in his teeth</u>.
>
> <u>The sugar that he had bought the previous day</u> was covered with ants.

Rule 5: *The* **is used with certain proper noun names of rivers, lakes, mountains, etcetera.**

the Mississippi River
the Nile River
the Rocky Mountains
the Pacific Ocean
the Hawaiian Islands
the Caribbean Sea
the Amazon Jungle

But note this isn't true with the words *lake* and *mount*, which precede the name.

Mount Kilimanjaro
Lake Michigan

Rule 6: When a proper noun is used as a modifier for another noun, *the* **always precedes the proper noun.**

the Smiths' house
the Egyptian pharaohs
the European Community

Rule 7: Articles are usually not used with parts of the body or clothing when the owner of the parts of the body or clothing is known.

In these cases a possessive adjective is usually used.

Julia cut <u>her</u> hair.

I wore <u>my</u> best pants.

If the owner of the body part or item of clothing is not known, an article may be used.

In the barn I found <u>an</u> old T-shirt.

One of David Lynch's films begins with the discovery of <u>a</u> human ear.

Rule 8: *The* **always precedes** *same.*

This story is almost exactly <u>the</u> <u>same</u> as a story I read last year by a different author.

PRACTICE 4: ARTICLES

Circle the correct answer choice for each question.

TOEFL – STRUCTURE

1. <u>One</u> of <u>a best</u> days <u>of</u> my life <u>was when</u> I had my first child.
   (A)   (B)   (C)   (D)

TOEFL – STRUCTURE

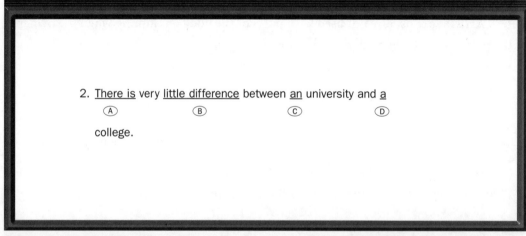

2. <u>There is</u> very <u>little difference</u> between <u>an</u> university and <u>a</u>
   (A)   (B)   (C)   (D)

college.

TOEFL – STRUCTURE

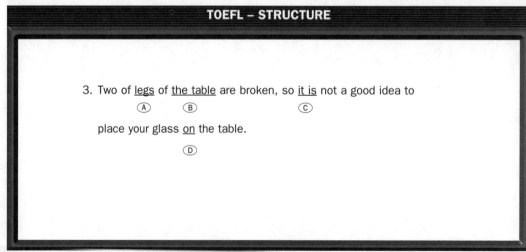

3. Two of <u>legs</u> of <u>the table</u> are broken, so <u>it is</u> not a good idea to
   (A)   (B)   (C)

place your glass <u>on</u> the table.
   (D)

KAPLAN

TOEFL – STRUCTURE

4. <u>Next week</u> we will <u>study more</u> about <u>Universe</u> and <u>our</u>

    Ⓐ   Ⓑ   Ⓒ   Ⓓ

solar system.

TOEFL – STRUCTURE

5. <u>The company</u> I work for <u>will pay</u> for my MBA as <u>long as</u> I get

    Ⓐ   Ⓑ   Ⓒ

accepted to one of <u>top schools</u> in the country.

                Ⓓ

PRACTICE 5: REVIEW QUESTIONS

Circle the correct answer choice for each question.

TOEFL – STRUCTURE

1. According _____ the dean, the enrollment is up since last semester.

    (A) with

    (B) to

    (C) by

    (D) in

TOEFL – STRUCTURE

2. The two courses couldn't be less _____.

    (A) not alike

    (B) unalike

    (C) alike

    (D) like

TOEFL – STRUCTURE

3. Everything she told me about the school turned _____ to be accurate.

    (A) in

    (B) out

    (C) for

    (D) down

TOEFL – STRUCTURE

4. Every fall, my allergies _____ really bad.

   (A) are

   (B) has been

   (C) is

   (D) will be

TOEFL – STRUCTURE

5. It is essential that he tells you what's on his mind and stop
   (A)   (B)   (C)

   playing these games with you.
   (D)

TOEFL – STRUCTURE

6. Almost every student brought their books to the first class.
   (A)   (B)   (C)   (D)

TOEFL – STRUCTURE

7. <u>During</u> the lecture, you <u>and</u> I can go get something <u>eating</u> if
   (A)   (B)   (C)

   you <u>like</u>.
       (D)

TOEFL – STRUCTURE

8. <u>Her</u> dress was <u>made up</u> of a rare material, the <u>likes</u> of which I
   (A)   (B)   (C)

   <u>had never seen</u> before.
        (D)

KAPLAN

TOEFL – STRUCTURE

9. <u>Driving</u> at night, I <u>can</u> barely see ten <u>foot</u> ahead <u>of me</u>.
    (A)   (B)   (C)   (D)

TOEFL – STRUCTURE

10. There <u>are</u> no reason you <u>can't do</u> better than you <u>have been</u> doing
        (A)   (B)   (C)

recently <u>on</u> your assignments.
     (D)

STRUCTURE POWER LESSON SEVEN
ANSWER KEY

Practice 1	Practice 2	Practice 3
1. B	1. C	1. B
2. B	2. C	2. B
3. C	3. A	3. A
4. C	4. D	4. B
5. D	5. C	5. A

Practice 4	Practice 5: Review
1. B	1. B
2. C	2. C
3. A	3. B
4. C	4. A
5. D	5. B
	6. C
	7. C
	8. B
	9. C
	10. A

Reading Power

The Reading Power practice exercises in this book will prepare you for the several different kinds of questions you should expect on the TOEFL CBT. By the time you finish this section of the book, your readiness for the test will have improved enormously.

However, to do really well on this section of the TOEFL, you will have to do a great deal of outside reading on many different topics. The TOEFL does not test test-taking skills—it tests language proficiency. There is a limit to how much test-taking skills can improve your TOEFL score. The point is this: to do really well on the Reading Comprehension section of the TOEFL CBT, you must do a lot of reading in English. So . . . get started!

Before you start to work on the Reading Power Practice exercises, read through "Reading Comprehension for the TOEFL CBT" on the following pages. These pages will give you more details on what to expect on the Reading Comprehension section of the computer-based TOEFL exam.

THE BIGGER PICTURE: READING BEYOND THE TOEFL

Depending on the major, American college students typically have to read 50 to 400 pages a week. Graduate students may have to read even more. Even students majoring in the sciences (which generally require less reading than the humanities) will spend the first two years of their academic careers taking courses outside of their major. In other words, a student in the American system cannot avoid courses in literature, philosophy, or psychology—which ask students to read a great deal.

This is why the TOEFL places such importance on students' reading skills. It is also why the passages in the TOEFL's Reading Comprehension section are about so many different topics; every student going through an American college or university—whether American or not— will have to do a lot of reading on many different topics.

Now that you know why the TOEFL tests reading skills, it's time to find out how you can prepare yourself for this section of the test as well as possible.

Reading Comprehension for the TOEFL CBT

Since July, 1998, the TOEFL has been administered on computer. The Reading Comprehension section of the TOEFL CBT differs from the paper-based TOEFL both in the way that test takers experience reading the passages and the way that they record their answers.

On test day, prior to taking the exam, you will have the opportunity to work through a tutorial, which will show you, step-by-step, how to use a mouse, how to scroll, and how to use the testing tools. In addition, before each of the four sections, you will be shown how to answer the types of questions that you will encounter in that section. The more comfortable you are with computers, the less you will have to worry about on test day!

In the following pages, we will discuss some unique features of the Reading Comprehension section of the TOEFL CBT.

COMPUTER LINEAR

The Reading Comprehension section is "computer linear." This means that you will receive a predetermined set of questions. You will get either 44 or 60 questions and the time allotted for the Reading Comprehension section will appear on the "Directions" screen prior to the actual test section. Your Reading Comprehension section will be either 70 or 90 minutes long.

Because the Reading Comprehension section is linear and not computer adaptive, you may skip questions and return to them later. However, we do not recommend skipping around; unlike the paper-and-pencil exam, you will not be able to see at a glance which questions you have skipped, and you are likely to become confused. It is better to work through the exam passage by passage.

CONTENT

The Reading Comprehension section tests a person's ability to read and understand passages written in a style that students at a North American university would typically encounter. The passages that appear on the TOEFL CBT are similar in content to those on the paper-and-pencil exam. The one difference is that they may be somewhat longer. However, the topic areas, such as physical and natural science and humanities, remain the same. Passages that discuss humanities topics, such as history, biography, and the arts, will focus on aspects of American culture. You will not be presented with passages on a historical figure from Sweden, a national holiday in Korea, or a musical style that is indigenous to South America, for example.

PASSAGE FORMAT

The passage will appear on the screen rather than printed on paper. You must practice reading off a computer screen to get comfortable with this way of reading. If you have access to the Internet, you should practice reading English texts on the Web (if you do not have a computer at home, check the local public library—many now have free Internet access).

All of the passages will require that you scroll in order to read them in their entirety. The best way to scroll is to click on the grey bar located to the right of the passage. Clicking on the grey bar will advance the text one full screen. If you try to scroll by moving the little scroll box or by clicking on the arrow at the top or bottom, you may lose your place. Be sure to practice scrolling in a word-processing program or on the Internet.

QUESTION FORMAT

The format of the questions on the TOEFL CBT is significantly different from that of questions on the paper-based format. On the paper-and-pencil exam, you are given four choices, from which you pick one and fill in the corresponding oval. On the computerized test, you will record your answer directly on the screen. Overall, Kaplan students who have taken both the paper-based and the computer-based test tend to agree that the Reading Comprehension section is now much easier, because you no longer have to hunt around for the correct line, sentence, or paragraph since it is either marked with an arrow or highlighted in bold print.

All question type examples in this chapter will refer to the following passage:

TOEFL – READING COMPREHENSION

Beginning

During the late 1880s, some failing farms were bought up and turned into resorts. Originally they were designed for Eastern European Jewish families who wanted to escape the overcrowded, polluted Lower East Side ghettos of New York City (this is how the region attained its nickname, "the Borscht Belt," so named for the Eastern European soup made from beets). Kuchaleyns, Yiddish for "cook-alones," were inexpensive bungalows where the guests supplied their own linens and did their own cooking. Usually ten families would share a single kitchen.

The Kuchaleyns served another purpose besides providing an opportunity to breathe fresh air. Marriage-minded young Jews (or more likely their anxious parents) saw these vacation days as a chance to meet other eligible young people and to get to know each other outside of the constraints of their neighborhood. The resort owners hoped to capitalize on the idea of courtship, bragging about matches made at their resorts.

Over time, these Kuchaleyns evolved to become more luxurious. Clients no longer had to cook for themselves and sheets were provided for the beds. Even so, the clientele continued to come from the New York City Jewish community and the social function of the resorts remained pretty much the same. Resort owners continued to take a direct role in match-making in a couple of ways. For one, they would spread rumors about what a "good catch" this or that one was. They also liked to present a view of overabundance of eligible young men. One owner, David Katz, would hire future doctors, dentists and lawyers to be his dining-room staff. Once a week he would call meetings to

cont. on next page

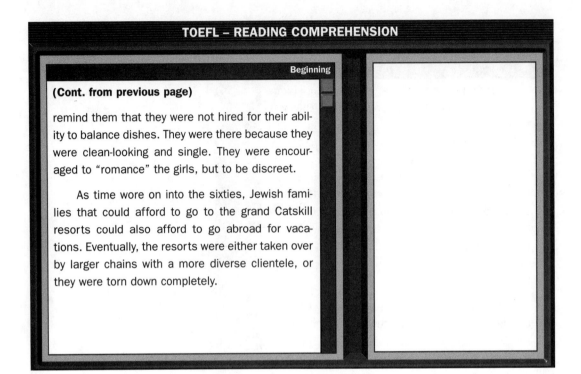

TOEFL – READING COMPREHENSION

Beginning

(Cont. from previous page)

remind them that they were not hired for their ability to balance dishes. They were there because they were clean-looking and single. They were encouraged to "romance" the girls, but to be discreet.

As time wore on into the sixties, Jewish families that could afford to go to the grand Catskill resorts could also afford to go abroad for vacations. Eventually, the resorts were either taken over by larger chains with a more diverse clientele, or they were torn down completely.

KAPLAN

Standard Multiple-Choice

In this question type, you will click on the oval next to the correct answer choice.

Example:

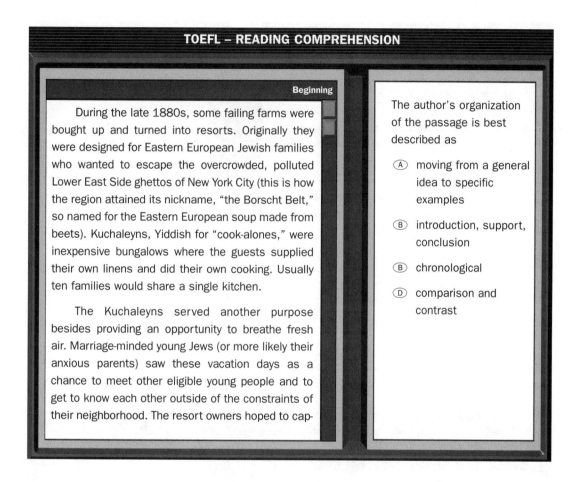

TOEFL – READING COMPREHENSION

Beginning

During the late 1880s, some failing farms were bought up and turned into resorts. Originally they were designed for Eastern European Jewish families who wanted to escape the overcrowded, polluted Lower East Side ghettos of New York City (this is how the region attained its nickname, "the Borscht Belt," so named for the Eastern European soup made from beets). Kuchaleyns, Yiddish for "cook-alones," were inexpensive bungalows where the guests supplied their own linens and did their own cooking. Usually ten families would share a single kitchen.

The Kuchaleyns served another purpose besides providing an opportunity to breathe fresh air. Marriage-minded young Jews (or more likely their anxious parents) saw these vacation days as a chance to meet other eligible young people and to get to know each other outside of the constraints of their neighborhood. The resort owners hoped to cap-

The author's organization of the passage is best described as

Ⓐ moving from a general idea to specific examples

Ⓑ introduction, support, conclusion

Ⓑ chronological

Ⓓ comparison and contrast

Click on Reference

In this question type, you will be given a vocabulary word or pronoun and asked to click on the word in a particular paragraph or section (identified by bold text) to which it refers. An example can be found below:

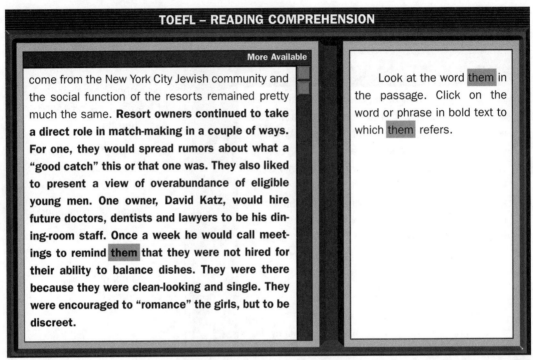

To answer, you can click on any part of the word or phrase in the passage. Your choice will darken to show which word you have chosen.

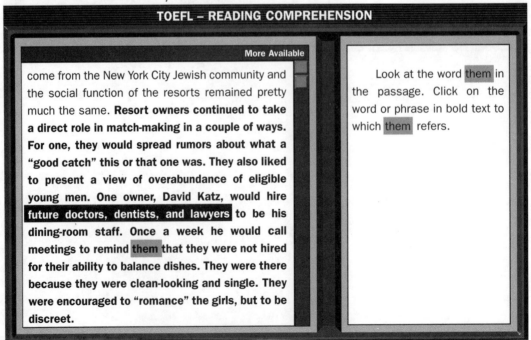

KAPLAN

Click on Sentence or Paragraph

Here, you will be given a question and asked to click on the sentence or paragraph in which the answer can be found. You will be presented with questions like the one below:

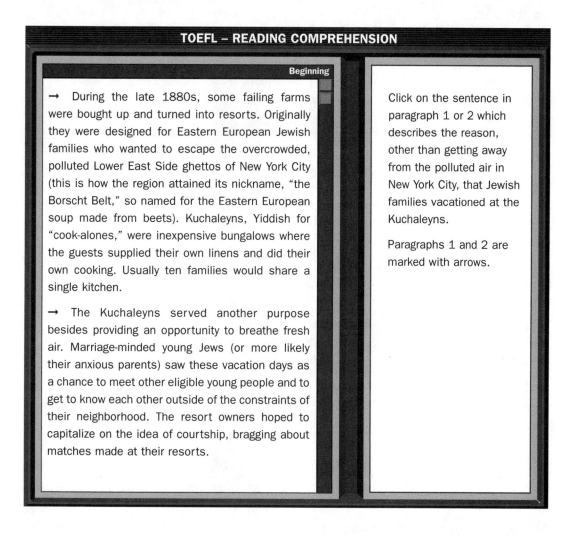

You can click on any part of the sentence in the paragraphs. The sentence will darken to show which answer you have chosen. The correct answer is darkened in the passage below.

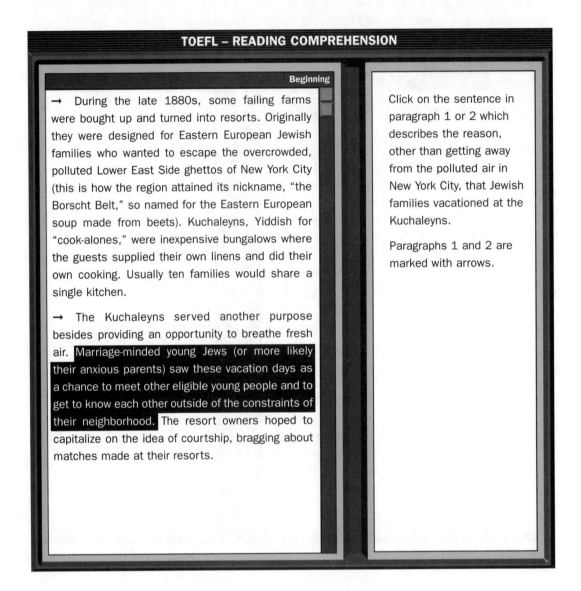

TOEFL – READING COMPREHENSION

Beginning

→ During the late 1880s, some failing farms were bought up and turned into resorts. Originally they were designed for Eastern European Jewish families who wanted to escape the overcrowded, polluted Lower East Side ghettos of New York City (this is how the region attained its nickname, "the Borscht Belt," so named for the Eastern European soup made from beets). Kuchaleyns, Yiddish for "cook-alones," were inexpensive bungalows where the guests supplied their own linens and did their own cooking. Usually ten families would share a single kitchen.

→ The Kuchaleyns served another purpose besides providing an opportunity to breathe fresh air. Marriage-minded young Jews (or more likely their anxious parents) saw these vacation days as a chance to meet other eligible young people and to get to know each other outside of the constraints of their neighborhood. The resort owners hoped to capitalize on the idea of courtship, bragging about matches made at their resorts.

Click on the sentence in paragraph 1 or 2 which describes the reason, other than getting away from the polluted air in New York City, that Jewish families vacationed at the Kuchaleyns.

Paragraphs 1 and 2 are marked with arrows.

Insert Sentence/Click on Square

You will click on a square to add a sentence to the passage for this type of question.

TOEFL – READING COMPREHENSION

Beginning

→ ■During the late 1880s, some failing farms were bought up and turned into resorts. ■Originally they were designed for Eastern European Jewish families who wanted to escape the overcrowded, polluted Lower East Side ghettos of New York City (this is how the region attained its nickname, "the Borscht Belt," so named for the Eastern European soup made from beets). ■Kuchaleyns, Yiddish for "cook-alones," were inexpensive bungalows where the guests supplied their own linens and did their own cooking. ■Usually ten families would share a single kitchen.

The Kuchaleyns served another purpose besides providing an opportunity to breathe fresh air. Marriage-minded young Jews (or more likely their anxious parents) saw these vacation days as a chance to meet other eligible young people and to get to know each other outside of the constraints of their neighborhood. The resort owners hoped to capitalize on the idea of courtship, bragging about matches made at their resorts.

The following sentence can be added to paragraph 1:

Most immigrant families who lived in this part of New York were not wealthy.

Where would it best fit in paragraph 1? Click on the square (■) to add the sentence to the paragraph.

Paragraph 1 is marked with an arrow.

Click on a square and the sentence will appear in the passage at that point. When the sentence is added, it will be shown in a dark box. You should read the passage to see if it makes sense with the new sentence. If not, try again by clicking on another square. The correct answer is:

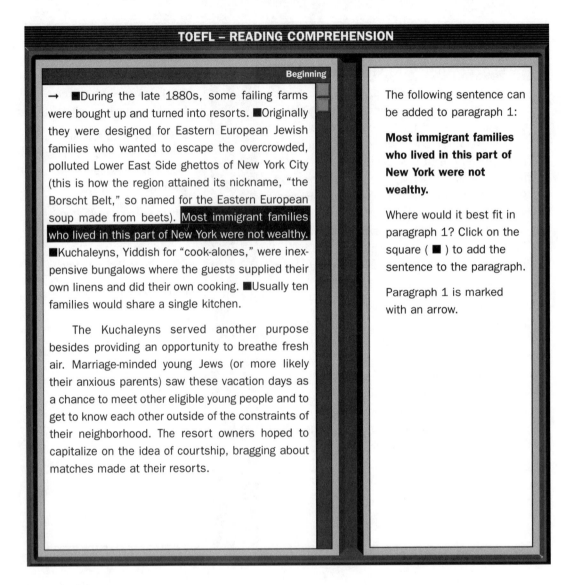

SCORING

The Reading Comprehension section of the TOEFL CBT is scored on a scale of 0 to 30.

SKILLS AND STRATEGIES

Skills Tested on the TOEFL CBT

Specific skills that you will practice throughout this section are:

- Reading for facts
- Reading for main ideas
- Reading for organization
- Reading for usage
- Reading for inference
- Answering negative fact questions
- Identifying references

Even though the Reading Comprehension section has been adapted for the computer, the same general skill is being tested as in the past—reading. Refer to the explanatory sessions that follow this section for more details about the skills listed above.

Strategies

Some tips for doing your best on the Reading Comprehension section are:

(1) Immediately scroll to the bottom of the passage in order to advance to the first question for each passage.

In order to see the first question, you have to scroll to the bottom of the screen. Once you have scrolled all the way through the text, you will see a box that says Proceed. Click on this box and you will advance to the first question. The reading passage is included with every question.

(2) Budget your time.

Do not spend too much time reading a passage. Nor should you waste time on any particular question. Once you know how much total time you have, you can figure out about how much time you can spend on each question. Generally, it is estimated that you will have about 2 minutes to answer each question (approximately 10 minutes to read the passage and answer five questions).

(3) Don't panic if there are a lot of words you don't recognize.

You do not need to know every word in a reading passage to answer the questions correctly. If you stay calm and make educated guesses, you can answer questions correctly even if you don't understand every word in the question. Reading in any language involves figuring out the meaning of new words from context.

(4) Click on the grey bar to advance through the text.

If you use the scroll bar, you may lose your place. If you click on the grey area above or below the scroll bar, the passage will advance or go back one whole screen.

(5) Avoid skipping questions.

Even though you are able to skip questions and return to them on this part of the test, you should avoid doing so. Unlike paper-and-pencil tests in which you can see immediately which questions you missed, in the computer version, you will have to click through all of the screens in between in order to find the question that you did not answer. If you find that there are a couple of questions in one section that are too difficult, you should skip the entire passage and come back to it later. It is easier to find a whole section of questions than just one or two.

(6) Answer all questions for a passage before moving on.

Answer every question for a reading passage before going on to the next passage. One thing you do not want to do on this section of the TOEFL is reread a passage—you simply do not have the time. If you leave a question unanswered in Passage 2, for example, and go on to Passage 3, you will forget what Passage 2 is about. You will have to reread Passage 2 before you can answer the question you left unanswered.

(7) Skim for organization and tone.

Don't read every individual word, one at a time. Group words together and look for key transitional words to get an overall feel for how the passage is organized and what the author thinks about what he or she is saying.

(8) Scan for facts and references.

You can find the information you are looking for by quickly scanning the passage for key words. Read the question, then look at the answer choices and look for words that correspond (don't get tricked, though; sometimes the TOEFL will throw in distractors!) One advantage to doing the Reading Comprehension section on the TOEFL CBT is that you no longer have to search and count to find "the word *you* in line 17." On the computer, if the question asks you to analyze a particular word, phrase, sentence or paragraph, it will be clearly marked with either bolding, highlighting, or an arrow.

A Note on the Practice Exercises

In the exercises that follow, we have attempted, to the fullest extent possible, to include all of the question types found on the Reading Comprehension section of the TOEFL CBT. However, it is impossible to accurately reproduce computerized question types in a paper-based format such as this book, and we recommend that you turn to the *Mastering the Computer-Based TOEFL* CD-ROM for more practice in a truly CBT-like environment.

Reading Power Practice

SESSION A: READING FOR THE MAIN IDEA

Main idea questions require you to summarize the basic topic of the passage as well as the purpose of the passage.

Main idea questions often take the form:

What is the main topic of this passage?

The best title for the passage is . . .

The main topic for this passage is . . .

The following suggestions will help you answer main idea questions accurately.

When you read the reading passage for the first time, you should:

(1) Note the topic sentence.
(2) Note the general tone of the passage.

After you have found a main idea question, you should:

(3) Scan the passage for key vocabulary that might indicate the author's attitude toward the topic.
(4) Read this part of the passage carefully to answer the question.

The steps recommended in this lesson work for many students. After trying our suggestions on the practice questions, if you find that you prefer to adapt them to suit your own style of test taking—go ahead!

Remember that the topic sentence alone will not contain the main idea. The main idea can only be generalized from the entire passage. It is only by following the entire passage from beginning to end and following the author's position that you will be able to determine the main topic of the passage.

SESSION B: DISCERNING THE MAIN TOPIC FROM THE MAIN IDEA

The TOEFL asks two types of questions related to the major focus of the passage, topic questions and main idea questions. Though they are similar, they do not mean the same thing.

Main Topic Questions

The *topic* is the subject being discussed in the reading passage. It is not necessarily the same as the argument or the point the author is making.

For example, in a reading passage in which the author is trying to persuade the reader that the 55-mile-per-hour speed limit should be changed:

- The topic is the 55-mile-per-hour speed limit.
- The author's point is that the 55-mile-per-hour speed limit should be changed.

Main topic questions are almost always asked in the form:

What is the main topic of the passage?

To answer main topic questions, you should:

(1) Read the first and last sentences carefully.
(2) Locate the topic sentence.
(3) If you are still not certain, scan the passage for repeated vocabulary. Repeated vocabulary often indicates the main topic of a reading passage.

Main Idea Questions

Main idea questions, first examined in Session A, differ from topic questions because they include the author's main point. In other words the main idea takes into account what the author is saying about the topic. Again, main idea questions take the form:

What does the author mainly discuss?

The best title for the passage is . . .

The main idea of this passage is . . .

Listed below is an example of the difference between the two categories, main idea and main topic.

Read the following passage for its main idea and its main topic.

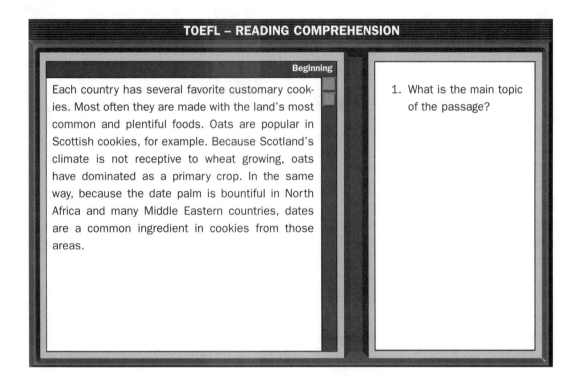

TOEFL – READING COMPREHENSION

Beginning

Each country has several favorite customary cookies. Most often they are made with the land's most common and plentiful foods. Oats are popular in Scottish cookies, for example. Because Scotland's climate is not receptive to wheat growing, oats have dominated as a primary crop. In the same way, because the date palm is bountiful in North Africa and many Middle Eastern countries, dates are a common ingredient in cookies from those areas.

1. What is the main topic of the passage?

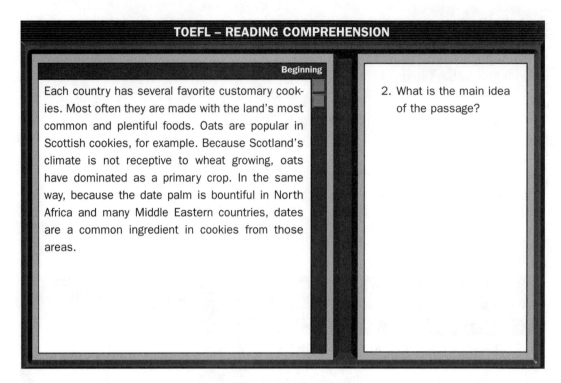

TOEFL – READING COMPREHENSION

Beginning

Each country has several favorite customary cookies. Most often they are made with the land's most common and plentiful foods. Oats are popular in Scottish cookies, for example. Because Scotland's climate is not receptive to wheat growing, oats have dominated as a primary crop. In the same way, because the date palm is bountiful in North Africa and many Middle Eastern countries, dates are a common ingredient in cookies from those areas.

2. What is the main idea of the passage?

The *topic* of the passage is: The ingredients in cookies from various geographical areas.

The *main topic* is the subject that the passage discusses. The *main idea* includes the main topic along with the point or position of the author.

The *main idea* is: Ingredients in cookies differ from region to region, depending on the country's most fundamental and abundant agricultural products.

Note that the main topic can usually be expressed with just a noun (for example, *cookies*). The main idea usually requires a sentence (subject + verb).

SESSION C: ANSWERING FACT-BASED QUESTIONS

The most common type of reading question on the TOEFL is the fact-based question. Fact questions require you to answer very specific information questions about the passage.

Here are some of the different ways that fact-based questions can be asked. Each statement would be followed by the four answer choices, only one of which would complete the statement correctly according to the passage.

Nimbostratus clouds are . . .

According to the article, nimbostratus clouds . . .

The passage states that all chimpanzees . . .

The author indicates that when nimbostratus clouds are visible, the weather . . .

Note the way each question is structured as well as the vocabulary it uses. You will often see words like according to, states, and indicates on this section of the TOEFL.

To answer fact-based questions, you should:

(1) Select from the question a key word or phrase.
(2) Scan the reading passage for this key word or phrase, or for words related to this key word or phrase.
(3) When you have found the key word or phrase in the passage, read this part of the passage carefully to answer the question.

TOEFL CBT Reading Comprehension questions show you the relevant sections of the passage so you will not have too much text to search through.

SESSION D: ANSWERING NEGATIVE FACT-BASED QUESTIONS

Negative fact-based questions offer three incorrect statements and one correct statement. Therefore, you are required to recognize the three correct statements about the passage and choose the one answer that is not true about the passage.

Negative fact-based questions usually take the form of one of the following statements:

According to the passage, all of the following are true except . . .

The author mentions all of the following except . . .

To answer negative fact-based questions, you should:

(1) Read the question carefully to determine the information you have to locate in the passage.
(2) Scan the passage to locate the answers that are true about the passage.
(3) Mark the answer that is not true about the passage.

This type of question usually takes longer to answer due to the need to find three correct statements in the passage. Slower readers may want to skip these questions until they have answered all of the easier types.

Remember, however, that for the Reading Comprehension section of the TOEFL CBT, you should make your best guess for all the questions belonging to one reading passage before going on to the next passage. If you move on to a new passage before completing your first passage, you will forget what you have read in this passage. When you return to the question about it, you will have to read the entire passage a second time—a very time-consuming process.

SESSION E: READING FOR INFERENCE

An *inference* is a conclusion based on information you have.

On the TOEFL, inference questions ask you to draw conclusions that are not explicitly given in the reading passage.

Below are two examples of inferences based on facts.

FACT:	All children acquire their first language before the age of four.
INFERENCE:	All six-year-old children speak a language.
FACT:	AT&T used to have a monopoly on telephone services in the United States.
INFERENCE:	There is currently more than one telephone company. (Used to means that something was true in the past, but no longer is.)

Inference questions usually take the form:

From the passage, it can be inferred that . . .

The author implies that . . .

To answer inference questions, you should:

(1) Read the question carefully.
(2) Read the answers to see what kind of answers you have available.
(3) Scan the passage to find where the information related to the inference can be found.
(4) Make assumptions about the information using what the passage says directly and what you already know about the topic.
(5) Select the best answer.

A good reader makes inferences while reading a text. You can improve your ability to answer inference questions by making inferences when you read the passage for the first time.

Inference questions require advanced reading skills. Previous knowledge of a topic (called *background knowledge*) will also help with inference questions. For example, a student with little knowledge of science will probably have difficulty trying to infer information from reading passages about science. For this reason, it is smart to learn a little about a lot of different topics by reading a wide variety of materials. This will give you background knowledge as well as a wide vocabulary.

SESSION F: READING FOR REFERENCE

Reference questions require you to identify the specific meaning or use of some word in the passage. The two main types of reference questions are vocabulary questions and questions about pronoun/possessive adjective reference.

A vocabulary question usually takes the forms shown below. Note that on the TOEFL CBT, these terms are shown in shaded boxes rather than italicized.

The term *anaplasty* is closest in meaning to . . .

King William's War refers to . . .

A question about pronoun or possessive adjective reference takes the form:

She refers to . . .

The word *their* refers to . . .

To answer reference questions you should:

(1) Read the context of the word or words carefully.
(2) Select the best answer.

Look at the following two examples of reference questions:

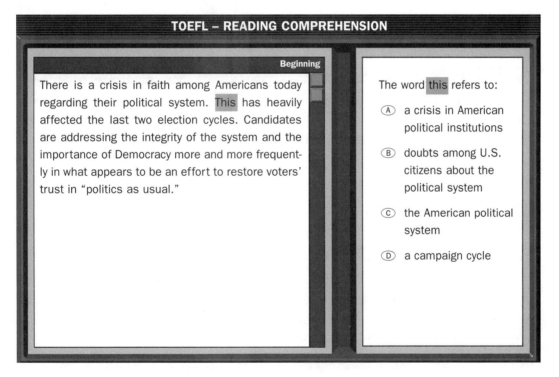

TOEFL – READING COMPREHENSION

Beginning

There is a crisis in faith among Americans today regarding their political system. This has heavily affected the last two election cycles. Candidates are addressing the integrity of the system and the importance of Democracy more and more frequently in what appears to be an effort to restore voters' trust in "politics as usual."

The word this refers to:

(A) a crisis in American political institutions

(B) doubts among U.S. citizens about the political system

(C) the American political system

(D) a campaign cycle

Although answer (A) contains the word *crisis*, which may distract you, answer (B) is correct. The crisis in faith mentioned in the first line is not within the political institutions themselves, but concerns doubts held by citizens about the system.

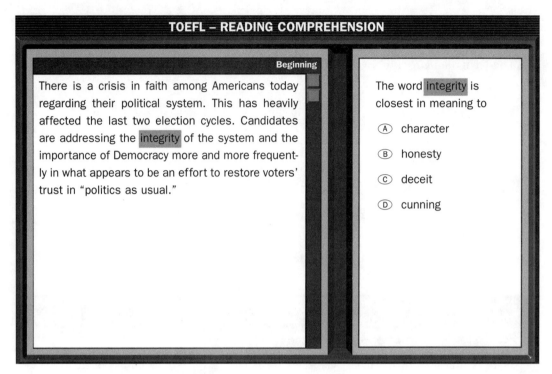

Here the correct answer is (B), *honesty*. Notice that the answer set gives two synonyms of integrity, *character* and *honesty*. Only one of these is correct in the context of the word in the reading passage. The TOEFL often presents this kind of distractor to the test taker.

Don't answer vocabulary questions too quickly. Sometimes the obvious synonym is a distractor—not the correct answer. Always check the answer you choose by seeing how the word is used in the reading passage.

SESSION G: READING FOR ORGANIZATION

Organization questions require you to understand the overall organization of the passage so that you can answer one of several types of questions. Organization questions are sometimes the most difficult kind of TOEFL reading question. For this reason, you may want to select your answer by eliminating the wrong answers first.

There are four types of organization questions. They are discussed separately below.

Basic Organization Questions

An organization question typically takes the form:

The author's organization of the passage is best described as . . .

(A) moving from a general idea to specific examples
(B) introduction, support, and conclusion
(C) chronological
(D) comparison and contrast

You should answer basic organization questions by:

(1) Determining what exactly the question requires you to answer.

(2) Reading the first and last paragraphs of the passage carefully, and identifying the topic sentence of the passage.

(3) Paying special attention to "linking words," such as *next, secondly, in conclusion,* etcetera.

(4) Eliminating the wrong answer choices until you have the best answer.

The Location of Specific Facts in the Passage

A location question would typically ask you:

Where in the bolded text does the author discuss the aging of neural transmitters?

You would then click on the appropriate phrase in the bolded section of the passage (see the "Click on Reference" question type in the "Reading Comprehension for the TOEFL CBT" section.)

You should answer specific-fact location questions by:

(1) Identifying a key word or words in the questions.

(2) Reading the bolded text, looking for the key word or its synonym.

(3) Eliminating the wrong phrases until you have the best answer.

Questions About Paragraphs That Precede or Follow a Passage

This type of question typically takes the form:

The paragraph after this passage would most likely be about . . .

The paragraph preceding this passage would most likely concern . . .

You should answer this type of organization question by:

(1) Going to the first paragraph of the reading passage if the question is about the preceding paragraph, or to the last paragraph of the reading passage if the question concerns the following paragraph, and reading that paragraph carefully.

(2) Keeping in mind the main idea of the passage as a whole, eliminating the wrong answer choices until you have the best answer.

Questions about the Kind of Larger Work in which the Passage Would Be Found

This type of question typically takes the form:

Where would this reading passage most likely be found?

(A) in an introductory textbook
(B) in a newspaper
(C) in a personal letter to a friend
(D) in a company memo

You should answer this type of organization question by:

(1) Reading the answer choices carefully.

(2) Skimming through the reading passage, noting characteristics such as tone, style, and main idea.

(3) Eliminating the wrong answer choices until you have the best answer.

In order to answer organization questions, it will be necessary for you to draw conclusions about ideas not explicitly given in the text. In this way, organization questions are very similar to inference questions.

If possible, you may want to leave organization questions until you have answered all the other types of questions for a reading passage. As you answer the other questions, you may come across the information needed to answer the organization questions. This is easier to do on the paper-based exam on the computer-based exam, as we have discussed.

SESSION H: READING FOR TONE

Your ability to judge the author's tone is sometimes tested on the TOEFL. In essence, this question is not very different from the tone questions used in the Listening Comprehension section (see Listening Power Lesson Two).

Tone questions frequently take the form:

The author's tone can best be described as . . .

You should answer a tone question by:

(1) Reading the answer choices carefully.

(2) Skimming through the reading passage, looking for words and ideas that indicate how the author feels about the topic or about the audience.

(3) Eliminating the wrong answer choices until you have the best answer.

PRACTICE 1

Read the passage provided and select the correct answer choice for each question.

TOEFL – READING COMPREHENSION

Beginning

Though adults breathe twelve times a minute, breathing is so automatic that the average person hardly ever thinks about it. But how does it happen? The breathing process is quite complex and controlled by the medulla of the brain, in an area called the "breathing center." The power required for breathing comes from the intercostal muscles and the diaphragm. During quiet, normal breathing, inhalation, or the intake of air, occurs when the intercostal or thoracic muscles (the muscles within the rib cage) contract and the three dimensions of the chest expand, allowing the expansion of the lungs. When the pressure inside the lungs increases, the air is exhaled. Interestingly, while inhalation during quiet breathing requires muscle contraction, exhalation does not. In circumstances in which more air needs to be exhaled than normal, such as when blowing out candles on a birthday cake, the abdominal muscles may contract to facilitate the exhalation.

While the basic breathing pattern remains the same, there can be variations depending on the location of the expansion during inhalation. Some people exhibit a large protrusion of the abdominal wall (they stick their stomach out), while others show more lateral expansion in the thoracic region. These two types of breathing are called diaphragmatic and thoracic respectively. A third type of breathing involves expanding the muscles of the extreme upper chest. People with this breathing pattern often lift their shoulders as they inhale. For this reason, this breathing type is known as clavicular (relating to the clavicle). People who breathe in this manner may have excessive tension in the throat and often feel as though they can't get enough air due to their shallow breathing.

1. What is the main topic of this passage?

   Ⓐ how to breathe

   Ⓑ variations in the breathing pattern

   Ⓒ the basic breathing pattern and its variations

   Ⓓ the muscles used during breathing

TOEFL – READING COMPREHENSION

Beginning

Though adults breathe twelve times a minute, breathing is so automatic that the average person hardly ever thinks about it. But how does it happen? The breathing process is quite complex and controlled by the medulla of the brain, in an area called the "breathing center." The power required for breathing comes from the intercostal muscles and the diaphragm. During quiet, normal breathing, inhalation, or the intake of air, occurs when the intercostal or thoracic muscles (the muscles within the rib cage) contract and the three dimensions of the chest expand, allowing the expansion of the lungs. When the pressure inside the lungs increases, the air is exhaled. Interestingly, while inhalation during quiet breathing requires muscle contraction, exhalation does not. In circumstances in which more air needs to be exhaled than normal, such as when blowing out candles on a birthday cake, the abdominal muscles may contract to facilitate the exhalation.

While the basic breathing pattern remains the same, there can be variations depending on the location of the expansion during inhalation. Some people exhibit a large protrusion of the abdominal wall (they stick their stomach out), while others show more lateral expansion in the thoracic region. These two types of breathing are called diaphragmatic and thoracic respectively. A third type of breathing involves expanding the muscles of the extreme upper chest. People with this breathing pattern often lift their shoulders as they inhale. For this reason, this breathing type is known as clavicular (relating to the clavicle). People who breathe in this manner may have excessive tension in the throat and often feel as though they can't get enough air due to their shallow breathing.

2. What type of breathing is NOT mentioned in this passage?

(A) clavicular

(B) oppositional

(C) diaphragmatic

(D) thoracic

TOEFL – READING COMPREHENSION

Beginning

Though adults breathe twelve times a minute, breathing is so automatic that the average person hardly ever thinks about it. But how does it happen? The breathing process is quite complex and controlled by the medulla of the brain, in an area called the "breathing center." The power required for breathing comes from the intercostal muscles and the diaphragm. During quiet, normal breathing, inhalation, or the intake of air, occurs when the intercostal or thoracic muscles (the muscles within the rib cage) contract and the three dimensions of the chest expand, allowing the expansion of the lungs. When the pressure inside the lungs increases, the air is exhaled. Interestingly, while inhalation during quiet breathing requires muscle contraction, exhalation does not. In circumstances in which more air needs to be exhaled than normal, such as when blowing out candles on a birthday cake, the abdominal muscles may contract to facilitate the exhalation.

While the basic breathing pattern remains the same, there can be variations depending on the location of the expansion during inhalation. Some people exhibit a large protrusion of the abdominal wall (they stick their stomach out), while others

3. How many times a minute do adults breathe?

 (A) 14

 (B) 12

 (C) 24

 (D) 16

Mastering the TOEFL CBT

TOEFL – READING COMPREHENSION

Beginning

Though adults breathe twelve times a minute, breathing is so automatic that the average person hardly ever thinks about it. But how does it happen? The breathing process is quite complex and controlled by the medulla of the brain, in an area called the "breathing center." The power required for breathing comes from the intercostal muscles and the diaphragm. During quiet, normal breathing, inhalation, or the intake of air, occurs when the intercostal or thoracic muscles (the muscles within the rib cage) contract and the three dimensions of the chest expand, allowing the expansion of the lungs. When the pressure inside the lungs increases, the air is exhaled. Interestingly, while inhalation during quiet breathing requires muscle contraction, exhalation does not. In circumstances in which more air needs to be exhaled than normal, such as when blowing out candles on a birthday cake, the abdominal muscles may contract to facilitate the exhalation.

While the basic breathing pattern remains the same, there can be variations depending on the location of the expansion during inhalation. Some people exhibit a large protrusion of the abdominal wall (they stick their stomach out), while others

4. According to the passage, which of the areas is most likely the location of the thoracic muscles?

Ⓐ the upper chest area

Ⓑ the abdominal area

Ⓒ the rib area

Ⓓ the digestive area

KAPLAN

TOEFL – READING COMPREHENSION

Beginning

While the basic breathing pattern remains the same, there can be variations depending on the location of the expansion during inhalation. Some people exhibit a large protrusion of the abdominal wall (they stick their stomach out), while others show more lateral expansion in the thoracic region. These two types of breathing are called diaphragmatic and thoracic respectively. A third type of breathing involves expanding the muscles of the extreme upper chest. People with this breathing pattern often lift their shoulders as they inhale. For this reason, this breathing type is known as clavicular (relating to the clavicle). People who breathe in this manner may have excessive tension in the throat and often feel as though they can't get enough air due to their shallow breathing.

5. Based on the reading, we can infer that the clavicle is

   (A) connected to the shoulder

   (B) in the neck

   (C) a muscle

   (D) in the chest

TOEFL – READING COMPREHENSION

Beginning

Though adults breathe twelve times a minute, breathing is so automatic that the average person hardly ever thinks about it. But how does it happen? The breathing process is quite complex and controlled by the medulla of the brain, in an area called the "breathing center." The power required for breathing comes from the intercostal muscles and the diaphragm. During quiet, normal breathing, inhalation, or the intake of air, occurs when the intercostal or thoracic muscles (the muscles within the rib cage) contract and the three dimensions of the chest expand, allowing the expansion of the lungs. When the pressure inside the lungs increases, the air is exhaled. Interestingly, while inhalation during quiet breathing requires muscle contraction, exhalation does not. In circumstances in which more air needs to be exhaled than normal, such as when blowing out candles on a birthday cake, the abdominal muscles may contract to facilitate the exhalation.

6. According to the passage, which muscles might you use when blowing out candles?

   (A) the diaphragm

   (B) the thoracic muscles

   (C) the abdominal muscles

   (D) the back muscles

TOEFL – READING COMPREHENSION

Beginning

While the basic breathing pattern remains the same, there can be variations depending on the location of the expansion during inhalation. Some people exhibit a large protrusion of the abdominal wall (they stick their stomach out), while others show more lateral expansion in the thoracic region. These two types of breathing are called diaphragmatic and thoracic respectively. A third type of breathing involves expanding the muscles of the extreme upper chest. People with this breathing pattern often lift their shoulders as they inhale. For this reason, this breathing type is known as clavicular (relating to the clavicle). People who breathe in this manner may have excessive tension in the throat and often feel as though they can't get enough air due to their shallow breathing.

7. According to the passage, what is a difficulty that clavicular breathers may experience?

Ⓐ tired shoulders

Ⓑ excessive tension in the throat

Ⓒ excessive tension in the neck

Ⓓ shallow breathing

TOEFL – READING COMPREHENSION

Beginning

Though adults breathe twelve times a minute, breathing is so automatic that the average person hardly ever thinks about it. But how does it happen? The breathing process is quite complex and controlled by the medulla of the brain, in an area called the "breathing center." The power required for breathing comes from the intercostal muscles and the diaphragm. During quiet, normal breathing, inhalation, or the intake of air, occurs when the intercostal or thoracic muscles (the muscles within the rib cage) contract and the three dimensions of the chest expand, allowing the expansion of the lungs. When the pressure inside the lungs increases, the air is exhaled. Interestingly, while inhalation during quiet breathing requires muscle contraction, exhalation does not. In circumstances in which more air needs to be exhaled than normal, such as when blowing out candles on a birthday cake, the abdominal muscles may contract to facilitate the exhalation.

8. Look at the word facilitate in the passage. Facilitate is closest in meaning to:

Ⓐ help

Ⓑ complete

Ⓒ start

Ⓓ stop

KAPLAN

Note: On the actual CBT test, the question that follows would instruct you to "click" on the text where you find the reference to the word in the shaded box.

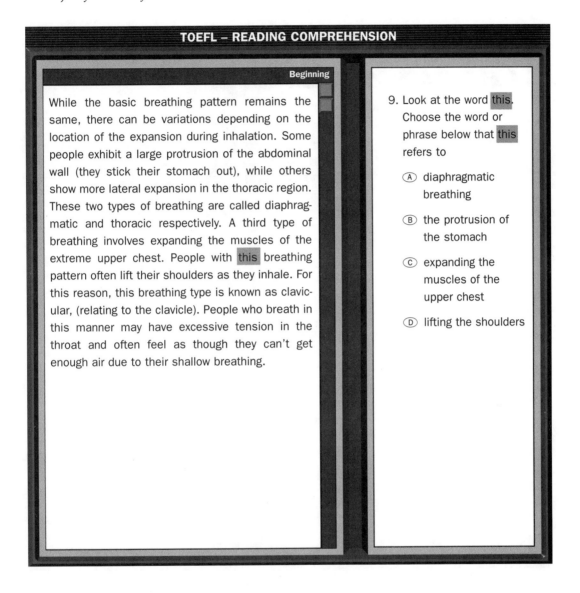

TOEFL – READING COMPREHENSION

Beginning

While the basic breathing pattern remains the same, there can be variations depending on the location of the expansion during inhalation. Some people exhibit a large protrusion of the abdominal wall (they stick their stomach out), while others show more lateral expansion in the thoracic region. These two types of breathing are called diaphragmatic and thoracic respectively. A third type of breathing involves expanding the muscles of the extreme upper chest. People with this breathing pattern often lift their shoulders as they inhale. For this reason, this breathing type is known as clavicular, (relating to the clavicle). People who breath in this manner may have excessive tension in the throat and often feel as though they can't get enough air due to their shallow breathing.

9. Look at the word this. Choose the word or phrase below that this refers to

(A) diaphragmatic breathing

(B) the protrusion of the stomach

(C) expanding the muscles of the upper chest

(D) lifting the shoulders

Note: On the actual CBT test, the question that follows would instruct you to "click" on the section of the text where you would insert the sentence.

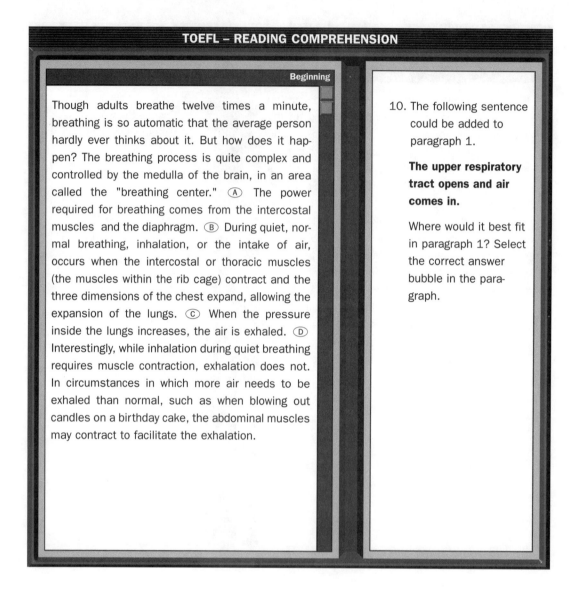

TOEFL – READING COMPREHENSION

Beginning

Though adults breathe twelve times a minute, breathing is so automatic that the average person hardly ever thinks about it. But how does it happen? The breathing process is quite complex and controlled by the medulla of the brain, in an area called the "breathing center." Ⓐ The power required for breathing comes from the intercostal muscles and the diaphragm. Ⓑ During quiet, normal breathing, inhalation, or the intake of air, occurs when the intercostal or thoracic muscles (the muscles within the rib cage) contract and the three dimensions of the chest expand, allowing the expansion of the lungs. Ⓒ When the pressure inside the lungs increases, the air is exhaled. Ⓓ Interestingly, while inhalation during quiet breathing requires muscle contraction, exhalation does not. In circumstances in which more air needs to be exhaled than normal, such as when blowing out candles on a birthday cake, the abdominal muscles may contract to facilitate the exhalation.

10. The following sentence could be added to paragraph 1.

The upper respiratory tract opens and air comes in.

Where would it best fit in paragraph 1? Select the correct answer bubble in the paragraph.

PRACTICE 2

Read the passage provided and select the correct answer choice for each question.

TOEFL – READING COMPREHENSION

Beginning

Extending the bounds of music beyond the restrictive formality of Classicism was the prime function of the musical period known as Romanticism. The Romantic period of classical music in the 19th century arose as a result of the Industrial Revolution and an increased sense of European nationalism. During this time, folk songs became admired as expressions of that nationalism, particularly in Germany, where nationalistic sentiments which had been politically suppressed could find a voice in music and other art forms. Musically speaking, rigid classical forms such as the sonata allegro form gave way to simpler more fluid styles that lacked formal unity. A piano sonata by Chopin, for example, might well be viewed as a series of short episodes rather than one distinct form with many parts.

One of the hallmarks of the Romantic period was the lieder, or vocal songs. Perhaps the most famous composer of lieder was Franz Schubert (1797–1828). In addition to nine symphonies, 22 piano sonatas, and many other pieces of music, he wrote over 600 lieder. He is best known for his artful creation of melodies and ingenious piano accompaniments which go beyond simply supporting the melody to depicting the text. Evidence of this can be seen in his earliest and most beloved lied, "Gretchen am Spinnrade" or "Gretchen at the Spinning Wheel." This setting of Goethe's *Faust* was composed in 1814. Some Schubert researchers even think that this is the lied that generated the genre of the romantic piano lied. The constant repetition of a simple motif in the piano accompaniment suggests the motion of the spinning wheel as well as the underlying mental agitation of Gretchen as she sings sadly for her lost love—"My peace is gone, my heart is sore."

The *Faust* lied was not the last Goethe poem Schubert set to music: by the end of his life, Schubert had completed over 60 of these settings.

1. What is this passage mainly about?

Ⓐ romantic music

Ⓑ Franz Schubert

Ⓒ lieder

Ⓓ *Gretchen am Spinnrade*

TOEFL – READING COMPREHENSION

Extending the bounds of music beyond the restrictive formality of Classicism was the prime function of the musical period known as Romanticism. The Romantic period of classical music in the 19th century arose as a result of the Industrial Revolution and an increased sense of European nationalism. During this time, folk songs became admired as expressions of that nationalism, particularly in Germany, where nationalistic sentiments which had been politically suppressed could find a voice in music and other art forms. Musically speaking, rigid classical forms such as the sonata allegro form gave way to simpler more fluid styles that lacked formal unity. A piano sonata by Chopin, for example, might well be viewed as a series of short episodes rather than one distinct form with many parts.

One of the hallmarks of the Romantic period was the lieder, or vocal songs. Perhaps the most famous composer of lieder was Franz Schubert (1797–1828). In addition to nine symphonies, 22 piano sonatas, and many other pieces of music, he wrote over 600 lieder. He is best known for his artful creation of melodies and ingenious piano accompaniments which go beyond simply supporting the melody to depicting the text. Evidence of this can be seen in his earliest and most beloved lied, "Gretchen am Spinnrade" or "Gretchen at the Spinning Wheel." This setting of Goethe's *Faust* was composed in 1814. Some Schubert researchers even think that this is the lied that generated the genre of the romantic piano lied. The constant repetition of a simple motif in the piano accompaniment suggests the motion of the spinning wheel as well as the underlying mental agitation of Gretchen as she sings sadly for her lost love—"My peace is gone, my heart is sore."

The *Faust* lied was not the last Goethe poem Schubert set to music: by the end of his life, Schubert had completed over 60 of these settings.

2. A title for this passage might be

   (A) The Romantic Period in Classical Music

   (B) German Nationalism as Seen in Romantic Music

   (C) Schubert's Lieder and Their Place in the Romantic Period

   (D) My Peace is Gone, My Heart is Sore

TOEFL – READING COMPREHENSION

Beginning

Extending the bounds of music beyond the restrictive formality of Classicism was the prime function of the musical period known as Romanticism. The Romantic period of classical music in the 19th century arose as a result of the Industrial Revolution and an increased sense of European nationalism. During this time, folk songs became admired as expressions of that nationalism, particularly in Germany, where nationalistic sentiments which had been politically suppressed could find a voice in music and other art forms. Musically speaking, rigid classical forms such as the sonata allegro form gave way to simpler more fluid styles that lacked formal unity. A piano sonata by Chopin, for example, might well be viewed as a series of short episodes rather than one distinct form with many parts.

One of the hallmarks of the Romantic period was the lieder, or vocal songs. Perhaps the most famous composer of lieder was Franz Schubert (1797–1828). In addition to nine symphonies, 22 piano sonatas, and many other pieces of music, he wrote over 600 lieder. He is best known for his artful creation of melodies and ingenious piano accompaniments which go beyond simply supporting the melody to depicting the text. Evidence of this can be seen in his earliest and most beloved lied, "Gretchen am Spinnrade" or "Gretchen at the Spinning Wheel." This setting of Goethe's *Faust* was composed in 1814. Some Schubert researchers even think that this is the lied that generated the genre of the romantic piano lied. The constant repetition of a simple motif in the piano accompaniment suggests the motion of the spinning wheel as well as the underlying mental agitation of Gretchen as she sings sadly for her lost love—"My peace is gone, my heart is sore."

The *Faust* lied was not the last Goethe poem Schubert set to music: by the end of his life, Schubert had completed over 60 of these settings.

3. Which of the following is NOT mentioned in the passage?

(A) Schubert's operatic works

(B) the Industrial Revolution

(C) Schubert's piano sonatas

(D) Chopin's piano sonatas

Note: On the actual CBT test, the question that follows would instruct you to "click" on the text where you would find the reference to/definition of the word in the shaded box.

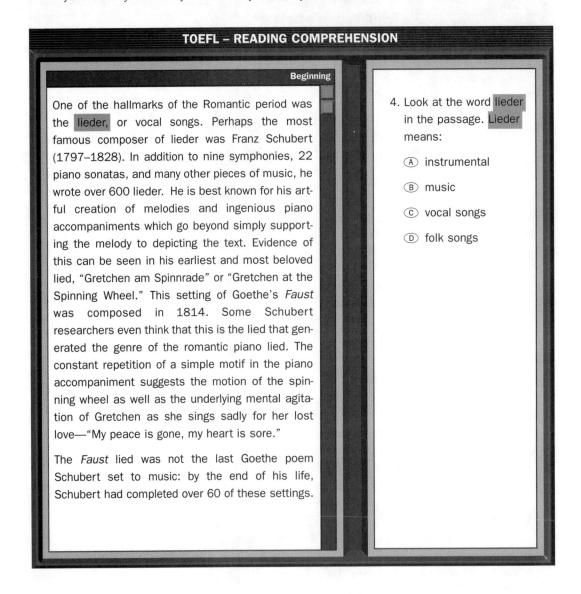

TOEFL – READING COMPREHENSION

Beginning

One of the hallmarks of the Romantic period was the lieder, or vocal songs. Perhaps the most famous composer of lieder was Franz Schubert (1797–1828). In addition to nine symphonies, 22 piano sonatas, and many other pieces of music, he wrote over 600 lieder. He is best known for his artful creation of melodies and ingenious piano accompaniments which go beyond simply supporting the melody to depicting the text. Evidence of this can be seen in his earliest and most beloved lied, "Gretchen am Spinnrade" or "Gretchen at the Spinning Wheel." This setting of Goethe's *Faust* was composed in 1814. Some Schubert researchers even think that this is the lied that generated the genre of the romantic piano lied. The constant repetition of a simple motif in the piano accompaniment suggests the motion of the spinning wheel as well as the underlying mental agitation of Gretchen as she sings sadly for her lost love—"My peace is gone, my heart is sore."

The *Faust* lied was not the last Goethe poem Schubert set to music: by the end of his life, Schubert had completed over 60 of these settings.

4. Look at the word lieder in the passage. Lieder means:

   Ⓐ instrumental

   Ⓑ music

   Ⓒ vocal songs

   Ⓓ folk songs

TOEFL – READING COMPREHENSION

Beginning

Extending the bounds of music beyond the restrictive formality of Classicism was the prime function of the musical period known as Romanticism. The Romantic period of classical music in the 19th century arose as a result of the Industrial Revolution and an increased sense of European nationalism. During this time, folk songs became admired as expressions of that nationalism, particularly in Germany, where nationalistic sentiments which had been politically suppressed could find a voice in music and other art forms. Musically speaking, rigid classical forms such as the sonata allegro form gave way to simpler more fluid styles that lacked formal unity. A piano sonata by Chopin, for example, might well be viewed as a series of short episodes rather than one distinct form with many parts.

5. According to the passage, why was Romanticism so embraced by the Germans?

(A) They had a romantic temperament.

(B) They liked folk songs.

(C) They wanted to rebel against Classicism.

(D) They wanted to express their nationalism.

TOEFL – READING COMPREHENSION

Beginning

One of the hallmarks of the Romantic period was the lieder, or vocal songs. Perhaps the most famous composer of lieder was Franz Schubert (1797–1828). In addition to nine symphonies, 22 piano sonatas, and many other pieces of music, he wrote over 600 lieder. He is best known for his artful creation of melodies and ingenious piano accompaniments which go beyond simply supporting the melody to depicting the text. Evidence of this can be seen in his earliest and most beloved lied, "Gretchen am Spinnrade" or "Gretchen at the Spinning Wheel." This setting of Goethe's *Faust* was composed in 1814. Some Schubert researchers even think that this is the lied that generated the genre of the romantic piano lied. The constant repetition of a simple motif in the piano accompaniment suggests the motion of the spinning wheel as well as the underlying mental agitation of Gretchen as she sings sadly for her lost love—"My peace is gone, my heart is sore."

The *Faust* lied was not the last Goethe poem Schubert set to music: by the end of his life, Schubert had completed over 60 of these settings.

6. Schubert's lieder were known for their

   (A) beautiful melodies

   (B) simple piano accompaniments

   (C) folk song-like melodies

   (D) complicated harmonic structure

TOEFL – READING COMPREHENSION

Beginning

One of the hallmarks of the Romantic period was the lieder, or vocal songs. Perhaps the most famous composer of lieder was Franz Schubert (1797–1828). In addition to nine symphonies, 22 piano sonatas, and many other pieces of music, he wrote over 600 lieder. He is best known for his artful creation of melodies and ingenious piano accompaniments which go beyond simply supporting the melody to depicting the text. Evidence of this can be seen in his earliest and most beloved lied, "Gretchen am Spinnrade" or "Gretchen at the Spinning Wheel." This setting of Goethe's *Faust* was composed in 1814. Some Schubert researchers even think that this is the lied that generated the genre of the romantic piano lied. The constant repetition of a simple motif in the piano accompaniment suggests the motion of the spinning wheel as well as the underlying mental agitation of Gretchen as she sings sadly for her lost love—"My peace is gone, my heart is sore."

The *Faust* lied was not the last Goethe poem Schubert set to music: by the end of his life, Schubert had completed over 60 of these settings.

7. "Gretchen am Spinnrade" was composed in

Ⓐ 1820

Ⓑ 1814

Ⓒ 1815

Ⓓ 1812

TOEFL – READING COMPREHENSION

Beginning

One of the hallmarks of the Romantic period was the lieder, or vocal songs. Perhaps the most famous composer of lieder was Franz Schubert (1797–1828). In addition to nine symphonies, 22 piano sonatas, and many other pieces of music, he wrote over 600 lieder. He is best known for his artful creation of melodies and ingenious piano accompaniments which go beyond simply supporting the melody to depicting the text. Evidence of this can be seen in his earliest and most beloved lied, "Gretchen am Spinnrade" or "Gretchen at the Spinning Wheel." This setting of Goethe's *Faust* was composed in 1814. Some Schubert researchers even think that this is the lied that generated the genre of the romantic piano lied. The constant repetition of a simple motif in the piano accompaniment suggests the motion of the spinning wheel as well as the underlying mental agitation of Gretchen as she sings sadly for her lost love—"My peace is gone, my heart is sore."

The *Faust* lied was not the last Goethe poem Schubert set to music: by the end of his life, Schubert had completed over 60 of these settings.

8. *Faust* was written by

   (A) Shakespeare

   (B) Goethe

   (C) Schubert

   (D) Chopin

TOEFL – READING COMPREHENSION

One of the hallmarks of the Romantic period was the lieder, or vocal songs. Perhaps the most famous composer of lieder was Franz Schubert (1797–1828). In addition to nine symphonies, 22 piano sonatas, and many other pieces of music, he wrote over 600 lieder. He is best known for his artful creation of melodies and ingenious piano accompaniments which go beyond simply supporting the melody to depicting the text. Evidence of this can be seen in his earliest and most beloved lied, "Gretchen am Spinnrade" or "Gretchen at the Spinning Wheel." This setting of Goethe's *Faust* was composed in 1814. Some Schubert researchers even think that this is the lied that generated the genre of the romantic piano lied. The constant repetition of a simple motif in the piano accompaniment suggests the motion of the spinning wheel as well as the underlying mental agitation of Gretchen as she sings sadly for her lost love—"My peace is gone, my heart is sore."

The *Faust* lied was not the last Goethe poem Schubert set to music: by the end of his life, Schubert had completed over 60 of these settings.

9. Look at the work motif in the passage. Motif is closest in meaning to

Ⓐ pattern

Ⓑ melodic theme

Ⓒ chord

Ⓓ reason

Note: On the actual CBT test, the question that follows would instruct you to "click" on the section of the text where you would find the information in question.

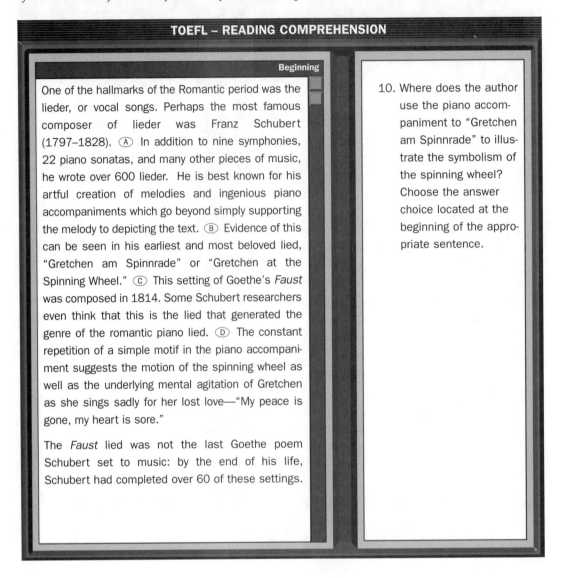

TOEFL – READING COMPREHENSION

Beginning

One of the hallmarks of the Romantic period was the lieder, or vocal songs. Perhaps the most famous composer of lieder was Franz Schubert (1797–1828). Ⓐ In addition to nine symphonies, 22 piano sonatas, and many other pieces of music, he wrote over 600 lieder. He is best known for his artful creation of melodies and ingenious piano accompaniments which go beyond simply supporting the melody to depicting the text. Ⓑ Evidence of this can be seen in his earliest and most beloved lied, "Gretchen am Spinnrade" or "Gretchen at the Spinning Wheel." Ⓒ This setting of Goethe's *Faust* was composed in 1814. Some Schubert researchers even think that this is the lied that generated the genre of the romantic piano lied. Ⓓ The constant repetition of a simple motif in the piano accompaniment suggests the motion of the spinning wheel as well as the underlying mental agitation of Gretchen as she sings sadly for her lost love—"My peace is gone, my heart is sore."

The *Faust* lied was not the last Goethe poem Schubert set to music: by the end of his life, Schubert had completed over 60 of these settings.

10. Where does the author use the piano accompaniment to "Gretchen am Spinnrade" to illustrate the symbolism of the spinning wheel? Choose the answer choice located at the beginning of the appropriate sentence.

PRACTICE 3

Read the passage provided and select the correct answer choice for each question.

TOEFL – READING COMPREHENSION

Beginning

Perhaps the most powerful woman in media today is Oprah Winfrey. To quote an old TV commercial, when she talks, people listen, and they've been listening in record numbers since her daytime talk show debuted in 1986. Since then, she has covered a broad range of topics, from family issues and drug abuse to celebrity profiles. A shrewd businesswoman, Oprah has inspired trends in the marketplace simply by mentioning a product on the air. On top of all this, she has battled with her weight and won while motivating many to "Make the Connection." Oprah has also championed literacy and inspired thousands to read. As a result, she has single-handedly propelled unknown authors to the top of the best seller list.

All this power did not come easily, however. Born in a small town in rural Mississippi on January 29th 1954, Oprah had a difficult childhood and endured sexual abuse. She eventually overcome it all and at age 19 she landed her first job as a radio reporter in Nashville Tennessee, where she attended college. In her sophomore year she became the first African American anchor at WTVF TV in Nashville. After that it was only a matter of time until she was hosting a talk show in Baltimore which led to her transfer to Chicago in 1984. Then, in 1985 she received an Oscar nomination for her role in *The Color Purple*.

Oprah is only the third woman in history after Mary Pickford and Lucille Ball to own a major studio from which she produces her talk show and numerous other projects. Most recently she produced and starred in a movie version of Toni Morrison's Pulitzer Prize winning novel *Beloved*. She is now ranked as the highest paid entertainer in America, according to *Forbes* magazine, and will soon be America's first African American billionaire.

1. The Oprah Winfrey Show began in

   Ⓐ 1984

   Ⓑ 1986

   Ⓒ 1973

   Ⓓ 1985

TOEFL – READING COMPREHENSION

Beginning

Perhaps the most powerful woman in media today is Oprah Winfrey. To quote an old TV commercial, when she talks, people listen, and they've been listening in record numbers since her daytime talk show debuted in 1986. Since then, she has covered a broad range of topics, from family issues and drug abuse to celebrity profiles. A shrewd businesswoman, Oprah has inspired trends in the marketplace simply by mentioning a product on the air. On top of all this, she has battled with her weight and won while motivating many to "Make the Connection." Oprah has also championed literacy and inspired thousands to read. As a result, she has single-handedly propelled unknown authors to the top of the best seller list.

2. Look at the word championed. Championed is closest in meaning to

   (A) won

   (B) fought against

   (C) ignored

   (D) supported

TOEFL – READING COMPREHENSION

Beginning

Oprah is only the third woman in history after Mary Pickford and Lucille Ball to own a major studio from which she produces her talk show and numerous other projects. Most recently she produced and starred in a movie version of Toni Morrison's Pulitzer Prize winning novel *Beloved*. She is now ranked as the highest paid entertainer in America, according to *Forbes* magazine, and will soon be America's first African American billionaire.

3. Look at the words major studio. Major studio refers to

   (A) a record company

   (B) a painter's workshop

   (C) a large production company

   (D) a place to record music

TOEFL – READING COMPREHENSION

Beginning

All this power did not come easily, however. Born in a small town in rural Mississippi on January 29th 1954, Oprah had a difficult childhood and endured sexual abuse. She eventually overcome it all and at age 19 she landed her first job as a radio reporter in Nashville Tennessee, where she attended college. In her sophomore year she became the first African American anchor at WTVF TV in Nashville. After that it was only a matter of time until she was hosting a talk show in Baltimore which led to her transfer to Chicago in 1984. Then, in 1985 she received an Oscar nomination for her role in *The Color Purple*.

Oprah is only the third woman in history after Mary

4. According to the passage, who wrote *The Color Purple*?

   Ⓐ Steven Spielberg

   Ⓑ Oprah Winfrey

   Ⓒ Toni Morrison

   Ⓓ The passage doesn't say.

TOEFL – READING COMPREHENSION

Beginning

Oprah is only the third woman in history after Mary Pickford and Lucille Ball to own a major studio from which she produces her talk show and numerous other projects. Most recently she produced and starred in a movie version of Toni Morrison's Pulitzer Prize winning novel *Beloved*. She is now ranked as the highest paid entertainer in America, according to *Forbes* magazine, and will soon be America's first African American billionaire.

5. Which of the following women did NOT own a production company?

   Ⓐ Lucille Ball

   Ⓑ Oprah Winfrey

   Ⓒ Mary Pickford

   Ⓓ Toni Morrison

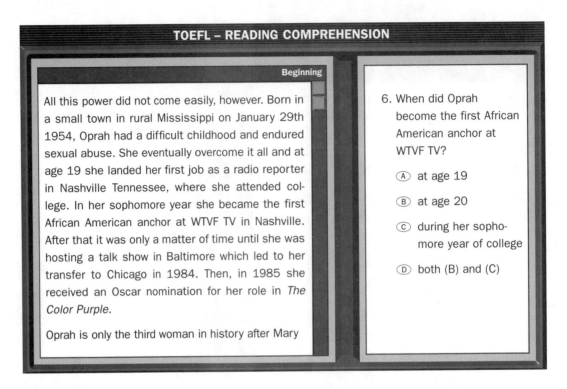

Note: On the actual CBT test, the question that follows would instruct you to "click" on the text where you would find the reference to the word in the shaded box.

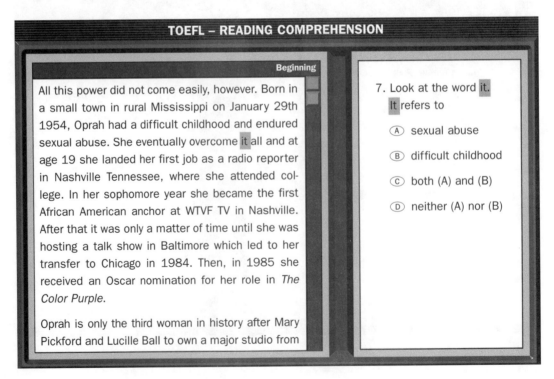

KAPLAN

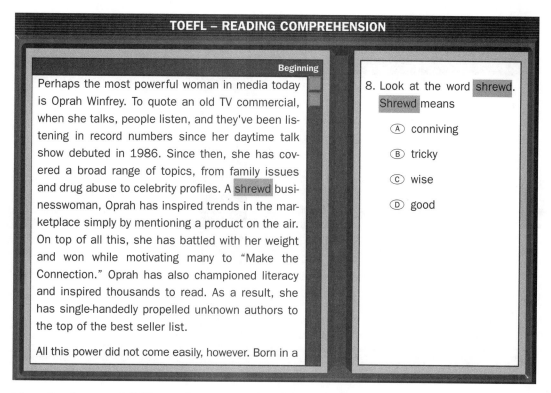

TOEFL – READING COMPREHENSION

Beginning

Perhaps the most powerful woman in media today is Oprah Winfrey. To quote an old TV commercial, when she talks, people listen, and they've been listening in record numbers since her daytime talk show debuted in 1986. Since then, she has covered a broad range of topics, from family issues and drug abuse to celebrity profiles. A shrewd businesswoman, Oprah has inspired trends in the marketplace simply by mentioning a product on the air. On top of all this, she has battled with her weight and won while motivating many to "Make the Connection." Oprah has also championed literacy and inspired thousands to read. As a result, she has single-handedly propelled unknown authors to the top of the best seller list.

All this power did not come easily, however. Born in a

8. Look at the word shrewd. Shrewd means

   (A) conniving

   (B) tricky

   (C) wise

   (D) good

Note: On the actual CBT test, the question that follows would instruct you to "click" on the text where you would find the reference to the word in the shaded box.

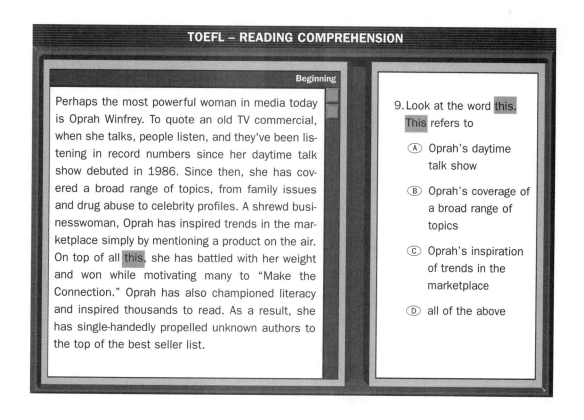

TOEFL – READING COMPREHENSION

Beginning

Perhaps the most powerful woman in media today is Oprah Winfrey. To quote an old TV commercial, when she talks, people listen, and they've been listening in record numbers since her daytime talk show debuted in 1986. Since then, she has covered a broad range of topics, from family issues and drug abuse to celebrity profiles. A shrewd businesswoman, Oprah has inspired trends in the marketplace simply by mentioning a product on the air. On top of all this, she has battled with her weight and won while motivating many to "Make the Connection." Oprah has also championed literacy and inspired thousands to read. As a result, she has single-handedly propelled unknown authors to the top of the best seller list.

9. Look at the word this. This refers to

   (A) Oprah's daytime talk show

   (B) Oprah's coverage of a broad range of topics

   (C) Oprah's inspiration of trends in the marketplace

   (D) all of the above

TOEFL – READING COMPREHENSION

Beginning

All this power did not come easily, however. Born in a small town in rural Mississippi on January 29th 1954, Oprah had a difficult childhood and endured sexual abuse. She eventually overcome it all and at age 19 she landed her first job as a radio reporter in Nashville Tennessee, where she attended college. In her sophomore year she became the first African American anchor at WTVF TV in Nashville. After that it was only a matter of time until she was hosting a talk show in Baltimore which led to her transfer to Chicago in 1984. Then, in 1985 she received an Oscar nomination for her role in *The Color Purple.*

Oprah is only the third woman in history after Mary Pickford and Lucille Ball to own a major studio from

10. Oprah was born in

   (A) a city in Mississippi

   (B) a small town in Tennessee

   (C) Baltimore

   (D) a small town in Mississippi

PRACTICE 4

Read the passage provided and select the correct answer choice for each question.

TOEFL – READING COMPREHENSION

Beginning

One of the most renowned Spanish architects of all time was Antoni Gaudi. Gaudi's emergence as one of Spain's preeminent artists at the end of the nineteenth century marked a milestone in the art world.

Gaudi's popularity helped to bring about the acceptance and rebirth of the Catalan language, which had been banned during the peak of Castilian literature and art. Gaudi shares his Catalonian background with two other famous Spanish artists, Pablo Picasso and Miro. The diverse ethnic background of the region greatly influenced the work of Picasso and Miro, as well as Gaudi. Thus, their works were a combination of an old history and an active, vivid imaginary world. This has sometimes been referred to as the "Catalan Mind." Yet it was perhaps Gaudi who had the greatest talent for bringing together diverse groups, ones which others viewed as being too diametrically opposed to be capable of coming together and co-existing amicably.

This was apparent not only in the artists and other individuals who surrounded him, but also in the varied styles and techniques he employed in his architecture. Much of his work can be seen in Barcelona, where his structures are known as a fine representation of modernism. He also used a great variety of color in his buildings, and this *art nouveau* is often associated with his own unique style of design.

All of these factors are what helped put him at the forefront of art movements to come: his unique ability to take on and transform traditional Spanish elements with the emerging diverse ethnic groups, merging these with his own fertile imagination, and consequently turning these forces into some of the greatest architecture the world has ever seen.

1. Antoni Gaudi's fame is due primarily to his world-famous

   (A) paintings

   (B) architectural structures

   (C) political skills

   (D) business acumen

TOEFL – READING COMPREHENSION

Beginning

One of the most renowned Spanish architects of all time was Antoni Gaudi. Gaudi's emergence as one of Spain's preeminent artists at the end of the nineteenth century marked a milestone in the art world.

Gaudi's popularity helped to bring about the acceptance and rebirth of the Catalan language, which had been banned during the peak of Castilian literature and art. Gaudi shares his Catalonian background with two other famous Spanish artists, Pablo Picasso and Miro. The diverse ethnic background of the region greatly influenced the work of Picasso and Miro, as well as Gaudi. Thus, their works were a combination of an old history and an active, vivid imaginary world. This has sometimes been referred to as the "Catalan Mind." Yet it was perhaps Gaudi who had the greatest talent for bringing together diverse groups, ones which others viewed as being too diametrically opposed to be capable of coming together and co-existing amicably.

This was apparent not only in the artists and other individuals who surrounded him, but also in the varied styles and techniques he employed in his architecture. Much of his work can be seen in Barcelona, where his structures are known as a fine represen-

2. Gaudi's first language was

Ⓐ Spanish

Ⓑ Castilian

Ⓒ Catalan

Ⓓ Portuguese

KAPLAN

TOEFL – READING COMPREHENSION

Beginning

Gaudi's popularity helped to bring about the acceptance and rebirth of the Catalan language, which had been banned during the peak of Castilian literature and art. Gaudi shares his Catalonian background with two other famous Spanish artists, Pablo Picasso and Miro. The diverse ethnic background of the region greatly influenced the work of Picasso and Miro, as well as Gaudi. Thus, their works were a combination of an old history and an active, vivid imaginary world. This has sometimes been referred to as the "Catalan Mind." Yet it was perhaps Gaudi who had the greatest talent for bringing together diverse groups, ones which others viewed as being too diametrically opposed to be capable of coming together and co-existing amicably.

3. Which of the following is NOT true about Pablo Picasso?

(A) He spoke Castilian as his first language.

(B) He was from the same area as Gaudi.

(C) He was from the same area as Miro.

(D) He incorporated his background in his paintings.

TOEFL – READING COMPREHENSION

Beginning

Gaudi's popularity helped to bring about the acceptance and rebirth of the Catalan language, which had been banned during the peak of Castilian literature and art. Gaudi shares his Catalonian background with two other famous Spanish artists, Pablo Picasso and Miro. The diverse ethnic background of the region greatly influenced the work of Picasso and Miro, as well as Gaudi. Thus, their works were a combination of an old history and an active, vivid imaginary world. This has sometimes been referred to as the "Catalan Mind." Yet it was perhaps Gaudi who had the greatest talent for bringing together diverse groups, ones which others viewed as being too diametrically opposed to be capable of coming together and co-existing amicably.

4. Miro has been viewed as being a prototype of

(A) the Castilian mind

(B) the Catalan mind

(C) a fantasy

(D) Spanish architecture

TOEFL – READING COMPREHENSION

Beginning

This was apparent not only in the artists and other individuals who surrounded him, but also in the varied styles and techniques he employed in his architecture. Much of his work can be seen in Barcelona, where his structures are known as a fine representation of modernism. He also used a great variety of color in his buildings, and this *art nouveau* is often associated with his own unique style of design.

All of these factors are what helped put him at the forefront of art movements to come: his unique ability to take on and transform traditional Spanish elements with the emerging diverse ethnic groups, merging these with his own fertile imagination, and consequently turning these forces into some of the greatest architecture the world has ever seen.

5. Gaudi's work is representative of

   Ⓐ *art nouveau*

   Ⓑ political strife

   Ⓒ archaic style

   Ⓓ Castilian heritage

TOEFL – READING COMPREHENSION

Beginning

This was apparent not only in the artists and other individuals who surrounded him, but also in the varied styles and techniques he employed in his architecture. Much of his work can be seen in Barcelona, where his structures are known as a fine representation of modernism. He also used a great variety of color in his buildings, and this *art nouveau* is often associated with his own unique style of design.

All of these factors are what helped put him at the forefront of art movements to come: his unique ability to take on and transform traditional Spanish elements with the emerging diverse ethnic groups, merging these with his own fertile imagination, and consequently turning these forces into some of the greatest architecture the world has ever seen.

6. Which of the following is true about Gaudi's architecture?

   Ⓐ He disdained color.

   Ⓑ He rejected whatever was considered innovative.

   Ⓒ He employed a wide range of colors.

   Ⓓ Most of his work has been destroyed.

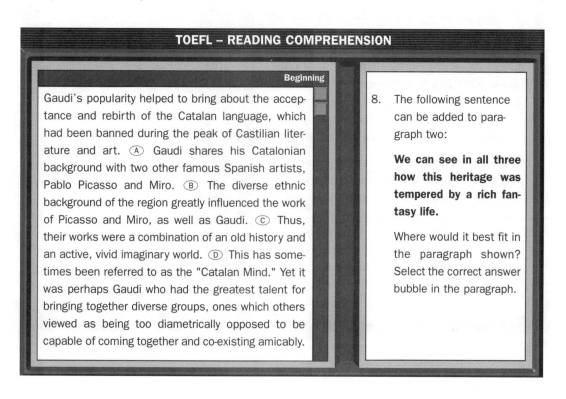

TOEFL – READING COMPREHENSION

Beginning

This was apparent not only in the artists and other individuals who surrounded him, but also in the varied styles and techniques he employed in his architecture. Much of his work can be seen in Barcelona, where his structures are known as a fine representation of modernism. He also used a great variety of color in his buildings, and this *art nouveau* is often associated with his own unique style of design.

All of these factors are what helped put him at the forefront of art movements to come: his unique ability to take on and transform traditional Spanish elements with the emerging diverse ethnic groups, merging these with his own fertile imagination, and consequently turning these forces into some of the greatest architecture the world has ever seen.

7. Which city is primarily associated with Gaudi today?

(A) Berlin

(B) Barcelona

(C) Castilia

(D) Spain

Note: On the actual CBT test, the question that follows would instruct you to "click" on the section of the text where you would insert the sentence.

TOEFL – READING COMPREHENSION

Beginning

Gaudi's popularity helped to bring about the acceptance and rebirth of the Catalan language, which had been banned during the peak of Castilian literature and art. (A) Gaudi shares his Catalonian background with two other famous Spanish artists, Pablo Picasso and Miro. (B) The diverse ethnic background of the region greatly influenced the work of Picasso and Miro, as well as Gaudi. (C) Thus, their works were a combination of an old history and an active, vivid imaginary world. (D) This has sometimes been referred to as the "Catalan Mind." Yet it was perhaps Gaudi who had the greatest talent for bringing together diverse groups, ones which others viewed as being too diametrically opposed to be capable of coming together and co-existing amicably.

8. The following sentence can be added to paragraph two:

We can see in all three how this heritage was tempered by a rich fantasy life.

Where would it best fit in the paragraph shown? Select the correct answer bubble in the paragraph.

TOEFL – READING COMPREHENSION

Beginning

One of the most renowned Spanish architects of all time was Antoni Gaudi. Gaudi's emergence as one of Spain's preeminent artists at the end of the nineteenth century marked a milestone in the art world.

Gaudi's popularity helped to bring about the acceptance and rebirth of the Catalan language, which had been banned during the peak of Castilian literature and art. Gaudi shares his Catalonian background with two other famous Spanish artists, Pablo Picasso and Miro. The diverse ethnic background of the region greatly influenced the work of Picasso and Miro, as well as Gaudi. Thus, their works were a combination of an old history and an active, vivid imaginary world. This has sometimes been referred to as the "Catalan Mind." Yet it was perhaps Gaudi who had the greatest talent for bringing together diverse groups, ones which others viewed as being too diametrically opposed to be capable of coming together and co-existing amicably.

This was apparent not only in the artists and other individuals who surrounded him, but also in the varied styles and techniques he employed in his architecture. Much of his work can be seen in Barcelona, where his structures are known as a fine representation of modernism. He also used a great variety of color in his buildings, and this *art nouveau* is often associated with his own unique style of design.

All of these factors are what helped put him at the forefront of art movements to come: his unique ability to take on and transform traditional Spanish elements with the emerging diverse ethnic groups, merging these with his own fertile imagination, and consequently turning these forces into some of the greatest architecture the world has ever seen.

9. Which of the following adjectives best describes Gaudi?

(A) broad-minded

(B) intolerant

(C) naive

(D) cautious

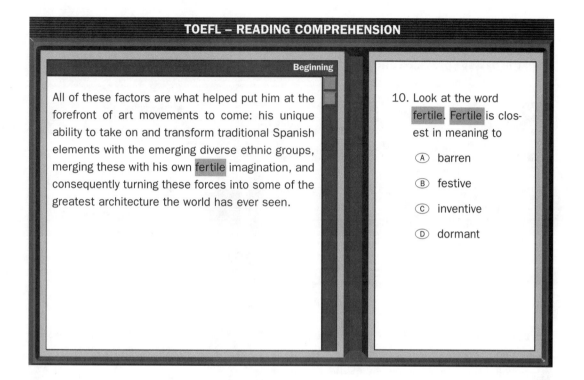

PRACTICE 5

Read the passage provided and select the correct answer choice for each question.

TOEFL – READING COMPREHENSION

Beginning

Alligators and crocodiles come from the same order. Both of them are large aquatic reptiles and are found in many parts of the world. Both can be very dangerous for humans as well as for most other forms of animal life.

Alligators, however, have physical qualities that differ greatly from those of the crocodile. For example, the alligator has a much broader snout that is almost triangular in shape. There are basically two types of alligators. The larger type is found in the United States in swamplands and bayous in Florida, Louisiana, and other states that border the Gulf of Mexico. It has also been sighted as far north as North Carolina. The smaller type of alligator is located in China, mainly near the Yangtze River. When young, the alligator has a brown or black body with gold rings, but by the time it reaches adulthood, its body is entirely black. The larger forms can reach up to 18 feet in length. Alligators are usually seen in the summer since they hibernate from October to March each year.

Crocodiles are seen less often in the United States because they live primarily in tropical zones. They have short legs and very powerful jaws. Unlike the alligator, the crocodile has a large tooth that always protrudes, even when its mouth is shut. Even though it is smaller than the alligator in length, generally from 6 to 10 feet, it is considered more aggressive and consequently more dangerous by most people. Although it is possible to see crocodiles in the swamplands of the United States, they are more frequently found along the Nile River in Africa, the West Indies, the Mediterranean coasts, and Central and South America.

1. The reading mainly discusses

  Ⓐ the largest aquatic animals

  Ⓑ the similarities and differences between alligators and crocodiles

  Ⓒ the chief qualities of alligators

  Ⓓ why both alligators and crocodiles are dangerous

TOEFL – READING COMPREHENSION

Beginning

Alligators and crocodiles come from the same order. Both of them are large aquatic reptiles and are found in many parts of the world. Both can be very dangerous for humans as well as for most other forms of animal life.

Alligators, however, have physical qualities that differ greatly from those of the crocodile. For example, the alligator has a much broader snout that is almost triangular in shape. There are basically two types of alligators. The larger type is found in the United States in swamplands and bayous in Florida, Louisiana, and other states that border the Gulf of Mexico. It has also been sighted as far north as North Carolina. The smaller type of alligator is located in China, mainly near the Yangtze River. When young, the alligator has a brown or black body with gold rings, but by the time it reaches adulthood, its body is entirely black. The larger forms can reach up to 18 feet in length. Alligators are usually seen in the summer since they hibernate from October to March each year.

Crocodiles are seen less often in the United States because they live primarily in tropical zones. They have short legs and very powerful jaws. Unlike the alligator, the crocodile has a large tooth that always protrudes, even when its mouth is shut. Even though it is smaller than the alligator in length, generally from 6 to 10 feet, it is considered more aggressive and consequently more dangerous by most people. Although it is possible to see crocodiles in the swamplands of the United States, they are more frequently found along the Nile River in Africa, the West Indies, the Mediterranean coasts, and Central and South America.

2. Which of the following statements is TRUE about both alligators and crocodiles?

Ⓐ They have a triangular snout.

Ⓑ They are found mainly along the Nile.

Ⓒ They are large aquatic reptiles.

Ⓓ They are generally harmless.

TOEFL – READING COMPREHENSION

Beginning

Alligators, however, have physical qualities that differ greatly from those of the crocodile. For example, the alligator has a much broader snout that is almost triangular in shape. There are basically two types of alligators. The larger type is found in the United States in swamplands and bayous in Florida, Louisiana, and other states that border the Gulf of Mexico. It has also been sighted as far north as North Carolina. The smaller type of alligator is located in China, mainly near the Yangtze River. When young, the alligator has a brown or black body with gold rings, but by the time it reaches adulthood, its body is entirely black. The larger forms can reach up to 18 feet in length. Alligators are usually seen in the summer since they hibernate from October to March each year.

3. Name two of the regions mentioned in which alligators can be found.

  (A) Africa and Florida

  (B) China and the United States

  (C) Louisiana and Florida

  (D) The Mediterranean and Florida

TOEFL – READING COMPREHENSION

Beginning

Alligators, however, have physical qualities that differ greatly from those of the crocodile. For example, the alligator has a much broader snout that is almost triangular in shape. There are basically two types of alligators. The larger type is found in the United States in swamplands and bayous in Florida, Louisiana, and other states that border the Gulf of Mexico. It has also been sighted as far north as North Carolina. The smaller type of alligator is located in China, mainly near the Yangtze River. When young, the alligator has a brown or black body with gold rings, but by the time it reaches adulthood, its body is entirely black. The larger forms can reach up to 18 feet in length. Alligators are usually seen in the summer since they hibernate from October to March each year.

4. Which of the following is FALSE about the adult alligator?

  (A) It has brown and gold rings around its body.

  (B) It is generally one color.

  (C) It can be 18 feet long.

  (D) It can be considered dangerous.

Note: On the actual CBT test, the question that follows would instruct you to "click" on the text where you would find the reference to the word in the shaded box.

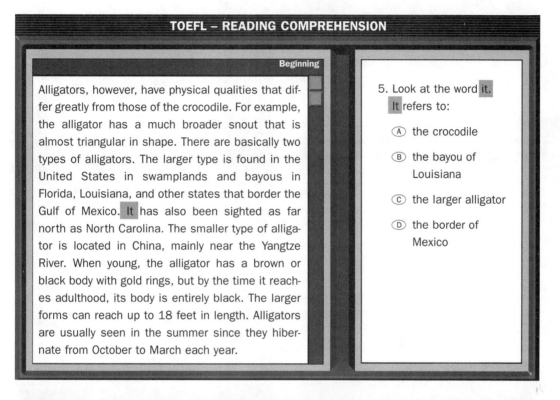

TOEFL – READING COMPREHENSION

Beginning

Alligators, however, have physical qualities that differ greatly from those of the crocodile. For example, the alligator has a much broader snout that is almost triangular in shape. There are basically two types of alligators. The larger type is found in the United States in swamplands and bayous in Florida, Louisiana, and other states that border the Gulf of Mexico. It has also been sighted as far north as North Carolina. The smaller type of alligator is located in China, mainly near the Yangtze River. When young, the alligator has a brown or black body with gold rings, but by the time it reaches adulthood, its body is entirely black. The larger forms can reach up to 18 feet in length. Alligators are usually seen in the summer since they hibernate from October to March each year.

5. Look at the word it. It refers to:

  Ⓐ the crocodile

  Ⓑ the bayou of Louisiana

  Ⓒ the larger alligator

  Ⓓ the border of Mexico

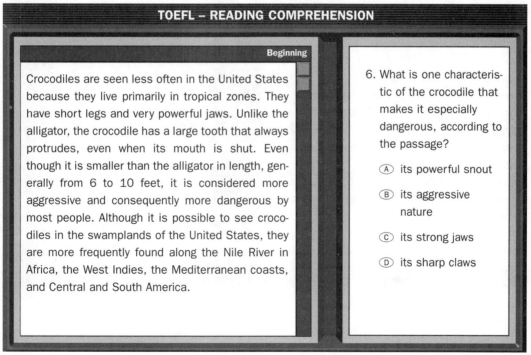

TOEFL – READING COMPREHENSION

Beginning

Crocodiles are seen less often in the United States because they live primarily in tropical zones. They have short legs and very powerful jaws. Unlike the alligator, the crocodile has a large tooth that always protrudes, even when its mouth is shut. Even though it is smaller than the alligator in length, generally from 6 to 10 feet, it is considered more aggressive and consequently more dangerous by most people. Although it is possible to see crocodiles in the swamplands of the United States, they are more frequently found along the Nile River in Africa, the West Indies, the Mediterranean coasts, and Central and South America.

6. What is one characteristic of the crocodile that makes it especially dangerous, according to the passage?

  Ⓐ its powerful snout

  Ⓑ its aggressive nature

  Ⓒ its strong jaws

  Ⓓ its sharp claws

TOEFL – READING COMPREHENSION

Beginning

Alligators and crocodiles come from the same order. Both of them are large aquatic reptiles and are found in many parts of the world. Both can be very dangerous for humans as well as for most other forms of animal life.

Alligators, however, have physical qualities that differ greatly from those of the crocodile. For example, the alligator has a much broader snout that is almost triangular in shape. There are basically two types of alligators. The larger type is found in the United States in swamplands and bayous in Florida, Louisiana, and other states that border the Gulf of Mexico. It has also been sighted as far north as North Carolina. The smaller type of alligator is located in China, mainly near the Yangtze River. When young, the alligator has a brown or black body with gold rings, but by the time it reaches adulthood, its body is entirely black. The larger forms can reach up to 18 feet in length. Alligators are usually seen in the summer since they hibernate from October to March each year.

Crocodiles are seen less often in the United States because they live primarily in tropical zones. They have short legs and very powerful jaws. Unlike the alligator, the crocodile has a large tooth that always protrudes, even when its mouth is shut. Even though it is smaller than the alligator in length, generally from 6 to 10 feet, it is considered more aggressive and consequently more dangerous by most people. Although it is possible to see crocodiles in the swamplands of the United States, they are more frequently found along the Nile River in Africa, the West Indies, the Mediterranean coasts, and Central and South America.

7. Which of the following is FALSE, in comparing alligators to crocodiles?

Ⓐ Alligators are shorter.

Ⓑ Crocodiles are shorter.

Ⓒ Alligators and crocodiles have several differences.

Ⓓ Their snouts are different.

PRACTICE 6

Read the passage provided and select the correct answer choice for each question.

TOEFL – READING COMPREHENSION

Beginning

In the age of alternative sources of energy, solar energy has come to the forefront. To harness energy from the sun, or solar energy, one must receive it either directly from the Sun or through very brief intermediate processes. An example of the latter is when crops which were grown using solar input are then used as fuel or biomass. Solar energy has many purposes, from heating cool buildings to racing cars. It can also be converted directly into electricity. Importantly, it is generally considered safe for the environment, since it produces almost no known hazards.

However, there are many criticisms of solar energy. It is often not a practical or viable alternative in cold climates or places that go without seeing the sun for long periods of time. It is also very difficult to transport. Power towers may used to store solar energy for a limited period of time, so when there is little or no sunlight in certain regions, this source of power cannot be utilized.

Thus, though many environmentalists and other proponents strongly advocate solar energy as a prime source of power, harvesting it and using it on a long-term basis is problematic. Until more of these basic problems have been ironed out, there seems to be little hope that this will turn into a major source of energy for our communities.

1. The main topic of this passage is

   Ⓐ the pros and cons of solar energy

   Ⓑ why solar energy has always failed

   Ⓒ the costs of using solar energy

   Ⓓ how the sun can be used

TOEFL – READING COMPREHENSION

Beginning

In the age of alternative sources of energy, solar energy has come to the forefront. To harness energy from the sun, or solar energy, one must receive it either directly from the Sun or through very brief intermediate processes. An example of the latter is when crops which were grown using solar input are then used as fuel or biomass. Solar energy has many purposes, from heating cool buildings to racing cars. It can also be converted directly into electricity. Importantly, it is generally considered safe for the environment, since it produces almost no known hazards.

However, there are many criticisms of solar energy. It is often not a practical or viable alternative in cold climates or places that go without seeing the sun

2. What is one of the uses of solar energy mentioned?

(A) starting an automobile in cold weather

(B) heating buildings

(C) making buildings cooler

(D) helping the economy

TOEFL – READING COMPREHENSION

Beginning

However, there are many criticisms of solar energy. It is often not a practical or viable alternative in cold climates or places that go without seeing the sun for long periods of time. It is also very difficult to transport. Power towers may used to store solar energy for a limited period of time, so when there is little or no sunlight in certain regions, this source of power cannot be utilized.

Thus, though many environmentalists and other proponents strongly advocate solar energy as a prime source of power, harvesting it and using it on a long-term basis is problematic. Until more of these basic problems have been ironed out, there seems to be little hope that this will turn into a

3. What is one of the major criticisms of solar energy?

(A) It's impossible.

(B) It's often impractical.

(C) It's inconceivable.

(D) It's inconsolable.

TOEFL – READING COMPREHENSION

Beginning

In the age of alternative sources of energy, solar energy has come to the forefront. To harness energy from the sun, or solar energy, one must receive it either directly from the Sun or through very brief intermediate processes. An example of the latter is when crops which were grown using solar input are then used as fuel or biomass. Solar energy has many purposes, from heating cool buildings to racing cars. It can also be converted directly into electricity. Importantly, it is generally considered safe for the environment, since it produces almost no known hazards.

However, there are many criticisms of solar energy. It is often not a practical or viable alternative in cold climates or places that go without seeing the sun

4. What is one of the major advantages that supporters of solar energy point out?

  (A) It's good for the environment.

  (B) It's harmful to the environment.

  (C) It's easy to use.

  (D) It's easy to obtain.

TOEFL – READING COMPREHENSION

Beginning

Thus, though many environmentalists and other proponents strongly advocate solar energy as a prime source of power, harvesting it and using it on a long-term basis is problematic. Until more of these basic problems have been ironed out, there seems to be little hope that this will turn into a major source of energy for our communities.

5. Look at the phrase ironed out. Ironed out means

  (A) worked out

  (B) exercised

  (C) wrinkled

  (D) exterminated

Note: On the actual CBT test, the question that follows would instruct you to "click" on the text where you would find the reference to the word in the shaded box.

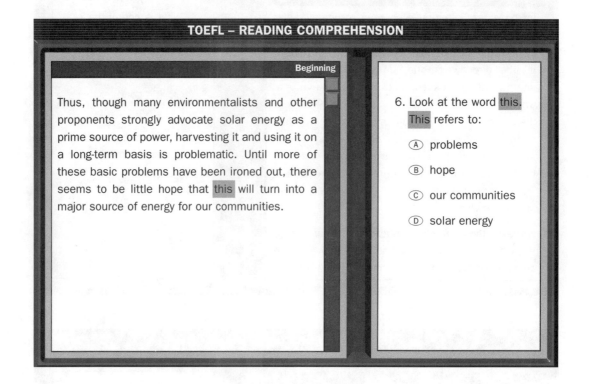

TOEFL – READING COMPREHENSION

Beginning

Thus, though many environmentalists and other proponents strongly advocate solar energy as a prime source of power, harvesting it and using it on a long-term basis is problematic. Until more of these basic problems have been ironed out, there seems to be little hope that this will turn into a major source of energy for our communities.

6. Look at the word this. This refers to:

   Ⓐ problems

   Ⓑ hope

   Ⓒ our communities

   Ⓓ solar energy

TOEFL – READING COMPREHENSION

In the age of alternative sources of energy, solar energy has come to the forefront. To harness energy from the sun, or solar energy, one must receive it either directly from the Sun or through very brief intermediate processes. An example of the latter is when crops which were grown using solar input are then used as fuel or biomass. Solar energy has many purposes, from heating cool buildings to racing cars. It can also be converted directly into electricity. Importantly, it is generally considered safe for the environment, since it produces almost no known hazards.

However, there are many criticisms of solar energy. It is often not a practical or viable alternative in cold climates or places that go without seeing the sun for long periods of time. It is also very difficult to transport. Power towers may used to store solar energy for a limited period of time, so when there is little or no sunlight in certain regions, this source of power cannot be utilized.

Thus, though many environmentalists and other proponents strongly advocate solar energy as a prime source of power, harvesting it and using it on a long-term basis is problematic. Until more of these basic problems have been ironed out, there seems to be little hope that this will turn into a major source of energy for our communities.

7. The author's organization of the passage is best described as

(A) presenting the pros and cons of solar energy and drawing a conclusion about it

(B) comparing and contrasting different types of solar energy

(C) introduction, support, and conclusion

(D) chronological

PRACTICE 7

Read the passage provided and select the correct answer choice for each question.

TOEFL – READING COMPREHENSION

Beginning

To many Americans, the name of Ethan Allen is more closely associated with a popular furniture chain located throughout the United States than that of a Revolutionary War hero. However, Ethan Allen was one of the most memorable and controversial of Revolutionists to emerge from that era.

Though born in Connecticut, Allen is long-remembered for being the most vocal supporter for the independence of the state of Vermont in the 1700s. In addition to his political aspirations, he was the war hero who helped form and served as leader of a group known as the Green Mountain Boys. Unlike many of his fellow Revolutionists, Allen was an outspoken atheist who was an advocate of deistic thought. Obviously, such a philosophy was widely criticized by many Christians. Still, undaunted by their scorn of his ideas, in 1784 Allen published a book on deism, entitled *Reason: The Only Oracle of Man*.

Along with his brother Ira, Allen became one of the major land speculators in New England in the second half of the 18th Century. The Allen brothers were instrumental in the formation of New Hampshire Grants, which served primarily to fight off New Yorkers who were trying to control the land located northeast of them. Thus, the New Hampshire Grants along with the Green Mountain Boys were reviled by the Governor of New York, who put a price on their heads. Fortunately, Allen was not captured, and returned to Vermont, declaring it an independent state, even though it was constantly in danger of being taken over by British troops.

In 1784, Allen withdrew from political life. At the time of his death five years later, Vermont was still an independent state and, of course, has remained so ever since.

1. According to the passage, during the Revolutionary War, Allen's atheist view was

   (A) advocated by the church

   (B) thought to be a notion centering on creation

   (C) a philosophy criticized by the Green Mountain boys

   (D) considered different from other Revolutionists

KAPLAN

TOEFL – READING COMPREHENSION

Beginning

To many Americans, the name of Ethan Allen is more closely associated with a popular furniture chain located throughout the United States than that of a Revolutionary War hero. However, Ethan Allen was one of the most memorable and controversial of Revolutionists to emerge from that era.

Though born in Connecticut, Allen is long-remembered for being the most vocal supporter for the independence of the state of Vermont in the 1700s. In addition to his political aspirations, he was the war hero who helped form and served as leader of a group known as the Green Mountain Boys. Unlike many of his fellow Revolutionists, Allen was an outspoken atheist who was an advocate of deistic thought. Obviously, such a philosophy was widely criticized by many Christians. Still, undaunted by their

2. In the first paragraph, the author infers that:

(A) most Americans are not familiar with American History

(B) Americans don't recognize the name of Ethan Allen

(C) most Americans equate Allen's name with furniture

(D) many Americans have read about Revolutionary War heroes

Note: On the actual CBT test, the question that follows would instruct you to "click" on the section of the text where you would find the information in question.

TOEFL – READING COMPREHENSION

Beginning

Though born in Connecticut, Allen is long-remembered for being the most vocal supporter for the independence of the state of Vermont in the 1700s. Ⓐ In addition to his political aspirations, he was the war hero who helped form and served as leader of a group known as the Green Mountain Boys. Ⓑ Unlike many of his fellow Revolutionists, Allen was an outspoken atheist who was an advocate of deistic thought. Obviously, such a philosophy was widely criticized by many Christians. Still, undaunted by their scorn of his ideas, in 1784 Allen published a book on deism, entitled *Reason: the Only Oracle of Man*.

Along with his brother Ira, Allen became one of the major land speculators in New England in the second half of the 18th Century. Ⓒ The Allen brothers were instrumental in the formation of New Hampshire Grants, which served primarily to fight off New Yorkers who were trying to control the land located northeast of them. Thus, the New Hampshire Grants along with the Green Mountain Boys were reviled by the Governor of New York, who put a price on their heads. Ⓓ Fortunately, Allen was not captured, and returned to Vermont, declaring it an independent state, even though it was constantly in danger of being taken over by British troops.

In 1784, Allen withdrew from political life. At the time of his death five years later, Vermont was still an independent state and, of course, has remained so ever since.

3. Where in the first two paragraphs shown does the author describe the reason for Allen's formation of the New Hampshire Grants? Select the answer bubble at the beginning of the appropriate sentence.

KAPLAN

TOEFL – READING COMPREHENSION

Beginning

Though born in Connecticut, Allen is long-remembered for being the most vocal supporter for the independence of the state of Vermont in the 1700s. In addition to his political aspirations, he was the war hero who helped form and served as leader of a group known as the Green Mountain Boys. Unlike many of his fellow Revolutionists, Allen was an outspoken atheist who was an advocate of deistic thought. Obviously, such a philosophy was widely criticized by many Christians. Still, undaunted by their scorn of his ideas, in 1784 Allen published a book on deism, entitled *Reason: The Only Oracle of Man*.

Along with his brother Ira, Allen became one of the major land speculators in New England in the second

4. Ethan Allen is most closely associated with the independence of which state?

Ⓐ Connecticut

Ⓑ Vermont

Ⓒ New York

Ⓓ New England

TOEFL – READING COMPREHENSION

Beginning

To many Americans, the name of Ethan Allen is more closely associated with a popular furniture chain located throughout the United States than that of a Revolutionary War hero. However, Ethan Allen was one of the most memorable and controversial of Revolutionists to emerge from that era.

Though born in Connecticut, Allen is long-remembered for being the most vocal supporter for the independence of the state of Vermont in the 1700s. In addition to his political aspirations, he was the war hero who helped form and served as leader of a group known as the Green Mountain Boys. Unlike many of his fellow Revolutionists, Allen was an outspoken atheist who was an advocate of deistic thought. Obviously, such a philosophy was widely criticized by many Christians. Still, undaunted by their scorn of his ideas, in 1784 Allen published a book on deism, entitled *Reason: The Only Oracle of Man*.

Along with his brother Ira, Allen became one of the major land speculators in New England in the second half of the 18th Century. The Allen brothers were instrumental in the formation of New Hampshire Grants, which served primarily to fight off New Yorkers who were trying to control the land located northeast of them. Thus, the New Hampshire Grants along with the Green Mountain Boys were reviled by the Governor of New York, who put a price on their heads. Fortunately, Allen was not captured, and returned to Vermont, declaring it an independent state, even though it was constantly in danger of being taken over by British troops.

In 1784, Allen withdrew from political life. At the time of his death five years later, Vermont was still an independent state and, of course, has remained so ever since.

5. According to the passage, Ethan Allen and his brother Ira were both

Ⓐ land speculators

Ⓑ writers

Ⓒ politicians

Ⓓ opponents of deism

KAPLAN

Note: On the actual CBT test, the question that follows would instruct you to "click" on the section of text where you would insert the sentence.

TOEFL – READING COMPREHENSION

Beginning

Though born in Connecticut, Allen is long-remembered for being the most vocal supporter for the independence of the state of Vermont in the 1700s. Ⓐ In addition to his political aspirations, he was the war hero who helped form and served as leader of a group known as the Green Mountain Boys. Ⓑ Unlike many of his fellow Revolutionists, Allen was an outspoken atheist who was an advocate of deistic thought. Ⓒ Obviously, such a philosophy was widely criticized by many Christians. Ⓓ Still, undaunted by their scorn of his ideas, in 1784 Allen published a book on deism, entitled Reason: the Only Oracle of Man.

Along with his brother Ira, Allen became one of the major land speculators in New England in the second

6. The following sentence can be added to the paragraph opposite.

   This belief centers around the notion that God created the universe, but since then, creation has had no role in what occurs in day-to-day life.

   Where would it best fit in the paragraph? Select the correct answer bubble in the paragraph.

TOEFL – READING COMPREHENSION

Beginning

Along with his brother Ira, Allen became one of the major land speculators in New England in the second half of the 18th Century. The Allen brothers were instrumental in the formation of New Hampshire Grants, which served primarily to fight off New Yorkers who were trying to control the land located northeast of them. Thus, the New Hampshire Grants along with the Green Mountain Boys were reviled by the Governor of New York, who put a price on their heads. Fortunately, Allen was not captured, and returned to Vermont, declaring it an independent state, even though it was constantly in danger of being taken over by British troops.

In 1784, Allen withdrew from political life. At the time of his death five years later, Vermont was still

7. What was the purpose of the New Hampshire Grants?

   Ⓐ to aid New Yorkers

   Ⓑ to free English living in the New World

   Ⓒ to protect New England land against New Yorkers who wanted it

   Ⓓ to fight Christianity

Note: On the actual CBT test, the question that follows would instruct you to "click" on the text where you would find the reference to the word in the shaded box.

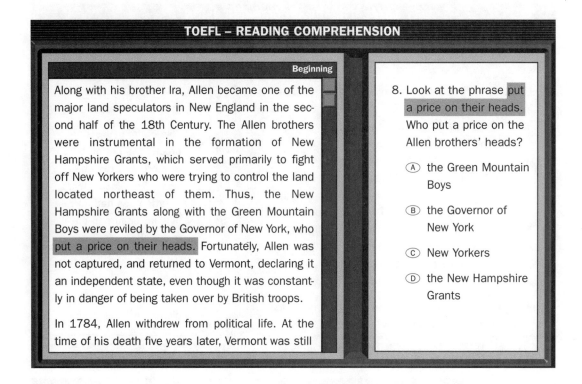

TOEFL – READING COMPREHENSION

Beginning

Along with his brother Ira, Allen became one of the major land speculators in New England in the second half of the 18th Century. The Allen brothers were instrumental in the formation of New Hampshire Grants, which served primarily to fight off New Yorkers who were trying to control the land located northeast of them. Thus, the New Hampshire Grants along with the Green Mountain Boys were reviled by the Governor of New York, who put a price on their heads. Fortunately, Allen was not captured, and returned to Vermont, declaring it an independent state, even though it was constantly in danger of being taken over by British troops.

In 1784, Allen withdrew from political life. At the time of his death five years later, Vermont was still

8. Look at the phrase put a price on their heads. Who put a price on the Allen brothers' heads?

- (A) the Green Mountain Boys
- (B) the Governor of New York
- (C) New Yorkers
- (D) the New Hampshire Grants

READING POWER PRACTICE EXERCISE
ANSWER KEY

PRACTICE 1	PRACTICE 2	PRACTICE 3	PRACTICE 4
1. C	1. A	1. B	1. B
2. B	2. C	2. D	2. C
3. B	3. A	3. C	3. A
4. C	4. C	4. D	4. B
5. A	5. D	5. D	5. A
6. C	6. A	6. C	6. C
7. B	7. B	7. C	7. B
8. A	8. B	8. C	8. C
9. C	9. B	9. D	9. A
10. B	10. D	10. D	10. C

PRACTICE 5	PRACTICE 6	PRACTICE 7
1. B	1. A	A. D
2. C	2. B	2. C
3. B	3. B	3. C
4. A	4. A	4. B
5. C	5. A	5. A
6. B	6. D	6. C
7. A	7. A	7. C
		8. B

Writing Power

At a Glance:

SESSION A: AN OVERVIEW OF THE ESSAY TEST

The first and most frequently asked question by ESL students who are confronting the TOEFL essay is: "What exactly is an essay?" This is a very good question, as essay organization and formation may vary greatly from one country to another. Quite simply, an essay is a written composition based on a particular topic. In the following writing sections, we will describe the kind of essay that the TOEFL examiners are looking for as well as provide you with the background you'll need to feel confident when you are faced with writing your TOEFL essay on the day of the exam.

Essay writing is a required part of every TOEFL CBT exam (as of July 1998). (The essay will, however, continue to be optional for the paper-based TOEFL.) Your essay score will be combined with the score from the Structure section to form one Structure/Writing score. On the day of the exam, you will be given one topic on which to base your essay and allowed

30 minutes to write your essay. Unlike with the rest of the new TOEFL, you will be able to choose whether you wish to write your essay on the computer or by hand.

The range for your score of the essay component is from 0 (lowest score) to 6 (highest score); your final Structure/Writing score will range from 0 to 30. The readers of your essay are English or ESL specialists and work under the direct supervision of a "reading manager." The two readers will rate your essay independently of each other. That is, neither will know the rating of the other, and your final grade will be an average of the two scores. If there is a difference of more than one point between the two, a third reader will also rate your essay. Your final score could be a 6.0, 5.5, 5.0, 4.5, 4.0, 3.5, 3.0, 2.5, 2.0, 1.5, 1.0, or 0 (for a paper that is blank or written in a language other than English, or one that in no way addresses the topic).

To help you prepare for the essay component, you should study the "Writing Topics" provided to you by ETS (Educational Testing Service) in its *TOEFL Information Bulletin for Computer-Based Testing*. By practicing essay writing prior to the day of the TOEFL, especially within the 30-minute time frame, you can greatly enhance your chances of doing well on this section of the test. There is a typing test included in the CD-ROM that will help you decide whether to use the keyboard or write your essay by hand (see the "User's Guide" in the beginning of this book for more details).

While becoming a proficient English writer may seem like a daunting task at first, there is no way to get around one very simple and basic truth: the only way to become a writer is to write and read as much and as often as you can. This may sound trite, but it is the fundamental key to improving your writing skills. Whereas it is important that you read and study examples of "good writing," unless you are willing to put in time and effort to write yourself, you will never become a competent writer of English. Great writers of English certainly did not become that way overnight; it obviously took a great deal of commitment, diligence, and time to perfect their craft. Thus, you—as an English as a Second Language writer and speaker— will need to be willing to invest an even greater effort into perfecting your English writing.

In the writing sections of this chapter, we will take you through steps that will help you learn how to organize your ideas, form an outline and develop organization, write a draft, and finally edit/proofread your essay. And yes, by the day of the test, you will need to know how to accomplish all of this in the 30-minute time frame that the TOEFL essay allows! But don't be discouraged. With dedication and perseverance, you will no doubt see results.

Your final essay must do the following in order for you to achieve the highest score possible:

(1) Your essay must effectively discuss the topic you have been asked to address.

It is vital that you read the assigned topic very carefully and not add or delete anything. This is one of the most common mistakes in writing an essay—by adding a few words, or conversely ignoring one or two significant ones, a test taker can easily digress from the assigned topic. Of course, the end result is failure to address the topic.

(2) Your essay must be well organized.

You must have an introduction (with a thesis statement), a body (with supporting details for your thesis), and a conclusion. Because essay organization is very important, this will be dealt with in greater detail later in this chapter.

(3) You must show consistent ease in your use of the English language.

This includes using correct grammar as well as the appropriate use of idiomatic language. Remember, you are trying to prove that your English skills are advanced enough for you to do as well as native English speakers in an American university class.

(4) You must prove to your readers that you possess a wide range of vocabulary and know how to use terms in an appropriate fashion.

In other words, be very careful with the words you choose and avoid redundancy of both words and ideas. You want to be conservative so that you can show how much vocabulary and how many different word forms you know.

You must be able to paraphrase some or all of the question asked or the quotation given. This shows that you have a broad vocabulary, that your reading comprehension is adequate, and that you can avoid redundancy in your writing. You will also need to be able to paraphrase your thesis in your conclusion to remind your readers of your main idea.

SESSION B: STANDARD ESSAY FORM

In general, an essay is made up of three basic components: an introduction, a body, and a conclusion. The length of an essay may vary greatly, but because you only have 30 minutes in which to prepare, write, and proofread your TOEFL essay, you should aim for an essay containing a maximum of four to five paragraphs (unless you are a highly accomplished English writer). Your first paragraph, the introduction, will introduce the main topic of your essay to your reader, and it typically ends with your thesis statement (the most important sentence in your essay). The next part of your essay is the body. The body provides detailed support to prove your thesis. The body will be made up of the main subpoints of your thesis, each with its own paragraph. Thus, your body will most likely consist of 2–3 paragraphs. Your final paragraph is your conclusion. These three basic parts are outlined below and discussed in greater detail in subsequent lessons.

I. Introduction

    A. Hook (to capture your reader's attention)

    B. General information on assigned topic (no details)

    C. Thesis (one-sentence statement of main idea plus viewpoint)

II. Body

    A. Sub-Point One

        1.Topic sentence

        2. Details supporting topic sentence

    B. Sub-Point Two

        1. Topic sentence

        2. Details supporting topic sentence

    C. (Possible) Sub-Point Three

        1. Topic sentence

        2. Details supporting topic sentence

III. Conclusion

    A. Paraphrase of thesis

    B. Summary of viewpoint

    C. General final statement/comment

SESSION C: TIME DIVISION FOR A 30-MINUTE ESSAY EXAM

One of the biggest dilemmas students face with essay examinations is how to make the best use of their time during the test. Certainly, the amount of time each student will need to make an outline, write the essay, and proofread will vary. However, all of these steps are necessary to produce a clear, organized essay with few grammatical errors. Below is a suggested way to divide the limited time you are given:

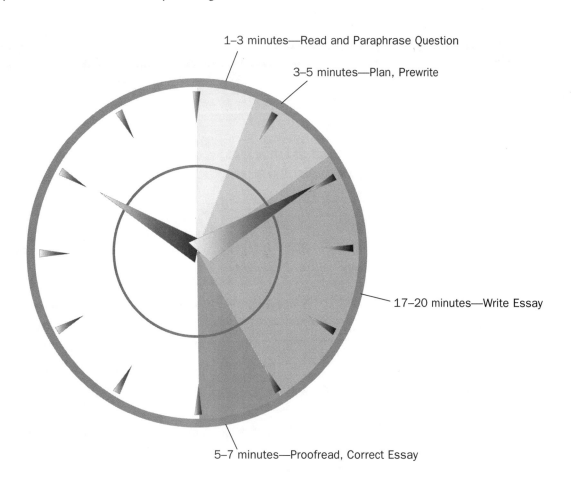

1–3 minutes—Read and Paraphrase Question

3–5 minutes—Plan, Prewrite

17–20 minutes—Write Essay

5–7 minutes—Proofread, Correct Essay

SESSION D: TYPES OF ESSAYS

The list below contains the most common types of essays found in an essay examination. After you have read your essay question and interpreted it, the next step is for you to decide what kind of essay you will need to organize and write. Determining the type of essay will help you write your thesis statement, decide how many body paragraphs are needed, know which transitions are appropriate to use, and much more.

Compare and Contrast Essay

This is one of the most typical forms of essay examinations. A comparison tells the ways in which a person, place, thing, event and so on are similar. A contrast points out differences. There are two common methods of organizing compare/contrast essays. Let's use the topic of "urban life vs. rural life" as an example:

(1) Body

    A. Similarities between urban and rural life

    B. Dissimilarities between urban and rural life

       OR

(2) Body

    A. Urban life: advantages and disadvantages

    B. Rural life: advantages and disadvantages

Persuasive Essay (Also Known as Personal Opinion Essay)

In the persuasive essay, you are trying to convince your reader to agree with a particular position or viewpoint you have expressed in your thesis. While adjectives and adverbs may sway your reader, the most effective way to bring your reader over to your side is through facts, detailed examples, and/or personal knowledge. Be sure to incorporate some aspects of the latter in the body of your persuasive essay.

This type of essay may be written in the first person and include: *in my opinion*, *it seems to me*, or *in my view*. However, even if you use the third person (and this is often considered to be more sophisticated), you can make your stand clear to your reader.

Descriptive Essay

The purpose of a descriptive essay is to present a detailed picture of a person, place, object, event, etcetera. To make the image as real as possible, you can use words or linguistic devices known as "imagery." These may be words that appeal directly to the reader's senses. That is, you can help your reader see, hear, taste, smell, or feel what it is you are describing by choosing vivid vocabulary. Avoid vague, general words such as *good*, *nice*, and *bad*, and replace these with more descriptive, specific terms. Metaphors (comparisons of two unlike items) are also often used in descriptions. Try to imagine that your reader has never experienced the object that you are describing; it is your job to bring this subject to life.

Cause and Effect Essay

To "cause" an action means to make something happen; the result or consequence of that action is the "effect." For example: "What are the chief causes of divorce, and how does it affect the children of the couple?" Typical transitions for this type of essay are: *as a result, as a consequence, consequently, therefore,* and *thus.*

Conditional sentence-type essay questions are sometimes classified as "cause and effect" as well. For example: "If you won a million dollars in the lottery, how would you spend the money? Describe in detail how you think your life would change as a result of your new-found wealth."

Interpretation/Analysis Essay

In the interpretation-type essay, you are given a short quotation (usually 1–3 sentences in length). You are asked to interpret the saying (i.e., paraphrase the author's message); then, either analyze or form your own opinion about the original quotation.

This kind of essay is rapidly growing in popularity, especially for essay entrance examinations to American universities and for many standardized tests. The time given for the essay test may vary from 15 minutes to two hours, depending on the school and/or the standardized test. Therefore, when you practice writing this type of exam, you should try several different time frames.

Illustrative Essay

Another type of essay is the one that is based on examples or illustrations to support the writer's thesis. For example: "What were the best classes you ever took? Give examples of at least two classes which you found outstanding, and explain why you chose these." Of course, illustration is an important component of many types of essay "body" paragraphs.

Process Essay

Process writing, generally speaking, provides instructions or details a process: that is, it tells the reader how to operate a VCR, apply to a school, build a bookshelf, learn a foreign language, etcetera. Therefore, while this writing style is quite common, it is not typically tested in an essay examination. On the other hand, it is not uncommon to be given this type of essay as an at-home assignment.

SESSION E: THE INTRODUCTION TO THE ESSAY

Like all first impressions, the introductory paragraph of your essay will leave a lasting imprint. Therefore, it is extremely important that it be well written. To favorably impress your readers, your introduction should contain the following:

Hook

How is a hook used in fishing? It dangles in front of its target (the fish) and tries to lure or captivate it. In much the same way, the "hook" in an essay is used to catch the attention of your audience. To accomplish this, begin your essay with an interesting, thought-provoking idea about the topic you have been assigned. Avoid asserting the obvious; that is, merely stating a fact that everyone knows is true. For example, "Learning a new language is difficult" is a fact known to be true by almost everyone, and, therefore, serves no useful purpose. Sometimes a quotation (or proverb) works well as a hook if it is particularly relevant to the thesis.

General Statements Regarding the Assigned Topic

Your introduction should only <u>introduce</u> the main ideas of your essay. This is not the place for you to provide supporting details, such as specific names, places, and dates. Save these for the body of your essay.

Thesis

The thesis is the most significant statement in your essay. It consists of one sentence only and is usually the last sentence of your introduction. A thesis must be a complete sentence (unlike a title). It should also be narrow enough for you to be able to discuss it within the short time frame allowed on the TOEFL and within a two- or three-paragraph body. Yet it must also be general enough for you to be able to write two to three sub-points on this topic.

Unlike some countries, in the United States, we do not state directly what we plan to do or say in our essay; for example, "I will write about . . . " is unacceptable in an American essay. If your essay is well written, your intentions should be obvious to your reader without your having to explicitly state them.

The thesis serves two basic functions. First, it states the main topic of your essay. Secondly, it provides a viewpoint or position that you, the writer, holds about this topic.

For example, this is not a thesis: "Smoking in restaurants in New York is illegal." It merely states a fact, but provides no position or opinion regarding this fact.

This is a thesis: "Not allowing smoking in restaurants in New York is highly unfair to the smoker and gives too much power to the nonsmoker." Here we are given both a topic (i.e., smoking in restaurants in New York is illegal) plus two clear opinions about this topic. Because this thesis states two positions regarding the topic, it will also help the writer to quickly and effectively set up the organization for the body of his/her essay. That is, the two sub-points have been clearly laid out in the introduction for both the reader and the writer.

Often students feel that there must be a "right" or "wrong" position that they should take on a given topic. Remember: You are entitled to your own opinion. The readers are only interested in whether you have logically, clearly, and effectively supported the position that you have taken.

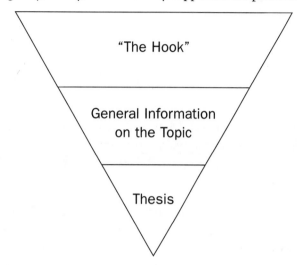

Practice One

Which of the following sentences is a thesis? If the sentence is a thesis, put a "T" in the space provided next to it. If it is not a thesis, put in "NT" in the space provided. Be prepared to discuss the reasons for your choices.

1. _____ Washington, D.C., is the capital of the United States.

2. _____ There are two basic reasons for the rise of divorce: the lack of communication skills and financial problems.

3. _____ Divorce is not legal in my country. Some people think it should be, some don't.

4. _____ Walking is the best exercise: it is great for one's health, and it doesn't cost anything!

5. _____ Traveling for fun and education.

6. _____ Because I wanted to learn how to speak English fluently, it was essential that I move to an English-speaking country.

7. _____ Financial woes and lack of free time are the major causes of stress today.

8. _____ The Beatles sold over a million records in the 1960s.

9. _____ The Beatles and the Rolling Stones were far more talented than the popular rock bands of today.

10. _____ Now, I am going to write about the reasons I moved to the United States.

To check your responses above, be sure the thesis statement:

- Contains one, and only one, complete sentence
- Provides a clearly defined main topic

- Takes a clearly stated position on the topic (instead of merely stating a fact)
- Doesn't explicitly state what you plan to do/say

Answers

1. NT
2. T
3. NT
4. T
5. NT
6. T
7. T
8. NT
9. T
10. NT

Practice Two

Take the following topics and questions, and turn them into theses. Remember that each thesis must be a complete sentence that clearly states your main idea and takes a position on this topic. Ideally, it will also set up the organization for the body of your essay. Doing this can save you a great deal of time when you write the body. It will also help you stay focused.

> EXAMPLE: Topic/Question: In many countries, the government practices censorship of television programs. Do you support this practice or not? Support your answer with specific examples.

> Possible Thesis: Government censorship of television programs is unfair and fiscally wasteful.

1. **Topic/Question:** If you had a choice, would you like to live forever? Explain why this does or does not appeal to you.

   Thesis:

   _____

   _____

   _____

   _____

2. **Topic:** Students attend a university or college for a variety of reasons. In your opinion, what should be the main purpose of a university education?

   Thesis:

   _____

   _____

   _____

   _____

3. **Topic:** When many people think of the United States, words such as *independent* and *free-spirited* come to mind. If you had to describe your country by its personality, what trait(s) would best describe it?

   Thesis:

   _____

   _____

   _____

   _____

4. **Topic:** Most people experience at least some degree of culture shock when they are getting accustomed to a new culture. What advice would you give to a friend of yours to help him get over culture shock? (You may write about your own culture or about the American culture.)

   Thesis:

   _____

   _____

   _____

   _____

5. **Topic:** It is necessary to be wealthy in order to be successful. Do you agree with this statement? Why or why not?

   Thesis:

   _____

   _____

   _____

   _____

Practice Three

Choose one of the questions from the above list (1–5) and write an introduction. Be sure to follow the steps laid out in the inverted pyramid diagram, and watch the time. Remember, on the actual test you will only have a very short time in which to compose your introduction.

SESSION F: THE BODY OF THE ESSAY

The main purpose of the body of your essay is to give support to your thesis (usually the last sentence of your introduction). To give sufficient support, you need to provide a minimum of two or three paragraphs in your body for an essay examination. However, a take-home essay generally has several body paragraphs.

All body paragraphs begin with a topic sentence. The topic sentence states the main idea of the body paragraph, a main sub-point of your thesis. For this reason, it may be said that after your thesis, topic sentences are the most important part of your essay.

Immediately following the topic sentence, you should provide clear, specific details to lend credence to the argument of your paper; specifically, to the topic sentence of that paragraph. To accomplish this, you should use specific dates, people, places, and/or events. You will most likely need more than one sentence to provide sufficient details for each point. Use transitions to introduce your examples (see list in appendix).

Generally speaking, the body paragraphs are longer than the introduction and conclusion. However, be sure that each body paragraph contains only one main sub-point. All the ideas included in each paragraph must fall under the broader topic sentence. That is, every new idea requires a new paragraph. Think of each sentence after the topic sentence ("the set") as a sub-set of it.

While you will want to use transitions within your body paragraphs, you also need to use them to connect one body paragraph to another. This is necessary to make your paper smooth and coherent. For example, if you are writing a compare/contrast essay, you may want to begin your second body paragraph with a transition phrase such as *on the other hand* or *in contrast*. Study the list of transition terms at the end of this chapter to determine which one(s) would be appropriate for the type of essay you are writing.

Practice One

Read the following sample essay body divisions, and think of possible topics for these divisions.

1. I. Introduction

    II. Body
       A. Past
       B. Present
       C. Future

    III. Conclusion

2. I. Introduction

    II. Body

        A. Infant

        B. Child

        C. Adult

        D. Old Age

    III. Conclusion

3. I. Introduction

    II. Body

        A. Emotional

        B. Mental

        C. Physical

    III. Conclusion

4. I. Introduction

    II. Body

        A. Urban

        B. Small Town

        C. Countryside

    III. Conclusion

5. I. Introduction

    II. Body

        A. Home

        B. Work

        C. School

    III. Conclusion

Practice Two

In the exercises below, take the topic provided and, working with a partner, create your own sub-topics.

    EXAMPLE: Topic: Best uses of home computers

            II. Body

                B. Entertainment

                C. Pay bills

1. Topic: The most practical college majors

    II. Body

        A.

        B.

        C.

2. Topic: Advantages to living in a foreign country

    II. Body
       A.
       B.
       C.

3. Topic: What a person must do to have a successful life

    II. Body
       A.
       B.
       C.

Practice Three

Choose one of the topics above, and write a 3-paragraph essay body on it. You have 20 minutes in which to write the body. You may choose either two or three sub-points (body paragraphs). Be sure that you begin with a topic sentence, and that all of the following sentences in that paragraph remain within the framework of your topic sentence. A new topic introduces a new paragraph.

SESSION G: THE CONCLUSION OF THE ESSAY

The conclusion of the essay is often neglected. One reason for this is that students often run out of time during the essay examination and never get beyond the body of their papers. Another factor is that students often do not know how or when to end their essay. Yet failure to end your essay is analogous to not finishing the final chapter of a book. Your reader is left with unanswered questions; you must put these to rest before you finish your paper. However, if you have gone through the recommended organization steps laid out in our earlier sections and practiced timed writing on your own, finishing your essay should become an easier task.

The following guidelines can help you improve your concluding paragraph:

*   Before writing your conclusion, reread your introduction (paying special attention to your thesis) and your topic sentences. This will refresh your memory as to the main idea and main subpoints of your paper.
*   Begin your conclusion with a paraphrase of your thesis. It is vital that you not repeat your thesis verbatim. Doing so is redundant and boring, and you miss the opportunity to show your readers the breadth of your vocabulary.
*   Follow with general statements. These should be a summary or evaluation of previously mentioned main thoughts.
*   Your last sentence should provide a final thought or comment concerning your main topic.

The following should be avoided in a conclusion:

- New information does not belong in a conclusion. You have neither the time nor the space to develop it further (this is what the body paragraphs are for).
- Avoid detailed information in support of your thesis. This, too, should be found in the body of the essay, after your topic sentences.
- Don't begin your conclusion with "to conclude" or "in conclusion." It is clear to your reader that this is your final paragraph and is obviously your conclusion. (You may, however, begin your conclusion with transitions like therefore, thus, to sum up, or in summary.)
- A conclusion should not be lengthy. In general, three or four sentences will suffice. This is especially true of a 30-minute essay examination conclusion.

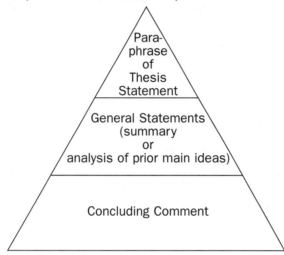

Diagram of a Typical Essay Conclusion

Practice One

Take the following thesis statements and paraphrase them so that they would fit into a conclusion. Remember that a paraphrase keeps the same ideas of the original statement, but uses your own words. When paraphrasing a thesis, it is often helpful to underline the key words in the original sentence. Be sure to use synonyms for these where possible. Also, be sure to include all of these main ideas in your rewrite. For example:

THESIS: Getting married and having children is not key to one's happiness.

PARAPHRASED THESIS: A person may find contentment in life even if (s)he never marries or has children.

1. **Thesis:** "If you want to live a long and productive life, you must exercise regularly and eat healthy foods."

    Paraphrased Thesis:

    _____

    _____

    _____

2. **Thesis:** "Because of the conveniences and the cultural opportunities available in the city, living there is superior to living in the countryside."

    Paraphrased Thesis:

    _____

    _____

    _____

    _____

    _____

3. **Thesis:** "The only ways to become a proficient writer are to read as much as possible and write whenever you can."

    Paraphrased Thesis:

    _____

    _____

    _____

    _____

    _____

SESSION H: WRITING ASSIGNMENTS

The following writing topics cover a variety of essay types (*compare and contrast, agree vs. disagree, interpretation, descriptive,* etcetera), and some of them combine more than one essay type. These assignments may be done in class or as a homework assignment, but they should always be done within a 30-minute time allotment.

1. What do you think is the most important invention of the 20th century? Choose only one. Provide specific details to support your choice.

2. Smokers should have the right to smoke whenever and wherever they please, without any restrictions. Do you agree or disagree with this statement?

3. Your university requires that you declare both a major and a minor. What would you choose for your major field, and what would you select for your minor? Explain your reasons for making these selections.

4. If you had a child who was not a native English speaker, would you prefer that she learn English through a bilingual education program, an English as a Second Language program, or regular English classes with native speakers? Choose one of these three methods, and explain why you would choose this method for your child.

5. Which is better: life in a big city or in a small town? Compare and contrast the advantages and disadvantages of these two.

6. What is the most important advice your parents gave you when you were growing up? Include what they taught you, how you learned this "lesson," and why it is important to you today.

7. "The death penalty should be abolished." Do you agree or disagree with this statement? Be specific in your supporting arguments.

8. You have been given a choice by your university to live in an on-campus dormitory or to live in your own apartment off campus. Which of the two would you choose and why?

9. Success is a very subjective term. How do you define success? In your essay, include both your definition and a description of a person whom you find to be successful.

10. Many American universities today have done away with grades. Do you think that grades are necessary? Why or why not?

11. Often, newcomers to a foreign country find it difficult to make friends with people who are natives of the country. What are some effective ways to make new friends in a foreign country? Provide specific suggestions and ways to achieve this goal.

12. What makes a great boss? Describe your ideal employer or boss, including specific personality traits, and state why these are vital to you.

13. Do you think physical education courses should be required for all university students? Take a position, and write a persuasive essay supporting your stand.

14. "Life seems to me like a Japanese picture which our imagination does not allow to end with the margin. We aim at the infinite and when our arrow falls to earth it is in flames."
   —*Oliver Wendell Holmes, 1932*

   Interpret the above quotation by Holmes and explain whether you agree or disagree with his metaphors on a person's life.

15. Is the American family structure similar to that in your country? Compare and contrast: What are the similarities? What are the dissimilarities? Be specific.

16. There are many environmental problems facing the world today. Some are primarily the responsibility of corporations and government. However, there are several steps an individual can take to help save the environment. Describe the steps that we can all can take to help improve the environment.

17. Interpret the following statement: "Unbridled freedom will ultimately abolish the very democracy it wishes to protect." What does this mean? Do you agree or disagree with the author of this quotation?

18. Describe the best teacher you ever had. What characteristics make this teacher stand out so strongly in your mind? Support your answer by including specific traits and/or anecdotes.

19. If you inherited $10 million, what would you do with the money? Limit your response to the two major ways you would spend or invest the money, and tell why you made these choices.

20. Do you think the national age for being able to drink alcohol should be lowered from 21 years of age to 18? Why or why not? Provide specific examples to support your response.

SESSION 1: PUNCTUATION GUIDELINES

The following is a general list of punctuation rules, beginning with the two most common types of punctuation: the period and the comma. It is important that you correctly use all of the types of punctuation; however, refrain from overuse of the types that are less frequently used in American English (such as the semicolon, colon, and dash).

Period

The period ends a complete sentence that is a statement.

> Classes will begin next week.

Comma

The comma has several functions and is very common. It is used:

(1) To separate clauses and phrases, especially after an initial dependent clause or a long prepositional phrase:

> If I were you, I would call her.

> At the beginning of next year, I'll start graduate school.

(2) To separate items:

> I shopped, watched videos, called friends, and took a nap on my day off.

(3) To introduce a direct quotation:

> He said, "I hope we can get tickets to the Yankees game."

(4) To separate appositives or nonrestrictive clauses:

> Ms. Jones, my physics professor, is on sabbatical.

(5) To separate two independent clauses joined by a conjunction:

> Bill was really exhausted, but he still managed to meet the deadline of the project.

Question Mark

Obviously, this is used at the end of the question.

What time is it?

Exclamation Point

This may be used to end a sentence statement, but it is rarely used because its purpose is to make a very strong point or to indicate great surprise.

Wow! That's amazing!

Semicolon

(1) This is used to separate two independent clauses, especially if one or both are short and if they are closely related ideas:

Jill runs ten miles a day; she's ready for the marathon.

(2) This separates groups of words when there are smaller groups within them set off by commas:

We visited Kyoto, a beautiful city; Seoul, also an interesting place; Honolulu, Hawaii; and several cities on the West Coast.

Colon

(1) This provides further explanation:

There are several reasons for my moving here: good job opportunities, a rich cultural life, and the chance to meet people from a variety of backgrounds.

(2) It can introduce a direct quotation (you may also use a comma in this situation):

The police shouted: "Stop. Put your hands up."

Dash

In general, this should be restricted to informal writing, and avoided on an essay examination. It is usually used to separate thoughts (often two short independent clauses).

Tell me what you want now—or I'll go ahead and decide without your input.

Apostrophe

(1) The apostrophe shows ownership or possession:

That is Kate's book.

(2) It also shows a contraction of two words:

That's her book; it's not mine.

Quotation Marks

(1) These are used to set off a direct quotation:

He said, "I'm a graduate student here." (Note that the period is inside the quotation mark.)

(2) In a few cases, these are used to indicate that a word or phrase is used in a way different from its traditional use or meaning or is slang:

He thought the idea was "far out."

(3) Quotation marks also indicate titles of chapters in a book, articles in a newspaper or magazine, or foreign words when you do not have access to italics.

Hyphen

(1) The hyphen indicates that a word will resume on the following line when you have run out of space at the end of the line (words should always be separated by syllables).

(2) It also separates compound words (most common in compound adjectives and compound nouns) which appear before the noun they describe:

I have a two-year-old son.

(But, "my son is two years old." In this example, the hyphens are omitted because "son" precedes "two years old.")

SESSION J: TRANSITION TERMS

The word *transit* means to move or pass from one place to another. Thus, the words and phrases we use to move smoothly from one idea to another one in an essay are called *transitions*. To create a coherent, smooth essay, you must use these terms, and use them correctly.

While not every sentence in an essay requires a transition, you must disperse a variety of them throughout the essay to link sentences and paragraphs to each other. The chart below states the purpose of the transition and provides you with a variety of similar ones to use. Avoid redundancy in your essay by choosing several different ones. In other words, don't use "however" every time you want to show contrast; instead, select as many different phrases as needed that serve the same function. Use commas to separate transitions from the rest of your sentence.

Purpose of Transition	Possible Transition Terms
to show likeness or add information	*also, too, besides, in addition, furthermore, moreover*
to show contrast	*however, but, on the other hand, conversely, yet, though, in contrast, nevertheless*
to introduce examples	*for example, such as, e.g., to illustrate, for instance*
to explain	*that is, in other words, i.e.*
to emphasize	*in fact, indeed, certainly, clearly, of course*
to generalize	*generally speaking, in general, overall, for the most part, usually, typically, in conclusion, in summary, to sum up*
to conclude or show result	*therefore, thus, consequently, as a result, as a consequence*
to indicate sequence or show order	*first, second, next, then, finally, lastly*

SESSION K: HOW TO BECOME A BETTER SPELLER

Although it is unlikely that a few misspelled words on the TOEFL essay will substantially lower your score, it is esssential that you have adequate spelling skills in order to be able to communicate your ideas effectively in English. In fact, frequently the word is so grossly misspelled that the reader has no idea what the writer is trying to say. Bad spelling has become a growing problem, not only with non-native English writers but also with people who speak English as their first language. Although "spell check" on a computer can help you with at-home assignments, it is of no use when you are writing your TOEFL essay.

Although becoming a proficient speller is a long-term process, there are several steps you can take right now that can greatly enhance your spelling ability. The following suggestions should help you get started today:

1. If you are unsure of the spelling of a word, always look it up in a dictionary (of course, this is not an option while you are writing your TOEFL essay). If you cannot find the word in the dictionary, simply ask a friend or a teacher. Keep a list in a notebook of words that you frequently have trouble spelling and practice writing these words correctly.

2. Don't worry too much about your spelling while you are actually writing the essay. That is, wait until you are editing (or proofreading) your paper to check the spelling. If you are really unsure of the spelling, replace the word with a synonym you are certain not to misspell. However, many spelling errors are simply the result of carelessness, and you should catch these when you are reading through your essay before submitting it. This applies to all in-class essays as well.

3. For words that you are unsure of, spell them out (or "sound" them) by syllables. In general, this should make them much easier to spell and you will be less inclined to omit necessary letters and endings. Of course, this means that you will have to work on your pronunciation skills too in order to become a better speller.

Important Terms to Know

Vowels/Consonants

Be sure that you know which letters are vowels and which ones are consonants. The letters *a, e, i, o,* and *u* are vowels. All others are consonants, with the exception of *y*, which can be either a vowel or consonant depending on its pronunciation. Usually it is a vowel when it comes at the end of a word—for example, *duty, why, busy,* etcetera. In general, *y* is a consonant when it begins a word or begins a syllable within a word—for example, *yard, Yale, youngster,* etcetera.

Prefix

A *prefix* is a letter or short group of letters added to the first of a sentence, to its "root" or "base" word. The purpose of a prefix may be to make a contrast out of the base word, or to add emphasis, among other things.

Some examples are: *imperfect, illegal, overworked,* etcetera. The following chart tells you the correct prefix for some common words.

While certain prefixes can ONLY be used with words that begin with a particular letter, that does NOT mean that every word that begins with that letter will use the same prefix.

For example, for a word to use the prefix *il*, it must begin with the letter *l*, such as *legal/illegal* (meaning "not legal"). On the other hand, many words that begin with the letter *l* use *un* as a prefix to mean *not*: for example, *licensed/unlicensed.* Consult your dictionary to be sure that you have chosen the correct prefix.

Words that use the prefix *im* to form the contrast must begin with the letters:

- *m (mature/immature)*
- *b (balance/imbalanced)*
- *p (patient/impatient)*

Words that use *ir* to form a contrasting term must begin with the letter *r.*

- *r (relevant/irrelevant)*

Other common prefixes are:

- to form the negative: *un, in, de, a, dis*
- to mean excessive: *over, extra*
- to repeat: *re*
- to indicate cross-movement: *trans*

ACTIVITY ONE

Fill in the space with the correct prefix. Check your dictionary if you are not sure.

1. _____ audible

2. _____ literate

3. _____ regardless

4. _____ partial

5. _____ phased

6. _____ segregation

7. _____ agreement

8. _____ eat (consume too much)

9. _____ write (write another time)

10. _____ curricular activities (activities beyond those which are required)

Suffix

A *suffix* is a letter or group of letters added to the end of a word. It often changes the part of speech (or word form) of the root word. Some examples are: *intelligent/intelligently*, *great/greatness*, and *universe/universal*. Recognizing suffixes and their use can also greatly help your grammar. For example, in the above, you should know that the ending *-ly* is almost always used to form an adverb, the ending *-ness* is almost always used for a noun, and the suffix *-al* generally forms an adjective.

Often students have trouble spelling words correctly when the root word ends in the letter *-y*. However, the following general rule should help: If the letter before the *-y* is a vowel, the *-y* remains unchanged. But, if the letter before the *-y* is a consonant, *-y* changes to an *i* before the suffix is added. Examples include: *boy/boys*, *enjoy/enjoys/enjoyment*, *study/studies*, and *carry/carries*.

Note the following exceptions: When adding *-ing*, the *y* is always kept (*carry/carrying*). Some other common exceptions: *day/daily*, *lay/laid/lain*, and *pay/paid* (but *payment*).

ACTIVITY TWO

Fill in the following by forming one word with the prompters given. Consult your dictionary if necessary.

1. happy + ness = _____
2. toy + s = _____
3. lazy + er = _____
4. fly + ing = _____
5. agree + ment = _____

6. total + ly = _____
7. marry + s = _____
8. place + ment = _____
9. colleague + s = _____
10. hurry + ed = _____

Additional Spelling Rules

One-Syllable Words

When adding an ending to a one-syllable word where the last letter is a consonant and the previous letter is a vowel, double the final consonant before adding your ending. This rule applies no matter what word form you are using. Examples include *jog, jogger/jog, jogging/jog/jogged*, etcetera.

ACTIVITY THREE

Form new words from the following roots and suffixes.

1. tip + er = _____
2. big + est = _____
3. dig + ing = _____
4. man + ed = _____
5. sad + er = _____

6. bat + er = _____
7. log + ed = _____
8. pan + ed = _____
9. nap + ing = _____
10. dip + er = _____

Words Ending in the Letter *E*:

When adding an ending to a word in which the last letter is *e*, drop the -*e* if the new ending begins with a vowel. For example, *mine/miner/mining*. However, if the new ending begins with a consonant, keep the -*e*. For example, *place/placement*.

Note: There are some important exceptions that you should try to memorize as they are common academic terms. Some of these are *argue/argument*, *judge/judgement*, *acknowledge/acknowledgment*, and *nine, ninth*.

ACTIVITY FOUR

Form new words from the following roots and suffixes.

1. rate + ing = _____
2. hope + ed = _____
3. advise + er = _____
4. take + ing = _____
5. sate + ed = _____

6. retire + ment = _____
7. tenure + ed = _____
8. courage + ous = _____
9. active + ist = _____
10. write + ing = _____

EI vs. *IE*

It is a good idea to learn the phrase that most American students learn when they are quite young to help them with these confusing letters: "*I* before *e*, except after *c*." It can also help to remember that you should use *ei* whenever the combination sounds like the letter *a*—for example, *neighbor*, or *weight*.

But again, there are many exceptions, many of which appear in academic vocabulary: *height*, *dietary*, *science*, *deity*, *either*, and *neither*.

ACTIVITY FIVE

Fill in the blanks with either *ei* or *ie*. Use your dictionary if necessary.

1. bel _____vers
2. rel_____f
3. consc_____nce
4. soc_____ty
5. v_____n

6. fr___ght
7. exper_____nced
8. ach_____vement
9. rec_____ve
10. conc_____vable

Adding Endings to Words with Two or More Syllables

You should double the consonant of words with more than one syllable if the new ending begins with a vowel, the combination of the last three letters is consonant-vowel-consonant, and the stress is on the last syllable of the original word. Examples include *begin/beginning/beginners.*

ACTIVITY SIX

Make new words from the following. Look very carefully at the final three letters and consult a dictionary for accent or stress if you are unsure.

1. permit + ed= _____
2. confer + ence= _____
3. excel + ent= _____
4. expel + ed=_____
5. admit + ance= _____

6. reject + ion=_____
7. submit + ed= _____
8. enroll + ment=_____
9. prefer + ence= _____
10. cancel + ed= _____

KAPLAN

SPELLING TEST: Put a "C" next to all correctly spelled words below, and an "I" next to the misspelled words; correct all the misspelled words. If you miss any of these, begin memorizing them, keeping a list, writing, and rewriting them until you have committed them to memory.

1. relucttance _____
2. freindship _____
3. mathmatics _____
4. grammer _____
5. psychiatry _____
6. phyics _____
7. Wedenesday _____
8. lisence _____
9. dormitory _____
10. registeration _____
11. psychical education _____
12. archeologey _____
13. fourty _____
14. forteen _____
15. travellers _____
16. meddical _____
17. referrence _____
18. Feberary _____
19. jurisprudence _____
20. bibiliography _____
21. anthroplogist _____
22. friendlyest _____
23. regretable _____
24. eviction _____
25. dictionaries _____
26. elderley _____
27. unreplaceaable _____
28. gymnasium _____
29. nieghborhood _____
30. libraries _____

Answers to Spelling Activities

ACTIVITY ONE
1. inaudible
2. illiterate
3. irregardless
4. impartial
5. unphased
6. desegregation
7. disagreement
8. overeat
9. rewrite
10. extracurricular

ACTIVITY TWO
1. happiness
2. toys
3. lazier
4. flying
5. agreement
6. totally
7. marries
8. placement
9. colleagues
10. hurried

ACTIVITY THREE

1. tipper
2. biggest
3. digging
4. manned
5. sadder
6. batter
7. logged
8. panned
9. napping
10. dipper

ACTIVITY FOUR

1. rating
2. hoped
3. adviser
4. taking
5. sated
6. retirement
7. tenured
8. courageous
9. activist
10. writing

ACTIVITY FIVE

1. believers
2. relief
3. conscience
4. society
5. vein
6. freight
7. experienced
8. achievement
9. receive
10. conceivable

ACTIVITY SIX

1. permitted
2. conference
3. excellent
4. expelled
5. admittance
6. rejection
7. submitted
8. enrollment
9. preference
10. cancelled

SPELLING TEST

1. I	11. I	21. I
2. I	12. I	22. I
3. I	13. I	23. I
4. I	14. I	24. C
5. C	15. I	25. C
6. I	16. I	26. I
7. I	17. I	27. I
8. I	18. I	28. C
9. C	19. C	29. I
10. I	20. I	30. C

SESSION L: WHY IS PROOFREADING IMPORTANT?

One of the most common mistakes students make when taking the TOEFL essay exam is using all of their 30 minutes to write their essay, but leaving very little or no time to proof-read (or check) for mistakes. This creates major problems. An essay that contains several grammatical errors, misspelled words, punctuation errors, and other careless mistakes will undoubtedly receive a low score.

The cliché "less is more" is often applicable here: students, for some reason, believe it is more important to write a long essay rather than a "correct" one, but this is not the case. Most students need a minimum of 5–7 minutes at the end of their essay test to look over their work and change anything that is not written correctly. At least half of the mistakes students make are careless ones. In other words, students tend to think more about the ideas they want to express, or the content, rather than the accuracy of how they state these ideas.

Once you finish your draft, take a moment (and a deep breath!), and reread your essay. Try to think of yourself as an outsider reading your paper so that you can view it more objectively and with a more critical eye. Most professional writers try to edit their work by rereading it once for content problems and a separate time for problems with mechanics (grammar, spelling, and punctuation). This is good advice for ESL writers as well. In fact, most of you will want to emphasize the mechanics part of editing over the content one, since this tends to be the area where most students have problems.

EDITING PRACTICE ACTIVITY

Read the following essays through once quickly, without writing anything; just get an overall idea of the content and subject matter. Now, read them a second time more carefully, and make corrections. You may want to use the proofreading symbols described below. Delete all unnecessary words and phrases. Remember, however, that sometimes there is more than one way to correct a sentence.

PROOFREADING MARKS KEY

γ or —— = delete

$\wedge$ = insert letter

L = put second letter in place of first letter

= = capital letter

/ = lower case

= add space

ESSAY ONE

TOPIC: Thanksgiving Holiday: An American Tradition

Undoubtlessly, they Americans celebrated Thanksgiving on the forth Thurday of each year. Therefore, this year is no exception to the rule.

It is difficult to say how old this holday really is; but rumor has it that it has been strated during the early days of colonization by the british who came to new england. These person known as Pilgrim wanted to do something to show thanks to the indians, so they decided to prepare a feast for them. ToDay American eat the same food that was ate by early settlers at the first Thanksgiving. Some of these is turkey, cornmeal dressings, cranberries and pumpkin pie.

Few American work on Thanksgiving Day. They spend the day with family and friend, watching parades and eating a lot good food!

ESSAY TWO

TOPIC: Why I Immigrated to the United States

As technology replace traditional agricultue society, the world became smaller and smaller. Because of modern technology, such like satellite television and computer, we get exposure to many different culture and way of thinking. Through this exposures, I decided that I wanted most to get to know better United States of America. This is main reason I move here last year.

My first consideration was for welfare of my family. I thoiught best opportunities for my children and their educations was to be here in this country. Because I get full-time research position at university here, my eldest son can go to the excellent school for free of cost. For my younger kids, it's great opportunitty for them to become fluently in english lnaguages. In addition, my wife is chinese language teacher and she can find works here too!

Each people have their own reason to come to another country besides these reason my family came. We are so much happy we did!

ESSAY THREE

TOPIC: Controversies over Recent "Advancements" in the Medical World

Many doctors and reserch scientist have gone on fire recent due to conflicts over ethics and medicical science. As a biochemistry, I am very awarely of this problem. Even though doctors, nurses and researachers works hard to try save lives and develop better technique, many people in society criticize them over religious and moral concerns.

Take for example Baby Fae case. Here, little 3 weeks old premature baby girl was brought to the hospital because she was out of breath. Her heart was so weak so the doctors had to do something right away. They transplanted heart of a baboon into her.

Her parents gave them permission to do it, but still many people were very upse and mad and angry.t. Unfortuantely, she died 5-hours after the operation. Even though the operation was lethal, some religious groups threatened to sue the hospital.

Another case was one in which two people got in argument with each another. A third man was accidentaly shot by mistake while cleaning his garage in the lung. They took him to hospital but he refuse to be treatment because his religion does not permit the tranfusions from bloods. He died--should the doctor have ignored his wishes and treated him anyway if it can save his life. These are not easy questions to answer.

Never before doctors and researchers have recieved so much criticism for thier work. Is it fair? Who should decide what is morally right for others? and what was not? These are tough lethal issues which society is curently trying to make solved.

EDITING PRACTICE ACTIVITY ANSWER KEY

ESSAY ONE

TOPIC: Thanksgiving Holiday: An American Tradition

Without fail (Undoublessly,) they Americans celebrated Thanksgiving on the forth Thursday of each year. Therefore, this year is no exception to the rule.

It is difficult to say how old this holiday really is; but rumor has it that it has been striated during the early days of colonization by the british who came to new england. These person known as Pilgrim wanted to do something to show thanks to the indians, so they decided to prepare a feast for them. Today American eat the same kinds of food that was ate were eaten by early settlers at the first Thanksgiving. Some of these are turkey, cornmeal dressings, cranberries, and pumpkin pie.

Few American work on Thanksgiving Day. They spend the day with family and friends, watching parades and eating a lot of good food!

ESSAY TWO

TOPIC: Why I Immigrated to the United States

As technology replaced the traditional agricultural society, the world became smaller and smaller. Because of modern technology, such as satellite television and computers, we have gained exposure to many different cultures and ways of thinking. Through this exposure, I decided that I wanted most to get to know the United States of America. This is

the
∧ main reason I move^d here last year.

My first consideration was for ^the welfare of my family. I thought ^the best opportunities for my children and their educations ~~was~~ were to be ~~here~~ found in this country. Because I ~~get~~ got a full-time research position at ^the university here, my eldest son can go to ~~the~~ an excellent school for free. ~~of cost?~~ For my younger kids, it's ^a great opportunity ~~for them~~ to become fluently in ^the english l^anguages. In addition, my wife is ^a chinese language teacher, and she can find work^s here too!

Each ~~people~~ person ~~have~~ has ~~their~~ his/her own reason to ~~come~~ move to another country besides these reason^s my family came. We are so ~~much~~ happy, ^that we did!

ESSAY THREE

TOPIC: Controversies over Recent "Advancements" in the Medical World

Many doctors and resе^arch scientist^s have ~~gone on~~ come under fire recent^ly due to conflicts over ethics and mediʒ^cal science. As a biochemistry, I am very aware^ly of this problem. Even though doctors, nurses and researɑchers work^s hard to try ^to save lives and develop better technique^s, many people ~~in society~~ criticize them over religious and moral concerns.

Take, for example, ^the Baby Fae case. Here, ~~little~~ ^a 3-week^s -old premature ~~baby~~ girl was brought to the hospital because she was ~~out of~~ gasping for breath. Her heart was so weak ~~so~~ ^that the doctors had to do something right away. They transplanted ^the heart of a baboon into her. Her parents gave them permission to do it, but still many people were very upse^t ^and ~~mad and angry~~.t. Unfortunately, she died 5 hours after the operation. Even though the operation was ~~lethal~~ legal, some religious groups threatened to sue the hospital.

Another case was one in which two people got in^-to an argument with each ~~another~~ other. A third man was accidentaly shot ~~by mistake~~ in the lung while cleaning his garage ~~in the lung~~ he was . They took him to ^a/the hospital, but he refuse^d to be ~~treatment~~ treat-ed because his religion ~~does~~ did not permit ~~the~~ blood tranfusions ~~from bloods~~. He died, ^Should the doctor have ignored his wishes and treat-ed him anyway if it ~~can~~ could have save^d his life. ? This is ~~These are~~ not ^an easy question^s to answer.

Never before ^have doctors and researchers ~~have~~ reci^eved so much criticism for thier work. Is it fair? Who should decide what is morally right for others? and what ^is ~~was~~ not? These are tough ~~lethal~~ ethical issues ~~which~~ that society is cur^rently trying to ~~make~~ resolve ~~solved~~.

SESSION M: WHY KEEP A JOURNAL?

You may be asking yourself the question above and wondering if writing down your thoughts in a journal can really help you on the TOEFL, and, more specifically, if it can help you with the essay section. The answer is YES!

Very few professional writers could have honed (or fine-tuned) their craft without journal writing. Not only do most writers claim that this was an important tool in their early days of becoming a writer, but it still plays a major role in their life as a writer. Why is this? Well, first of all, in journal writing you can write freely without the fear of someone looking over your shoulder and holding a red pen, ready to swoop down and start correcting. Writing freely and frequently will help you to get to the stage of sounding like a native speaker in your written communication much faster. That is, your writing will sound more natural, and "native-like fluency" is one of the criteria used to judge the essay section of the TOEFL.

How can you begin? Your first step is to buy something (such as a small, spiral notebook) that you can carry with you easily, for whenever or wherever you get that urge to jot down a few thoughts or feelings. DON'T edit your work! That is not the purpose of journal writing. Your goal is to become a more relaxed, less self-conscious writer, and eventually to carry this skill over to more academic-type assignments.

Below are some suggestions for journal writing topics. But, of course, these are merely suggestions—you can write about anything you desire. If you want to ask someone to look over your writing, that is fine—just remind the person that you are not looking for a critique of your grammar and spelling, just sharing your thoughts with a friend.

You will be amazed by how quickly this technique helps you with your written expression, at the same time as it enables you to become more fluent and less hesitant in your verbal communication.

Journal Topic Suggestions

1. Pick a photograph out of a magazine or newspaper. What words come to your mind? Why did you choose this particular picture? Free-associate any words or phrases that you think of when you look at this. Jot these down, in any order, and don't edit.

2. Associate ideas with words. Think about the word *liberty*—what images do you see? Now describe those images in your notebook.

3. Close your eyes. Think about the word *family*—Who do you see first in your mind? Describe that person. What does that person look like? What is she wearing? What is she doing? Write down any other words that come to you when you see this person.

4. Go to a crowded area in your city (a train station, a park on a Saturday afternoon, a shopping mall, etcetera). Find a place to sit and observe for about fifteen minutes. Don't write anything during this time. Now, write down everything that you can remember about the last 10–15 minutes—the people, the sounds, the smells, etcetera.

5. Your very first day of school when you were a youngster—what was it like? Write down every single thing you can recall about that day (positive, negative, and even neutral memories).

6. Describe some difficulty or conflict you have been faced with in the past year. What was it? How did you deal with it? Do you feel that this is resolved now? What kinds of things did you learn from this experience?

SESSION N: TOEFL ESSAY CHECKLIST

The following guidelines should be practiced routinely when you are going over your essays after you have made a rough draft. You should practice using these while you are preparing for the TOEFL Writing section in advance, at home or in your TOEFL class. Because you have so little time when you are actually taking the essay section (30 minutes), you will want to use these steps repeatedly BEFORE you take the test so that by the actual test day they will have become almost "second nature" to you.

As is mentioned in the "Why Is Proofreading Important?" section, most professional writers check their work for content and mechanics separately. You are advised to do the same.

Mechanics Checklist

Begin here, since many English as a Second Language writers, especially those at the intermediate–advanced level, have more problems with grammar than they do with content. You should be able to answer "yes" to the following questions after you've checked through your essay:

1. Do all sentences have a complete subject and a complete verb (no fragments)?

2. Do all subjects and verbs agree with each other in number (i.e., singular or plural)?

3. Do all pronouns have an antecedent? If so, do they agree in number and gender with their antecedent?

4. Do all single count nouns have an article preceding them?

5. Did you use correct punctuation? (Make sure you have no run-on sentences)

6. Are all structures parallel?

7. Did you check for spelling errors? (follow the spelling guidelines in this book)

Content Checklist

1. Is your introduction brief and relatively general, not more than four or five sentences?

2. Does your essay clearly address the topic that you have been assigned?

3. Does the introduction include a one-sentence thesis?

4. Do your body paragraphs begin with a topic sentence?

5. Does each paragraph stay within the topic stated in the topic sentence?

6. Did you use transition terms to connect your ideas smoothly?

7. Did you use specific examples to support your thesis and topic sentences (i.e., particular names, dates, places, events, etcetera.)?

8. Does your conclusion restate your main ideas, rather than introduce new concepts?

9. Did you avoid redundancy (i.e., repeating verbatim that which you have already stated)?

Appendix:
Countries Offering Computer-Based TOEFL Test Format*

Albania	Chile	Kiribati	Niger	St. Kitts and Nevis
American Samoa	Colombia	Kuwait	Nigeria	St. Vincent
Angola	Comoros	Kyrgyzstan	Northern Mariana Isl.	Suriname
Antigua & Barbuda	Congo	Latvia	Norway	Swaziland
Argentina	Costa Rica	Lebanon	Oman	Sweden
Armenia	Croatia	Lesotho	Panama	Switzerland
Aruba	Cyprus	Liberia	Papua New Guinea	Syria
Australia	Czech Republic	Lithuania	Paraguay	Tahiti
Austria	Democratic Republic	Luxembourg	Peru	Tajikistan
Azerbaijan	of the Congo	Macedonia	Philippines	Tanzania
Bahamas	Denmark	Madagascar	Poland	Togo
Bahrain	Djibouti	Malawi	Portugal	Tonga
Barbados	Dominican Rep.	Malaysia	Puerto Rico	Trinidad & Tobago
Belarus	Ecuador	Mali	Qatar	Tunisia
Belgium	Egypt	Malta	Reunion	Turkey
Belize	El Salvador	Marshall Islands	Romania	Turkmenistan
Benin	Equatorial Guinea	Martinique	Russian Federation	Uganda
Bermuda	Guinea-Bissau	Mauritania	Rwanda	Ukraine
Bolivia	Guyana	Mauritius	Saint Lucia	United Arab Emirates
Bosnia & Herzogovina	Haiti	Mexico	Samoa	United Kingdom
Botswana	Honduras	Micronesia	Sao Tome & Principe	United States
Brazil	Hungary	Moldova	Saudi Arabia	Uruguay
Brunei Darussalam	Iceland	Mongolia	Senegal	U.S. Virgin Islands
Bulgaria	Indonesia	Morocco	Seychelles	Uzbekistan
Burkina Faso	Ireland	Mozambique	Sierra Leone	Venezuela
Burundi	Israel	Namibia	Singapore	West Bank
Cameroon	Italy	Nepal	Slovakia	Yemen
Canada	Ivory Coast	Netherlands Antilles	Slovenia	Yugoslavia
Cape Verde	Jamaica	Netherlands	Solomon Islands	Zambia
Cayman Islands	Jordan	New Caledonia	South Africa	Zimbabwe
Central African Rep.	Kazakhstan	New Zealand	Spain	
Chad	Kenya	Nicaragua	Sri Lanka	

Countries Offering Computer-Based TOEFL Test Format*

Algeria	China	Korea	Pakistan	Vietnam
Bangladesh	Hong Kong	Laos	Parts of Africa	
Bhutan	India	Macao	Taiwan	
Cambodia	Japan	Myanmar	Thailand	

*At the time this book went to press. For an updated list consult the ETS TOEFL Web site at http://www.toefl.org.

SEE THE "USER'S GUIDE FOR THE COMPUTER-BASED TOEFL CD-ROM" IN THE FRONT OF THIS BOOK FOR SYSTEM REQUIREMENTS AND INSTRUCTIONS ON HOW TO USE THE SOFTWARE.

SOFTWARE LICENSE/DISCLAIMER OF WARRANTIES

COPYRIGHT INFORMATION FOR CD-ROM

Technical Support for this CD-ROM is available Monday through Friday 6 A.M.–6 P.M. EST at 1-970-339-7142. When calling Tech Support, please refer to the ID number (406203-02) on the disk.